THE BEGINNING
FILMMAKER'S
GUIDE

**EVERYTHING YOU NEED
TO KNOW TO MAKE
YOUR FIRST FILM**

RENÉE HARMON

MJF BOOKS
NEW YORK

Published by MJF Books
Fine Communications
Two Lincoln Square
60 West 66th Street
New York, NY 10023

The Beginning Filmmaker's Guide

ISBN 1-56731-384-1

This edition published by arrangement with Walker Publishing Company, Inc.
To order the paperback editions of *The Beginning Filmmaker's Guide to Directing* or
The Beginning Filmmaker's Business Guide, call Walker Publishing at 1-800-289-2553.

The American Film Institute, which provided the sample grant application on pages 189-192, is funded by the National Endowment for the Arts.

Book Design by Claire Vaccaro

Manufactured in the United States of America on acid-free paper
MJF Books and the MJF colophon are trademarks of Fine Creative Media, Inc.

10 9 8 7 6 5 4 3 2 1

The Beginning Filmmaker's Guide

The
Beginning
Filmmaker's
Guide to
Directing

Contents

Acknowledgments

I wish to thank Mary Kennan Herbert, at Walker and Company, for her interest in *The Beginning Filmmaker's Guide to Directing,* her belief in the book, and her encouragement.

I wish to thank Ed, my husband, and Cliff and Cheryl, my children, for their patience with me while the book was being written.

I wish to thank all the actors and crew who work with enthusiasm, tenacity, and diligence on my films, and the directors—most of all James Bryan, director, and Bill Luce, art director—who make the impossible possible.

I wish to thank the many aspiring filmmakers who, attending my lectures, provide me with insight as to what kind of information is valuable to them.

. . . . . .

Preface

We are witnessing a rapidly expanding motion picture market that, to be sure, provides product not only for the numerous multiple-screen theaters springing up all over the country, for cable, TV, and domestic video, but for the growing video market overseas as well. Consequently interest in filmmaking has never been stronger. You may be among the many talented, skilled artists who need only that one break to get a foothold in the motion picture industry. You may be ready to get a project off the ground and onto the screen.

The Beginning Filmmaker's Guide to Directing has been tailored to your specific needs. This book has been designed for you—the writer, actor, or cinematographer who wishes to enter the directing field. You have talent, vision, and tenacity; all you need are some commonsense, down-to-earth guidelines, some nuts-and-bolts advice to lead you in the right direction. You need the advice of a professional moviemaker, one who is actively engaged in producing and directing low-budget feature films.

This book has grown out of my own experiences as filmmaker and lecturer. I am familiar with the problems you—the beginning director with only limited funds at your disposal—will face.

So let's get to work. Pick up your slate, and . . . "Scene 1, Take 1."

Part One

Introduction

You—the writer, the actor, the cinematographer, the producer—own a motion picture script. You have something to say and *know* how it should be said. You have a mental image, and you know how it should be expressed. Almost physically you experience the mood of your script and the rhythm of its scenes. You are possessed by a vision demanding to come alive in the matrix seen on the screen. So you slave over a budget, you get investors, and if you are fortunate you'll arouse some distribution interest. You are ready to turn your vision into reality . . .

You sign a director. And all of a sudden, something strange and disturbing happens. The director, imposing his or her own vision onto the motion picture, turns it into a *project,* while the matrix you had envisioned and loved fades into the background. In front of your eyes, your film turns out very different from the one you had expected and battled for. This does not necessarily mean that the film is inferior to the one you had pictured in your mind. The director, most likely, is as excited about the motion picture as you are, but his or her vision of it may not correspond to yours.

By now you are positive that you, and only you, ought to direct your picture. You are the only person able to bring your mind's image to the screen.

Hold your horses.

Unless you are a *skilled* director, chances are that your film, regardless of the validity of your vision, will end up a failure—an amateur's attempt at best, not the viable expression of cinematic art it deserves to be. Don't forget, you are *not* a director as yet, but an expert in any one of the other cinematic areas; therefore, you look at the motion picture to be directed from your point of view, not the director's.

You, the screenwriter, expect to see the scenes you have written on the screen.

You, the actor, intend to explore the characters' emotional life.

You, the cinematographer, are ready to create unforgettable visual moments.

You, the producer, are tired of handing your vision over to a "bunch of creative nuts" who see you merely as an accountant, not the artistic force you are.

But: It is the *director* who is fully aware that the writer, actor, and cinematographer are but parts of the cinematographic *expression* being forged from a multitude of elements. It is the director who is responsible for expressing the film's story, theme, and mood in a *visual way*.

Obviously you, the beginning director, must study this visual approach to your matrix. You must learn all about a new, exhilarating, and often frustrating craft. Whether you choose to attend a film school or prefer to learn by observation working for a production company, you must be familiar with the basics of directing a motion picture. You must know about the structure of a viable motion picture script, you must know about acting *and* actors, you must know about music and sound. Most important, you must know about camera angles, setups, and moves, as well as editing techniques. Only then will you be able to bring your vision, your message, and your personal style to the screen.

Yet gaining proficiency is not a matter of memorizing a list of basic rules, it is the ability to gain mastery of technical skills, for these are the channels of your creative power. Marcel Proust put it very clearly: "But in art excuses count for nothing—good intentions are of no avail." In other words, talent and creativity count little if not backed up by craft.

Unfortunately some beginning directors rely too heavily upon the myth that their personal style and expertise in one of the related cinematic fields will pull them through their first directing assignment. They are the ones who believe in other myths as well:

I do not have to know anything about camera setups, movements, or angles. I let the cinematographer worry about those.

Wrong. Deciding about camera work is one of the most exciting aspects of directing a motion picture. By all means consult with your cinematographer. Listen to his or her advice; the cinematographer is an expert and knows what to do. But the decision is up to *you.* You give your motion picture its look and feel; after all, camera work does play an important part in giving a film its specific mood.

I do not have to worry about any mistakes. It's the editor's job to correct them.

If you failed to *cover,* if you failed to *match,* and if you misdirected on-screen movements (screen directions)—in short, if you as director have not done your homework—there is little an editor, even the best one, can do.

I will save time and money by using three cameras simultaneously.

Agreed, multimillion-dollar productions, even television films, employ the three-camera system. But you should not follow suit unless you own and operate a money-printing machine.

I do not have to shoot a full-length film. I'll produce a trailer and will interest an established production company in a coproduction.

Directors who believe in this myth will make the most costly mistake in their careers. Again and again during my lectures I have to look at happy faces and listen to excited voices telling me: "I've just completed my trailer—well, it cost about twenty thousand dollars—and now I'll show it around to investors and production companies." The sad fact is, though these beginning directors have sunk all their assets into the project or gone into debt, all this money is lost. No reliable production company will join forces with a neophyte, no investor will risk one penny on an unfinished motion picture regardless of how impressive the trailer is, if a novice director helms the project.

On the other hand, you'll have some chance of finding a distributor who will come up with the postproduction money if your motion picture is at least available in a raw cut.

I'll take my film (or script) to one of the film markets—Cannes, France; Milan (MIFED), Italy; Los Angeles—where I will meet people and interest them in my project.

Save your money. No one, except a few con artists out for a free drink, will even talk to you. You won't get admission to any of the exhibition halls. Admission (by ticket only) is reserved to exhibitors, distributors, and film buyers.

Take my advice, and don't ever rely on any of the above myths. They won't get you anywhere. Rely on your creative ability, and have the *craft* to back you up as you take step after step in pursuit of success. The motion picture industry does not abound with creative, talented, and *skilled* film-makers. Eventually you will succeed.

But don't get discouraged if your progress seems slow. Don't we all know about the "overnight success" that took ten years to be achieved? Be ready for setbacks; accept failures as a learning experience; *and don't give up.*

Hang in there, and you'll make it as a filmmaker and director. So let's start working.

The Director

and the

Screenplay

You have written or optioned a motion picture script. You are all fired up; you must see the exciting story on the screen. You can't wait to commence shooting. I know the feeling; I have been through it many times.

But now is the time to wait. Stand back. Gain some distance from the images churning in your mind. Wait until you are able to look at your script with—hopefully—unbiased "director's eyes." Remember, audiences do not attend motion pictures because of the actor's sensitive interpretations, the cinematographer's admirable work, or the director's skill. No, audiences attend motion pictures because they want to see a *gripping story*—a story that you, the director (unbeknownst to them), have brought in *on time* and *on budget.*

Since this book is about directing a motion picture, it covers only the essentials a beginning director ought to know about script structure. There are a number of excellent books on script writing on the market, and you should familiarize yourself with some of them.

In this chapter we will discuss the following:

Basic budgetary considerations
Script construction

Dialog
Screenplay development
   Rewriting original script in *visual* language
   Rewriting scenes into a shooting script (combined
      shot list/camera setup list)

Basic Budgetary Considerations

First you'll have to decide whether or not your script may be too demanding for the beginning director's admittedly meager budget.

Does the story require car chases, helicopter shots, or any other extensive action scenes?

Stunts are time consuming and will add shooting days to your budget. You ought to consider the cost of stunt vehicles and stuntmen, and last but not least the fact that your liability insurance will skyrocket the moment stunts have been added to the script.

Are the required special effects too ambitious for your budget?

If done ingeniously, special effects do not have to cost an arm and a leg. (Some advice on this will come in chapter 9.)

Is the script too verbal?

Remember, unlike a stage play, a motion picture is a visual medium. Therefore ask yourself, "Where should I substitute or strengthen verbal expression by the use of visual expression?"

Do you really need a cast of thousands?

Most likely you will be able to omit or consolidate some of the characters in the script.

Are too many different and/or expensive locations required?

If possible, forgo any location that demands an extensive travel budget. Try to find an equally satisfactory location close to home. If the expensive location will add to the film's production values, by all means splurge on it, but find ways to limit your use of the location. (More advice about this may be found in chapter 2.)

Script Construction

Each screenplay (script) has a beginning, a middle, and an end, or—if you will—Act I, Act II, and Act III as customary in a stage play, only the action is not nearly as evenly distributed as in a stage play. The screenplay offers a short beginning (Act I), a lengthy middle (Act II), and a short ending (Act III). You, the beginning director, should consider limiting your screenplay to ninety minutes on-screen time. Each additional five or ten minutes will increase your budget, and often the added expenditure does not justify the end product. Considered this way, a script looks something like this:

20 pages beginning
65 middle
15 end

Your script should contain no fewer than 100 and no more than 110 pages to cover the 90 minutes on-screen time. The rule of thumb is, one page of script equals one minute on-screen time. It is important to remember that the same basic script structure, as discussed in the pages that follow, applies to all films, not to suspense-type motion pictures only.

After you have made your decision about the script's budgetary requirements and its viability, you should ask yourself some pertinent questions:

- Does the screenplay as written show and anticipate the story's mood and atmosphere?
- Have the Who and Where been established clearly?
- Does the script contain any twists, and are those placed correctly?
- Do What and Why grow out of the relationship between the main characters, or have they been imposed on this relationship for the purpose of creating an exciting plot?
- Has the main question been asked correctly, or does it give rise to a split goal?
- Is the subplot strong enough?
- Does Act II keep on developing, or does it lag?
- Have you built a strong ending, and answered the main question?

ESTABLISHING MOOD AND ATMOSPHERE

Unlike a television show, which zaps the viewer immediately into the story, the motion picture can afford a more leisurely approach. A TV show *must* grab the viewers' attention quickly, or they will switch channels. However, a viewer who has bought a movie ticket or has rented a videotape is more patient. (Of course, when your motion picture is being shown at the various film markets, you must interest prospective buyers within the first fifteen minutes. They will look at the first ten to fifteen minutes and the last ten minutes of a feature film. Still, you'll have plenty of time to establish mood and atmosphere.)

But we are getting ahead of ourselves. Let's go back to the beginning that sets the mood of your motion picture. For the purpose of illustration we'll use the script of my motion picture *Jungle Trap.** This is the background of the plot:

About fifty years ago a number of Peruvian investors turned a sacred Mali burial ground, located in the Amazon jungle, into a luxury hotel resort. Shortly after the hotel was completed, the Malis attacked. They killed the staff and guests and destroyed the hotel. They in turn were annihilated. The jungle claimed the hotel again. A group of anthropologists travels to the site to recover an ancient Mali ritual mask. Upon arrival, the anthropologists find the hotel in perfect condition, fully staffed but devoid of guests. The scientists stay in the hotel, unaware that they are living in a phantom place and being served by apparitions. The moment they realize the truth, they are trapped as ghostly Mali warriors attack them.

On the emotional level the plot deals with Chris, a photojournalist, who sees her marriage to Josh, the leader of the expedition, on the verge of destruction as he falls in love with his young and beautiful native assistant, Leila.

This is how the original script read:

Establishing Shot of City.
(Various angles. Cut to an imposing building. A car stops in front of it. CHRIS *gets out, walks toward the building, and enters. Establish sign: "Museum of Natural History.")*

---

*Jungle Trap, a Ciara Productions film, 1991.

Interior Museum. Hallway.
(Camera pans along the pristine, whitewashed walls that display a collection of South American Indian sculptures. CHRIS *approaches. Camera moves in and holds on* CHRIS *as she stops in front of a warrior's mask.)*

You can tell, this beginning did its very best *not* to establish any mood. Rewritten, however, it did give the audience an anticipatory sense of the spine-tingling mood that permeates this motion picture:

(Dark screen. The swishing, rumbling sound of an approaching storm sweeps over us as slowly, ever so slowly, a number of indistinguishable shapes emerge from the darkness. The storm grows more violent. Faces, machetes, masks, and fists flash—intercutting and superimposing one another—in quick succession across the screen. The shapes become more and more distinct, until ultimately the Shock Zoom of a shrunken head, grinning, attacks the viewer. A high, piercing sound drowns out the storm.

Then, all of a sudden, silence takes over. Camera pulls back, revealing the shrunken head neatly displayed in a glass case. Camera pulls back farther to take in CHRIS. *She stops for a beat in front of the glass case, shakes her head. Camera pans with her as she continues down the hallway to a door marked "Director of South American Displays.")*

Now the beginning, obviously, is more in the line with the needed sense of eerie anticipation.

ESTABLISHING WHO AND WHERE

Some scripts make the mistake of revealing the What (what is going to happen) and Why (the motive for the main character's actions) just a little too early. Yes, the audience must know about the What and Why, but first it has to meet the main characters (Who) before it will care about what is happening to them. *Jungle Trap* features three main characters:

Chris, a photojournalist and anthropologist
Josh, her husband, an anthropologist
Leila, Josh's young assistant

The relationship between the main characters (Who) and their environment (Where) should be made known as early as possible. It is this relationship that explains the Why.

PLACING TWISTS

If the script contains any twists, they must be placed correctly.

• *Twist at the end of Act I:* An event occurs that sets up the main plot (What) and the main characters' motives subplot (Why). These motives lead the protagonist's (hero's) goal and the antagonist's (villain's) countergoal. This twist asks the main question: "Will _____ achieve this or that?"

• *Twist 1 in the middle of Act II:* Keeps the story going, possibly turns it in a different direction, and repeats the main question.

• *Twist 2 at the end of Act II:* Pulls the story toward Act III and to the plot's climax and denouement.

ESTABLISHING THE MAIN PLOT

The What and Why of the story must grow out of the relationship between the main characters, not just be imposed on it for the purpose of creating an exciting plot. In *Jungle Trap* Josh is very much taken with his young and beautiful assistant. Chris fears for her marriage. Leila is after Chris's husband *and* her job at the museum. The What and Why set the story in motion:

What the story is about determines the main plot and the film's line of action. *Why* determines the main characters' motives, leading to goal and countergoal. *Why* establishes the film's subplot and examines its theme.

The What in *Jungle Trap* sets the main plot in action: the anthropologists commence their expedition in search of the sacred Mali warrior mask.

As we look at the Why, we discover that Chris and Leila are the pivotal characters. It is their Why that supplies them with goals:

Chris's goal: I want to save my marriage by showing Josh that I'm a better woman and better scientist than Leila is.

Leila (countergoal): I want to destroy Chris's marriage by destroying her reputation as a scientist.

FRAMING THE MAIN QUESTION

If the main question has not been asked correctly, it will give rise to a split goal. Chris's character, in contrast to the aggressive Leila, has been established as pliable and soft. Her goal, as mentioned earlier, is:

> I want to save my marriage by showing Josh that I am
> a better woman and better scientist than Leila is.

If Chris's goal were to be stated this way:

> I want to save my marriage.
> I want to get hold of the ceremonial mask.

then we would be faced with a split goal. A split goal pulls a story in two different directions. The above split goal would result in the main question: "Will Chris save her marriage?" This main question, however, would end the film at the end of Act II, when Josh asks Chris for a divorce.

STRENGTHENING THE SUBPLOT

The subplot reveals the human element of your story. It gives your story depth and keeps your characters from becoming cardboard figures; it demands the audience's empathy. Here are some guidelines:

• The subplot must be part of the story, not a story by itself. While the main plot tells the story, the subplot focuses on the relationship between people. Often the subplot is the stronger and more interesting one, but it is the plot that causes the actions the characters take, and as such it holds the film together. (For example, in *Kramer vs. Kramer* the subplot deals with the couple's relationship to each other; the plot deals with the custody case.)

• Once you have clarified your plot-subplot structure you will have to check the structure of the subplot. The subplot has the same structure as the main plot, with a beginning, a middle, and an end. It also has twists of its own.

• The subplot twists should be placed as closely as possible to their respective main plot twists. If you are struggling with a script, most likely you are facing faulty main plot–subplot integrations.

BUILDING THE MIDDLE

(Act II)

Act II is the area where your screenplay should develop into an increasingly gripping matrix. At times, unfortunately, Act II may drag after an interesting beginning (Act I). Besides main plot and subplot twists and the integration of both, you need the following to keep Act II alive and kicking:

• Momentum (graduation, suspense)
• Foreshadowing
• Dark moment
• Highlight scenes
• Obstacles and conflicts

Momentum   Momentum simply means that a story gains in strength. This is achieved by the application of *graduation* and *suspense*.

Graduation   Check your story: Are *all* events on the same high or low interest level, or do they vary in strength? The interest level must move up, even though you should give your audience plateaus when "nothing much happens." The final (and highest) graduation should lead into the Dark Moment and from there into the last twist that propels the story into Act III. In *Jungle Trap* the final graduation begins when the Mali ghost warriors attack the hotel, and ends in the twist when Chris and Leila, the only survivors, have to join forces to escape being killed.

Suspense   While graduation keeps the audience's interest alive, it is overlapping suspense that holds Act II together. Act II consists of a series of overlapping suspense sequences, each headed by a goal that has to be either frustrated or satisfied. The point is that a new overlapping suspense sequence begins before the denouement of the previous one. For instance:

- Suspense sequence A: Chris suspects the hotel is a phantom place.
- Goal: I want to find out whether my suspicion is correct.
- Suspense sequence B: The anthropologists fear an attack by the ghost warriors.
- Goal: We will have to protect ourselves.

Make certain that suspense sequence B has been set in motion before the denouement of suspense sequence A has been delivered.

The denouement of the various suspense sequences *must* be delivered at the end of Act II. Then only the main question remains to be answered.

Never fail to make your characters' expectations of the outcome clear to your audience. Remember, your audience *expects* some outcome. It is fun (and makes for an exciting film) to manipulate this expectation:

- The denouement does not happen as anticipated: surprise.
- The audience—at this point—does not expect a denouement: shock. (This technique was used to great effect in the original *Halloween*.)
- The denouement happens as expected: satisfaction.

It is obvious that an always satisfied anticipation becomes as boring as a continually frustrated expectation becomes annoying.

Foreshadowing Foreshadowing is another integral part of momentum. Any event needs to be foreshadowed twice. Audiences should not become aware of foreshadowing. They should remember, however, after the foreshadowed event has taken place.

Dark Moment The twist at the end of Act II features the Dark Moment, when everything seems lost. It is imperative that at this point the main plot twist and the subplot twist are closely integrated, and that the main plot twist moves the story in a different direction. The Dark Moment in *Jungle Trap* occurs when everyone but Chris and Leila has been killed.

Highlight Scene A highlight scene resembles a plot within a plot. The highlight scene is an excellent device to keep the middle of a motion picture from dragging. It is most effective if it occurs immediately after Twist 1.

- The highlight scene ought to be an integral part of your film; it should not take off on a tangent of its own.
- The highlight scene should not last more than five to seven minutes.
- A highlight scene, starting from a point of departure, features a beginning (Act I), a middle (Act II), and an end (Act III). A twist occurs at the end of Act II.

In *Jungle Trap* I used the following highlight scene:

- *Point of Departure:* Chris is convinced that she and the anthropologists are trapped in a phantom place.
- *Beginning:* After Josh and Leila laugh about her "insane" phobia, Chris tries to get help. By radio she tries to make contact with the outside world.
- *Twist:* Chris reaches a ham operator, who shrugs her SOS off as a bad joke.
- *Middle:* Chris, assisted by a number of supernatural incidents, convinces the anthropologists about the impending danger.
- *Twist:* Ready to defend themselves, the anthropologists barricade the lobby's entrance and windows.
- *Dark Moment:* In front of their eyes the hotel begins to crumble. Jungle overgrows the lobby, and there is no place for them to hide.
- *End:* The anthropologists expect the warriors to attack. The attack does not happen (audience expectation has been frustrated — surprise and heightened suspense), and the anthropologists live through a night of waiting and fear.

The highlight scene has a subplot: finally Chris and Josh find the courage to discuss their marriage honestly.

Obstacles/Conflicts   Obstacles are barriers that keep a character from reaching his or her goal. Obstacles are important as they give you, the beginning director, the chance to "prove character in action" — that is, a character has to react to obstacles in keeping with *his or her established personality*. A braggart will not react humbly. A sensible person will not turn reckless, unless the secondary trait of recklessness has been established (foreshadowed) prior to the event.

Obstacles are closely connected to conflicts. All conflicts need to be established clearly, and at times they may need to be foreshadowed. Never expect your audience to guess at who is in conflict with whom or what, *but spell it out.* Only three conflict patterns are possible:

Man against man
Man against nature
Man against himself

If your script lacks suspense, I recommend that you investigate the obstacle/conflict area. Ask yourself:

Has obstacle or conflict been established early enough to cause audience anticipation?

Do the opposing forces have an equal chance to reach their goal? If not, your script will lack suspense. If John and Jerry court Miss Beautiful, but all advantages are on John's side, no suspense is evoked. But if the chance of success is equally distributed between the two, then we, the audience, are interested in the outcome of the competition.

Are goal and countergoal clearly stated, and are both focused upon the same area? Mary and Beth are both up for the starring role in an off-Broadway play. The girls are equally compelled to win the role, but they have never met, and do not know of each other's existence: same goal, but no conflict, and therefore no suspense. But if Mary and Beth are friends, and devious Beth does everything in her power to discredit sweet Mary, then we have a countergoal, with conflict and suspense.

CREATING THE STRONGEST END

(Act III)

The twist of Act II leads *immediately* into Act III. I recommend that this twist be the strongest of the entire script. Once Act III has started,

- Do not introduce any new characters
- Do not introduce any new events
- End your subplot before the climax of Act III begins.

Let the climax unfold quickly. Do not extend it by another conversation, by another action scene or horror effect. Make certain that the main question has been answered and that all loose ends have been tied up.

A word of warning to you the writer-director: as you set out to write your screenplay, don't concern yourself about script structure—except beginning, middle, and end. Let your excitement pull you ahead. Have fun; forget about twists, as well as dialog and highlight scenes, for the moment. It is especially futile to worry about main plot and subplot integration until the first draft of your screenplay has been written. However, by the time you are ready to tackle the shooting script, it is imperative that all humps have been straightened out. A vague or faulty structure will cause editing problems and delays, as you and your editor frantically try to give your film plot logic and a clear sense of relationship.

DIAGRAM OF SCRIPT STRUCTURE

Act I

- Visualize the mood of your film in the very beginning.
- Establish the Where (place and time).
- Establish the Who (main characters).
- A plot twist changes the existing conditions and sets the story in motion. It establishes:
    a. The main plot (the film's line of action)
    b. The subplot (the film's theme)
        1. Main goal: Protagonist's goal
                      Antagonist's countergoal
        2. Subgoal: Protagonist's and antagonist's subgoals (or secondary character's main goals) lead to conflict.
- The twist in Act I poses the main question: "Will _____ achieve _____?" The main question cannot be answered until the denouement of Act III.

Act II

- Act II begins immediately after the twist of Act I and its ramifications have been established.
- Now is the time to check for:
    a. Momentum (graduation and overlapping suspense sequences)
    b. Obstacles and conflicts

- About the middle of Act II, the main plot twist (Twist #1) occurs. This twist coincides with subplot twist #1 of Act II. The subplot twist should be set shortly before or after the main plot twist.
- It is effective to set a highlight scene in close proximity to main plot twist #1 and subplot twist #1. The highlight scene keeps a script from dragging. It has the same basic structure as the script:
  a. Beginning, middle, and end
  b. A clearly established *point of departure*
  c. Twists that lead from one act to the next
  d. A dark moment
- Main plot twist #2 and subplot twist #2 propel the story into Act III. These twists are the strongest ones in the film.

Act III

- Do not:
  a. introduce any new characters
  b. introduce any new events
- End your subplot before the climax begins. The climax focuses on the main plot only.
- Let the climax build up swiftly.
- Tie up all loose ends.
- Answer the main question.

Dialog

Now your script is finished. But you are not yet ready to commence shooting; your homework has not been finished. All dialog demands close scrutiny.

- Keep all speeches *short*. If some of the speeches are too long, divide them between two or more characters.
- Characters should *not* sound alike.
- Keep your dialog lean; trim off any unnecessary description, stilted words, or elegant turns of speech. Develop an ear for the everyday speech the average person uses.
- Have the dialog consistent with the area and/or time your film takes place. A Massachusetts fisherman speaks differently from a New York taxi driver or a Hollywood parking valet.

- Dialog should reflect the character's emotional state.
- Dialog—at times—should reveal conflict.
- Be aware that motion pictures are a *visual* art form; what your character says is not as important as what your character thinks or feels. Choose camera-trained actors who are able to express thoughts and emotions in a subtle way.
- Let your dialog reveal emotion. Permit differences in the way your characters:
  1. Comprehend and look at things
  2. Think and feel

Don't ever forget about a dialog's emotional content.

Dialog is not easy to write. I cannot stress enough that it should *speak well*. Quite often, lines that read well may sound stilted and too polished once actors speak them. Ask your writer to rewrite dialog. The rewrite should take place during preproduction. Please do not surprise your actors with rewritten pages the moment they enter their dressing rooms.

Once dialog resembles everyday speech, it should reveal:

Character
Emotional state of mind
Emotional relationship
Conflict (if appropriate)

TRAITS AND MANNERISMS

(Characterization)

Most scriptwriters stress a character's traits and mannerisms. Some writers are very specific in the way they describe their characters. William may see an old man like this: "Jonathan stands like a tree that refuses to be felled. His eyes, in a face beaten by years in sun, wind, and biting snow, search the horizon with still-youthful vigor. Only his hands, now gnarled from hard work, reveal the ebbing strength of his body." And Elinor may state: "The old man, Jonathan, tries to keep going, but his body is ready to give up."

Regardless how much—or little—characterization a writer bestows upon his script, my advice is, forget about characterization for now. Go back to characterization once you are ready to cast the film. At this point go easy on what the writer has written about looks, traits, and mannerisms, and leave yourself open to whatever the actors' interpretation may be. Writers notoriously are not the best actors, and their character descriptions might lead you down the primrose path of cliché. But once you are involved in the casting process, *do* take traits and mannerisms seriously. After all, believable and creative characterization helps to shape the visual impact of your motion picture.

Traditionally, characterization provides the audience with clues to:

Physical traits/mannerisms
Personal traits/mannerisms
Emotional traits

Well, let this be all for now. In chapter 5, "The Director and Actors," we will tackle the problems of characterization.

Screenplay Development

The director's real homework starts once the script has been structured, and possibly rewritten, to your satisfaction. You will work on:

- Shooting script
- Once locations have been set:
    1. Continuity (in cooperation with the script supervisor*)
    2. Shooting and camera setup list.

And always keep in mind: you, the director, are responsible for the artistic and budgetary viability of your motion picture.

The following is a scene from *Jungle Trap*. It shows the script as written by the screenwriters.

---

*The script supervisor is responsible for taking notes throughout the production. These notes include directional notes such as "camera left, look" or "carried purse on right arm." Directional notes are important for the matching of shots in various angles (one shot flowing logically and smoothly into another).

Interior Hotel. Hallway. Night.
(On CHRIS and OBY, the bellhop, approaching. OBY carries CHRIS's duffel bag. He opens a door and motions CHRIS to enter.)
Interior Hotel. Chris's Room. Night.
(CHRIS enters, followed by OBY. OBY places the duffel bag on her bed. CHRIS stands motionless as her eyes travel from corner to corner of the room.)

OBY: I hope the room meets with your approval, madame.

CHRIS: Yes, it does. Thank you.

(She takes off her shoulder bag. She opens it. But suddenly her attention is caught by some perfume bottles and makeup items on the dressing table.)

CHRIS: But someone . . . apparently . . . lives here.

(OBY smiles. It is a plastic, half-mocking, half-threatening smile.)

OBY: Living is a metaphor . . . the idea is an abstraction.

CHRIS: Remove these things, please.

(OBY walks over to the dressing table. He collects perfume bottles, powder box, and lipsticks. Again he smiles.)

OBY: Living is . . . relative.

(By now CHRIS, searching through her shoulder bag, has found a dollar bill. Ready to hand it to OBY, she turns. But OBY has disappeared. In his place a rocking chair rocks back and forth gently. CHRIS closes her eyes. As she opens them, the rocking chair has disappeared. OBY, hand outstretched, smiles at her. CHRIS hands him the dollar bill.)

CHRIS: I seem to be seeing things . . . I'm exhausted.

OBY: Your journey was long and arduous.

(He pockets the money.)

OBY: Merci, madame.

(OBY leaves. At the door he turns.)

OBY: Dinner will be served at eight o'clock.

CHRIS: Thank you.

(Tired to her bones, she sits on the bed. She opens the duffel bag, and as she does, her gaze travels to the dressing table. Sparkling and glistening tauntingly, the perfume bottles and makeup items are back on the dressing table. CHRIS closes her eyes. As she opens them, she sees the makeup items are gone.)

CHRIS: I'm seeing things . . . Well, I better start unpacking. Hope they don't expect me to dress for dinner.

(She pulls some slacks and shirts out of her duffel bag. All of a sudden there is a puzzled expression on her face. She digs deeper into the bag, gets hold of something, pulls it out. A shrunken head grins at her. CHRIS stifles a scream as laughter echoes softly through the room.)

The following is the same scene after the director—at times helped by the screenwriter—has written the visual translation of the original script.

Interior Hotel. Hallway. Night.
300* *(On CHRIS and OBY, the bellhop, approaching. OBY carries CHRIS's duffel bag. He opens one of the doors and motions CHRIS to enter.)*
Interior Hotel. Chris's Room. Night.
(Note—Light plot: soft, almost diffused basic lighting, contrasted by slashing shadows and bright highlights on the dressing table.
301 *(CHRIS enters. OBY follows her. Pan with him as he walks to the bed and places CHRIS's duffel bag on it. Smiling a plastic, half-mocking, half-threatening smile, he turns to CHRIS.*
302 *Pull in on CHRIS. Medium Shot. She looks around.*
303 *CHRIS's point of view [POV]. The bed, shadows slashing across it. Hand-held camera to dressing table and the mirror. OBY's reflection hovers like an evil shadow.*
304 *Back on CHRIS. A slight shiver runs through her body. She crosses her arms protectively. But then, lifting her chin, she forces herself to calm down. Immediately something else catches her attention.*
305 *CHRIS's POV. The open window, curtains moving slightly in the night breeze [hand-held camera].*
306 *Back on CHRIS, Medium Shot, then Pull Back.)*

---

*Three-digit numerals preceding directions refer to camera setups.

Voice-over (VO) OBY: I hope the room meets with your approval . . .

(OBY *steps into frame.*)

OBY: . . . madame.

(CHRIS's *eyes are still focused in the direction of the window.*
[NOTE—Watch eye level and direction])

CHRIS: Yes, it does . . .

(*She turns to* OBY.)

CHRIS: . . . thank you.

(*Searching for a tip,* CHRIS *opens her shoulder bag, but—again—she becomes distracted.*)

307 (CHRIS'S *POV. Hand-held camera on dressing table. Bright highlights glitter on perfume bottles, on a powder box, and on two or three* opened *lipsticks.*

308 *Back on* CHRIS *and* OBY.)

CHRIS: But someone . . . apparently . . . lives here.

OBY *(smiles):* Living is a metaphor . . . the idea is an abstraction.

CHRIS: Remove these things, please.

309 (*Pan with* OBY *as he walks to the dressing table.* OBY *collects the makeup.*)

OBY: Living is . . .

(*Pan with* OBY *as he walks back to where* CHRIS *stands.*)

OBY: . . . relative.

(*By now* CHRIS *has found a dollar bill. She turns to* OBY.

310 *Tight Medium on* CHRIS, *startled.*

311 CHRIS's *POV.* OBY *has disappeared. In his place a rocking chair rocks back and forth gently. We hear a slight creaking sound. Flash cuts: hand-held camera [NOTE—For editing: flash cuts increase in speed]*

312 *On* CHRIS

313 *On rocking chair*

314 *On* CHRIS

315 *On* OBY, *extreme closeup [CU]. He smiles.*

315A *Low angle on* OBY

315B *High angle on* OBY

315C *Zoom Shot on* OBY, *and hold on* OBY. *His voice seems to come from far away.)*

OBY: Your journey was long and arduous.

316 *(Back on* OBY *and* CHRIS. *She hands him a dollar bill.* OBY *pockets the money.)*

OBY: Merci, madame. Dinner will be served at eight o'clock.

*(*OBY *walks out of frame. Pull Out as* CHRIS *walks toward the bed. Suddenly she stops, her body tenses.*

317 CHRIS's *POV. The dressing table. The makeup items are back [hand-held camera]. The perfume bottles glitter harshly.*

318 *Back on* CHRIS. *First puzzled, then frightened.*

319 *Back on the dressing table. It is empty [hand-held camera].*

320 *Pan with* CHRIS *as she walks to the bed, flops down on it. For a beat she sits motionless, hands folded in her lap, head down, her back rounded. Then she stretches, and—every movement showing how tired she is—she opens her duffel bag. She yawns, curls up next to her duffel bag.)*

CHRIS: Hope they don't expect me to get dressed for dinner.

(Grinning to herself, she stretches again and finally begins to pull some clothes—slacks and shirts—out of the bag. She digs deeper into her bag.)

CHRIS: Where is my . . .

(She continues searching for something.)

CHRIS: . . . must have forgotten it. So what . . .

(She digs deeper into her duffel bag. Stops. She reaches for something, and—a puzzled expression on her face—begins to explore it.

321 CU *on* CHRIS's *hand holding an item.*

322 *Tight Medium as* CHRIS *pulls something out of her duffel bag.*

323 *Shock Zoom on a shrunken head, grinning in* CHRIS'S *hand.*
324 *Medium Shot on* CHRIS. *Still holding the shrunken head, she stifles a scream.*
    Soft laughter echoes through the room.)

As you compare the visual script with the original script you will notice:

• On the page the visual script appears longer than the original script. Don't worry that your film may run over the cost-effective ninety minutes' length. On-screen minutes are based upon the original script, not the visual script.

• The dialog was not changed. It was lean and precise to begin with, but has been *integrated* with camera and actors' movements. Chris's lines about "seeing things" have been omitted and replaced with visual elements.

• All visual elements were expanded upon.

• Camera movements and setups plus the appropriate numbers have been decided upon and written in. Many directors do not add numbers and camera setups at this time, but work on the script's visual elements only. They prefer to write a more extensive shot list (shooting script).

This particular scene does not require intricate camera moves. I felt the otherworldliness had to be created by Oby's smile and a lighting plot that contrasted soft basic lighting with harsh shadows and burning highlights. Since this scene did require a lengthy light setup, I saved time by going easy on camera moves and setup, and by using a hand-held camera whenever possible.

Shooting Script

(Combined Shot List/Camera Setup List)

Do not write your shot list until you have your locations contracted. Once you have your locations, you may be forced to adjust or simplify some elements of your shooting script. Now is the time to work closely together with your cinematographer, as you pay close attention to the *time element* involved in shooting each scene:

- How much time is required to set up the basic light plot for a location?
- How much time is required to adjust lights for each camera setup?
- How much time is required to shoot each segment of every scene?
- Have you allowed plenty of rehearsal time for intricate actor-camera moves?

For you, the beginning director who will, most likely, begin your career directing a low (very low)-budget film, it is imperative that you set a brisk—but achievable—time schedule for each shooting day.

I recommend that you neither stress out your actors and crew by breathing down their necks, nor lose authority by permitting too leisurely setups. For a nonunion film the following time schedule should work well:

7–9 A.M.	Setup time.	Lighting crew, prop and set crew setup. Makeup for actors. AD works with actors on lines. Director and cinematographer discuss day's work. Consult with script supervisor.
9 A.M.–2 P.M.	Shoot	
2–3 P.M.	Lunch break	
3–8 P.M.	Shoot	

Such a strenuous shooting schedule applies to the nonunion, weekend shoot *only*. If you are to shoot five days in a row you'll have to readjust your schedule to a somewhat easier pace. A union film (SAG [Screen Actors Guild] actors but nonunion crew) has schedule requirements (meal penalty, overtime, TDY*) that change somewhat from area to area. In case you are shooting a SAG film, have your production manager check out individual requirements.

---

*TDY stands for "temporary duty," a military expression that has become popular in the film industry. It is used to describe travel, lodging, and meal expenses en route to locations and sometimes on location as well.

SHOT LIST

The following shot list (shooting script) shows the various camera setups and camera moves needed in the scene. In this scene we have four camera setups. Setup I is at the door, setup II is at the dressing table, setup III refers to the hand-held camera sequence, and setup IV takes place at the bed. As you will notice, the camera setup numbers are not in consecutive order; they do not follow the scene's logical flow, but take into consideration only where the action takes place. For example, camera setup I (at the door) begins with Oby's and Chris's entrance and ends with Oby's exit—that is to say, includes all action taking place at the door.

Camera Setup I   (one hour)

301   *(OBY and CHRIS enter room*
302   *Camera moves in on CHRIS*
304   *On CHRIS*
306   *On CHRIS. Camera Pull Back.*
308
310
312
314
318
316
308   *On CHRIS and OBY—Pan as OBY walks to door.)*

Camera Setup II   (dressing table)   (one hour)

303
317
315
309   *(Pan with OBY as he goes to dressing table.*
311   *On rocking chair*
313   *On rocking chair)*

Camera Setup III   (hand-held on OBY)   (a few minutes)

315, 315A, 315B, 315C

Camera Setup IV   (bed)   (one hour)

316   *(Pan with* CHRIS *as she walks to the bed.*
320
322
324
321   *CU on item in duffel bag.*
323   *Zoom Shot on shrunken head.)*

The Director

and the

Budget

Motion picture budgets have skyrocketed during the past few years. A budget of $40 million for a production mounted by a major studio sounds quite reasonable these days. Before we discuss your budgetary responsibility as a beginning director, it might be beneficial to scrutinize your film's distribution possibilities.

Distribution of Small Films

It is more than unlikely that you will be entrusted with a budget that carries a $5 million tag. Your film, if you are fortunate, will have to be produced on a budget of, say, $250,000 to $500,000. While such an amount sounds adequate for a small film, it is, in actuality, hardly sufficient to produce a film sellable in today's market. There are many small, artistically and technically excellent films around, as well as a host of mediocre action and horror films. These are the projects that will give you your first chance to direct. While a few of these films will enjoy a short theatrical distribution in the United States, the majority will never do so.

Escalating advertising and promotional costs are the reason behind the theatrical nonexistence of small films. Typically one third of the cost of a film has to be earmarked for promotion. About $10 million for a major studio production, and from $500,000 to $2 million for the average small, independently distributed film, are considered to be reasonable advertising (PR) budgets.

But don't despair, don't give up your dreams of producing and directing your film. A small but healthy overseas market exists for your product. Admittedly, Japan, France, England, Canada, and Germany are not very receptive to small independents. But other European territories as well as Africa and the Far East provide a number of enthusiastic buyers, who look for the Hollywood label (United States–produced films) but are unable to spend a great deal of money. (The producer doesn't have to worry about language barriers. The respective buyers will dub the film, but the producer has to supply the buyers with sufficient numbers of black-and-white "stills" for lobby display and promotion.) Films are bought for theatrical as well as TV release, and for the lucrative video rental market. During the past few years Africa and the Far East have seen an explosion in the latter market and are looking for action, adventure, and horror films.

If a low-budget film is fortunate enough to find a small domestic theatrical* distribution company that will book it on a limited run (a week here, another week there), this film will make more money in the foreign market than would the U.S. theatrical undistributed film, and it has a good chance to be picked up by one of the bigger domestic video rental distributors. At times small independent distributors, counting on the lucrative video rental release, are ready to lose money on the limited theatrical run of a picture. Without domestic theatrical release a small, low-budget film has little chance to interest a big video rental distributor. It may, however, be lucky enough to be accepted by one of the small ones.

The point I wish to make is this: do not set your hopes on your film's breaking box office records. (Yes, I have heard about "sleepers"—they are rare, very rare exceptions.) Don't expect your film to become a success, even a mild one, but be happy and satisfied if it finds some overseas distribution and a small niche among the domestic video rental releases. If you think about the many pictures remaining on the shelf, you may consider yourself fortunate to have your film out, have it compete with others, and have it

---

*"Theatrical" refers to exhibition in motion picture theaters.

make your name known a little. Who knows—somewhere down the line you may be directing a major picture for Columbia, Universal, Warner Brothers, or Paramount.

Budgets for Small Films

And now to the other side of the coin. A budget of even $250,000 may be out of line for you. You have no way of ever raising such an amount.

Don't give up.

A budget of this size refers to a film shot on 35mm raw stock, or as it is commonly called in the industry, a "35 film," but a sellable film shot on tape can be made for a fraction of that amount. To be honest, a taped film will be made for *home video use* only. And again, to be honest, the video rental distributors are still shying away from taped features. Still, if your film is artistically and technically sound, you will be able to interest some foreign video rental buyers and one or another of the small domestic home video distribution companies. (We will learn more about taped feature films later in this chapter.)

Remember, it is important to get your film *out in the market.* Don't sit at home thinking, "I hope I get a budget," or "I wish I knew some investors," or even worse, "One of these days . . ." *Get out and do your film!*

It is a sad truth that whenever a motion picture—regardless of the size of the budget—runs "over," the director has to take the blame for it. It doesn't matter that the film went over budget because the star—being late, requesting too many takes—held up the shooting schedule, or the producer had not done his or her homework, or unforeseen expenditures were unavoidable. The truth is, *all* accusing fingers will point at you, the director. It is, therefore, a good idea to become familiar with the budget items directly—at times indirectly—under your control:

Camera rental	Special effects
Raw stock	Actors
Editing	Stunts
Locations	

Discuss costs with the producer and agree on sums to be spent. Please don't join the ranks of those directors who firmly believe that the producer, being a money machine, has unlimited funds at his or her disposal.

CAMERA RENTAL

You'll save a great deal of money by utilizing weekend rates. Have your equipment (camera, lenses, magazines, tripod, sound and light equipment, etc.) picked up on Friday after 5 P.M., and return it before 10 A.M. Monday morning. If you are — and most likely you will be — on a tight budget, weekend rates are heaven sent. Ask your cinematographer to arrange for equipment rental, since he or she knows the rental places and is familiar with their equipment. Needless to say, all items must be returned *before* 10 A.M. Monday, or you'll have to pay for another day's rent. And don't forget to reserve your equipment about four weeks ahead of your first shooting day.

Make certain that the producer has arranged for equipment insurance. Any camera damage for which the production company has to pay will skyrocket your budget.

Do *not* permit a crew member to attempt any repair should equipment break down. The production company will be held responsible for damages resulting from the repair attempt. For this very reason it is imperative that you obtain the name and *home* telephone number of the rental house's owner or manager. In case of equipment breakdown, the rental house is responsible for the exchange, and the exchange has to take place *quickly.*

Make certain that the cinematographer has all the necessary items such as lenses, filters, magazines, etc. needed for the weekend shoot. You do not wish to waste shooting time while the production assistant rushes back to the rental house to pick up a forgotten item. At times, rather than wait, find alternative ways of shooting.

Before taking the camera out, have your cinematographer check it out thoroughly. Ignore any claims the rental house makes as to previous tests and equipment reliability.

- Check for camera scratches and light leaks by running a small amount of film through the camera and examining the *undeveloped* film for scratches.

- Focus a strong light on the *loaded* camera and develop the raw stock to show any light leaks in the equipment. This, of course, has to be done days ahead of your first shooting date.
- Check for blurred projection. In this case the camera shutter is out of synchronization.
- If the film goes in and out of focus, something is wrong with the camera's pressure plate.
- When using more than one camera check that individual frames and sprocket holes match. If they do not, the frame line will jump during the projection of the edited film.

Check microphones and recorders for any unusual noise. In editing most difficulties arise because of poor sound quality.

Reserve your expensive 35mm BL sync camera for dialog scenes only. Dialog scenes should take place on interior shots (indoors), where the sound environment can be controlled. If you must shoot a lengthy dialog exterior (outdoors), you will have to contend with unwanted sounds disturbing the scene. You should be able to correct some (not all) of them during the editing process by adding canned (recorded) sound that is in harmony with the environment. You may add traffic if the dialog takes place at a street corner, the roar of surf for your beach scene, and have birds chirping whenever you film a romantic garden scene. A more cost-efficient way, nevertheless, is the use of rear projection. (We will discuss rear projection a little later.)

If you are faced with a short dialog scene, you may decide to shoot MOS (without sound)* and dub the dialog in later; you do this by cutting "loops" of the actor's lines, which the actors must be able to lip-sync, and that are then edited in later. I would recommend this technique only if you have to loop a word here and there, since there is a noticeable difference between sync and looped sound.

For any scenes that require very little or no dialog, you will do well to use a nonsync camera. Such a camera is far less expensive than the BL sync camera, and you save setup time by eliminating the sound equipment.

---

*In the early thirties a German director used to say "motion, *mitout* sound," thus the term MOS.

THE THREE-CAMERA SYSTEM

If you are faced with tricky action shots (fights, car chases, car crashes, etc.), then—but only then—is the time ripe to rent three cameras. Forget about the fact that major productions use the three-camera system whenever the spirit moves them. Let me remind you, the three-camera system should be used for *action* scenes only; then, of course, three cameras are mandatory, since you may have only *one* chance to get a certain moment on film.

But let me explain why (besides the cost) the three-camera system won't work for you, the beginning director:

Three cameras are set up to shoot simultaneously a Full Shot, a Medium Shot, and a CU. Generally speaking, this does not work well, since actors move differently in each shot. The actor has sufficient space for movement in a Full Shot, less in a Medium Shot, and very little—if any—in a CU. Also, the actor's facial expression is far more subtle in the CU than in the Medium Shot.

The Full Shot, Medium Shot, and CU camera setups are effective for fight scenes. Most fight scenes are combinations of numerous *very short* takes, and you will use Neutral Shots (closeups of faces, fists, knives, etc.) to transit from one shot to the next.

For action scenes (car hits, car tumbling down a cliff, car exploding, etc.) you will set up your cameras at various angles. One camera shoots the action from front, the other two cameras shoot from the sides. Since none of these shots match in terms of direction (we will discuss camera movement and direction in Part II), this technique does represent an editorial problem, which you may overcome easily by adding Neutral Shots, such as CUs of faces, hands gripping a steering wheel, or a foot pumping brakes.

For three-camera shots you will rent an inexpensive non-sync 35mm combat camera.

RAW STOCK

Unexposed film is called raw stock. One minute of film takes ninety feet of 35mm raw stock and forty-five feet of 16mm raw stock. Add to that the ensuing lab costs (developing and 1 light work print, which is used to edit the rough cut), and raw stock constitutes a major expense.* Many beginning directors and producers are fond of shooting 16mm or even Super 8mm. I would like to discourage this practice. Of all the films I produced I shot only one in 16mm, and it was the one film that turned out to be a headache.

Granted, if you shoot 16mm you'll save on raw stock and lab cost. Granted, you can blow up a 16mm print into a 35mm print (not inexpensive), but there is always the chance that such an answer print will look grainy, and unless you have framed your 16mm meticulously, you'll be faced with very unattractive empty spots on either side of the frames, since a 35mm frame is *oblong* and a 16mm frame is *square.*

SHOOTING RATIOS

A shooting ratio of ten to one (on good days, five to one) is considered acceptable for the average low-budget film. You the beginning director with only a limited budget at your disposal would do well to limit yourself to a three-to-one shooting ratio—that is, you'll shoot *three* takes for every *one* take to be seen on-screen.

Theoretically you'll shoot 270 feet of 35mm raw stock for every minute seen on the screen. All of us, without any doubt, are aware that theory and practice are birds of different feathers. No producer will tie you, the director, to the stake of the three-to-one rule. Nevertheless, the three-to-one rule is a bitter reality; three to one is all you can *afford* to shoot. Decide, therefore, how much raw stock you can expend on each scene. Action scenes do require at least three (if not more) takes—one rule of thumb is to give each action scene about five takes—but dialog scenes should be brought in in two takes. This explains why you *must* employ skilled *motion picture* actors only. Forget about the brilliant actor you saw last month at a little theater performance; forget about your niece the aspiring actress who needs a break; forget about your writer who always dreamed about acting; and do hire skilled *motion picture actors* who:

Know how to hit a mark in front of a camera.

---

*The film you have shot will be developed in the lab, then stored in a vault. You will receive a work print, which the editor uses.

Know about moving and performing in front of a
   camera.
Know about the angles they have to use when in front
   of a camera.
Know how to express thought and emotions.

Any skilled motion picture actor will bring in a credible performance in the first take. But do take a second one for security. Having only one take is too risky.

EDITING

You'll save considerably on raw stock and lab costs if you "edit in the camera." But let me clear up a common misconception. Editing in the camera does not indicate that you will shoot scenes in the same sequence as they will appear on the screen. You are, after all, shooting a professional motion picture, and not a home movie. Editing in the camera means that you *won't* follow the traditional progression of shots:

Master Shot of entire scene (Full Shot) followed by:
Medium Shots (either Two-Shots or Reversal Shots of
   dialog and/or business) followed by:
Closeups of actors and/or objects

Once in a while the traditional way of shooting has its place, even for you the beginning director, but generally you'll edit in the camera by following your airtight shooting script that lists camera angles and movements. A tight shooting script is mandatory for the smooth flow of each day's shooting. It eliminates last-minute inspiration that may cause setup changes. Discuss the shooting script at length with your cinematographer, and pay close attention to such potential problem areas as "matching" and "directions" (both will be discussed in chapter 3).

Since we will discuss editing later, suffice it to say that you should work closely with the script supervisor, during preproduction and once the project is "on the floor." Meticulously kept records will save much editing waste later on.

LOCATIONS

If at all possible, avoid travel time and overnight stays. Both bear on a limited budget heavily. Do avoid travel from one location to the next during one day's shooting. For instance: You have planned a morning shoot in front of a small town's old-fashioned courthouse. Next on the agenda—right after lunch—is a beach location where your two young leads discuss Aunt Hilda's inheritance. It takes about two hours to travel from the courthouse to the beach. So why not scratch the beach location and substitute it with a location close by—say, one of the picturesque, tree-lined streets near the courthouse? Couldn't the dialog about Aunt Hilda take place just about anywhere?

Or: One of the scenes in your film takes place in the hallway of a college; the next scene—a short one—will be shot in an attorney's office. Why load up all your equipment? Why chase actors and crew from one place to the next? Why not "dress up" a college office appropriately?

Or: You have to shoot two living-room scenes. One takes place in the Browns' living room; the other takes place in the Smiths' living room. Both families are of equal socioeconomic background. Avoid going to two different locations for your interior shots. Have your art director set up both locations in the same house.

Avoid too many exterior locations. Agreed, you must have a number of exterior shots; they open your film and help set its mood. But exteriors are time consuming. If no action takes place, and if no particular atmosphere is needed, why not buy stock shots for your run-of-the-mill Establishing Shots of a place?

Avoid night shots. Night shots do require more equipment, including a generator, and are time consuming to set up. Still, night shots do add considerably to a film's mood, especially a suspense or horror film. Fortunately, the problem of expensive night shots can be overcome by shooting "day for night." All you need are special filters and plenty of sunshine, for it is the sunshine that translates to the most gorgeous moonlit night on the screen. Needless to say, if you want dark corners and threatening shadows to create a mood of apprehension, you have no other choice but to opt for a nighttime shoot. In case you need rain, you can rent a rain machine; if you hanker for fog, you can choose from a number of fog makers on the market.

By all means *do* utilize expensive locations, may these be a movie ranch for your action and car chase scenes, or the fabulous interior of an old mansion. Do not skimp on picturesque locations; they do add production value to your film, and they hide all the other corners you may have cut. Expensive locations can, and will, give your low-budget film the air of a major production. But: utilize your expensive location in a conservative way.

Shoot plenty of Establishing Shots, moving shots, as well as group scenes on the location, but choose a substitute location for all your lengthy dialog scenes. This is the way you do it:

Exterior, Expensive Location   Have your actors move into a Medium Shot against heavy foliage before their dialog commences.

Exterior, Inexpensive Location   Place your actors in front of heavy foliage (your backyard) in a Medium Shot, and shoot the dialog scene. Note that an exterior dialog scene should be shot only if there is little or no sound interference. You may opt for an interior shot instead and have your art director set up the foliage background in a studio. But let me warn you, there will *always* be a slight problem in lighting the scene. Outdoor light *is* different from indoor light. It may be more efficient to take a slide of the foliage background at the expensive location, go on an insert stage, and use the slide for rear projection, as such re-creating the original location. I have used this technique successfully several times. On the screen it was impossible to tell where the actual location ended and the substituted location (rear projection) began.

Interior, Expensive Location   Shoot all the establishing and moving shots you could possibly use (you need these for transitional shots between segments). Bring some of your own props, such as chairs, bric-a-brac, pictures, and move your actors in front of them. Finish the take in a Medium Shot.

Interior, Inexpensive Location   Have your art director paint a few flats to match the wall of the expensive location, place your props as these had been placed at the expensive location, move your actors in front of them, and shoot. Or take a slide of the expensive location and utilize the insert stage. Another word of warning: be aware that the small fan used to keep the slides cool *does* make a slight humming sound, so you will need some appropriate canned sounds to mask the hum.

MORE ADVICE

Discourage your cinematographer from installing scaffolding, wooden or steel beams attached to the ceiling to support lights. Admittedly, such lighting is extraordinary *if* you are on a sound stage that offers catwalks, but on location you should avoid this type of lighting. Setting up scaffolding is very time consuming, and the damage that scaffolding *will* do to walls and ceilings adds considerably to the producer's damage budget. Stand firm; scaffold lighting is *out*.

Building tracks is another time-consuming habit dearly beloved by some cinematographers. Commonly tracks are built to accommodate a camera that moves back or forth, while actors engaged in dialog walk in front of it. You, the beginning director, do not need tracks, but you *do* need a cinematographer who (with the help of a shoulder harness) is blessed with a steady hand. Seat him or her on a wheelchair pulled by a grip (you can rent a wheelchair at any place that rents medical supplies), and—presto—you do your tracking shots simply, easily, and cost effectively.

Always apply for location permits. In Los Angeles and New York (and any other large city) you will apply for permits at the appropriate city administrative office. The permits are very reasonable, but they do require that the production company shows *proof of insurance*. The producer (or production manager) has to list:

Number of cars to be parked
Number of people (cast and crew) on location
Use of generator, if applicable
Special effects, car chases, stunts, gunfights

In case you film car chases and/or gunfights, a fire marshal *must* be hired by the production company. If you have contracted for a location that has no fire hydrant close by, a fire truck and driver must be provided as well.

If you are filming at an exterior location way out in the sticks, please make certain that your production company provides a Port-a-Potty for cast and crew.

Check with your production manager to make *certain* that all location permits have been obtained. You do not want to arrive at your location, only to be sent home by the police. Incidentally, you need location permits for both exterior and interior locations.

Recently, at least here in Los Angeles, an interesting money-producing game has cropped up. Suddenly from the house to the right of your location, a boom box blasts, while in the backyard to your left someone keeps a chain saw in motion. If you want to shoot you'll have to pay for peace and quiet. But the moment you wave your location permit, the noisemakers are out of business.

SPECIAL EFFECTS

We will discuss this important area in chapter 9.

ACTORS

Since actors are the director's most important, pressing, and exciting responsibility, chapter 5, "The Director and Actors," has been devoted to them.

CREW

Here we are getting into a gray and often slippery area. Theoretically the crew is not the director's responsibility. It is the producer who, advised by the production manager and cinematographer, will hire the crew. Yet it is you, the director, who is responsible for their efficiency. Obviously, an inefficient crew will cause shooting delays. You should—gently—suggest to the producer that he or she:

- Hire only well-qualified personnel.
- Not rely completely on resumes, but talk to previous employers.
- Hire college students as assistants. Give them a chance to work and to learn.
- Stay away from smooth-talking drifters, who abound in this business.

STUNTS

The producer will hire the stunt coordinator, who, in turn, will hire the stuntmen. But it is you, the director, who together with the producer and stunt coordinator—are responsible for any mishap. Insist that the producer hire a well-qualified and experienced stunt coordinator. *Insist* (as will the insurance company) on sufficient insurance. *Insist* (as will the agency that is responsible for location permits) that a fire marshal, water truck, and driver be in attendance in case of car chases or car crashes. Though it is not mandatory, insist that a knowledgeable first-aid person be on the location whenever you film chases, fights, and shoot-outs.

The Taped Feature Film

And now to the taped feature film I mentioned previously. It is possible to bring in a taped feature film for about $30,000—a fraction of the cost of a 35mm or even 16mm film. But let me warn you, even if a taped film is technically and artistically as sound as any 35mm film, you will face difficulties in finding a well-established domestic video rental distributor, for the simple reason that your taped film had no theatrical distribution. But your film, no doubt, will find a comfortable niche in the smaller foreign video rental market, and it may even get a shot at the domestic market.

For you, the beginning director, it is imperative that you have a film out in the market. So why not tape your project?

We discussed financing at the beginning of this chapter, and as you will agree, it is unusual if not impossible for the beginning director-producer to secure financing—even a sum as small as $30,000—for a project. No one, not even kind Aunt Lucille, feels impelled to invest in your cinematographic future. But you believe in yourself, your friends believe in themselves. So get together a group of skilled and enthusiastic artists (a writer, a producer, a cinematographer, an art director, some lead actors) and finance your project the credit card way, as each of you contributes his or her services and a few thousand dollars.

A tape project will expose the involved artists' names and work to the market. A tape project, if artistically and technically sound, *will* find its market. Here are the advantages of a tape project over a film project:

• Three costly items are eliminated from the start. Using ¾" tape (and this *is* the format you will use) is not costly at all. Moreover, if a take doesn't meet your standards you'll erase it and start anew. Even better, you do not have to wait for "dailies" to see your mistakes. By viewing a scene immediately, you can make corrections on the spot.

You do not have lab expenses:

Developing and 1 light print

Negative cutting

Answer print

You do not have expensive sound-lab costs.

• Lighting is not as extensive and as complicated as it is in films. You will save on lighting equipment rentals and on crew.

• Opticals (not inexpensive on film) cost nothing if done during the taping, and titles (another costly item) cost next to nothing if done via character generator during the editing process.

• Some terrific special effects and even animation can be done on tape.

But don't even dream of saving money by enlisting your faithful camcorder. To have the technical edge over other projects, you must give the picture the *look* of a 35mm film by using the very best taping and editing equipment available. You may do well to earmark the main portion of your budget for equipment rentals and editing.

It is best to stay away from renting camera, sound equipment, and lights separately. Also, who knows whether your cinematographer is *really* familiar with the rented equipment? During the first few shooting days much time might be lost in learning about the camera.

I'd suggest that you hire a package that includes not only a cinematographer and assistant—who will be responsible for sound and lighting—but also camera, sound equipment, and lights. In Hollywood such a package can be rented for about $1,200 to $1,500 per day. (You do not pay for equipment insurance.) And, of course, since you will be shooting between ten and twelve days, you will negotiate for a discount.

Find out whether the cinematographer who owns the package is versed in taping commercials, industrials, and—hopefully—feature films. Stay away from one who specializes in weddings and family gatherings; such a person lacks the experience you need.

Editing a taped film, no question about that, is expensive. Editing time, including the operator, may range from $35 to about $115 per hour. (You will arrange for a discount.) Your taped film requires—after extensive pre-editing—about fifty to seventy editing hours.

You should supervise the editing process and do the pre-editing yourself. For this purpose have the ¾" tape—adding time codes—transferred to a ½" tape. Time codes, numbers that count minutes and (in rapid succession) seconds, are the key to pre-editing. Rent a VCR that comes equipped with a counting device, and going over and over your tapes, do your pre-editing at home.

This task, nerve-racking at first, will go smoothly as soon as you have become accustomed to the insane dance of numbers in front of your eyes. You will write down:

Reel #
Number count on VCR
Time code
Scene synopsis

PRE-EDITING LIST FOR TAPED FILM

Reel #	Number count on VCR	Time code	Synopsis
R 10	211	5:7–6:28	Est. high rise
R 3	85	32:53–33:06	Lil at bus stop
		Kitchen Scene	
R 3	155	2:35–4:22	"I have good news . . ."
R 3	170	4:30–5:40	CU
R 3	186	55:06–56:02	Lil walks to corner Medium Shot

Why Low-Budget Motion Pictures
Go Over Budget

Director Has Not Done His or Her Homework.

Director Has Not Done His or Her Homework.

Director Has Not . . .   You get the idea!

Ego Clashes   A great many films go over budget because ego clashes cause lengthy (and stubborn) arguments on the set. Ego problems may exist between:

Director and writer
Director and producer
Director and cinematographer
Director and actor
Director and production manager
Actor and actor

Leave your ego at home. Know when to compromise or even give in, and when to stand firm. Don't forget it is you, the director, who helms the project. To keep the shoot flowing smoothly, try to gauge personalities during the preproduction period. Keep an ear and eye open for any personality quirks that may cause difficulties later on.

The person you most likely may encounter difficulties with is the production manager. Undeniably it is his or her responsibility to keep the show rolling, to avoid delays, and to get all scheduled setups "into the can." This responsibility naturally offers built-in opportunities for clashes. First of all, let the production manager know that while you appreciate all this help, you are the one at the helm once the production is on the floor. Recognize that it is he or she who is in full command of crew, catering, transportation, location permits, location arrangements, procuring of raw stock, equipment rental, and liaison with lab and sound lab—in short, all elements that will help or hinder your responsibility of *directing* the film. Do not permit the production manager to infringe on your responsibility. Second, win his or her respect by having done your homework, and by bringing in the scheduled setups for each day. Third, make it clear that you are equally concerned about bringing the film in on time and on budget.

Rewrites on the Set   Among the most annoying and time-wasting devices are those last-minute "inspired" rewrites on the set. Actors bristle the moment they see changes. Don't blame them. They have created a character based on the original text. Any change may make their interpretation opaque.

Rewrites on the set are especially damaging to a suspense film, in which action and dialog are so closely hinged together that changes may obscure the plot.

All rewrites should be done during the preproduction period.

Actors   Actors unskilled in motion picture acting techniques can ruin a low-budget motion picture's shooting schedule.

Unskilled Key Personnel   If any of your key personnel should prove to be unskilled or overly argumentative, you have no choice but to replace this person with one better suited.

Too Many Takes On One Scene   Know when to splurge and know when to conserve expensive raw stock. Don't expect every scene to be perfect; minor flaws—if you have shot enough coverage—will be taken care of in editing. At times, clever use of coverage may save your day, by straightening out a potential problem, such as I experienced in making one of my films:

One of our actresses, a lovely girl, had been cast for her beauty, not for her skill in front of the camera. Repeatedly she blew her lines, moved out of frame, could not hit her mark. Raw stock was wasted; time was wasted. Before things could get any worse, we took some (silent) reaction shots of her, and—and since this particular scene took place in a small restaurant— we took the opportunity to shoot many reaction shots of the extras assembled there. Then we had our actress read her lines into a recorder. In editing, her beautiful face was shown to best advantage, while her taped lines were edited over the townsfolk's reactions.

Poorly Scheduled Light Plot Setup   If intricate light plots and setups have been scheduled for the beginning of a shooting day, you can count on one or even two hours' delay. Once these two hours are wasted, it is impossible to catch up. If you are faced with an intricate light plot:

· Set up the day *before* the scheduled shot.

- Set up the day of the shot, but film at a different area of your location while the setup takes place.

Lack of Alternate Locations   Shooting outdoors, you may lose precious time if you are rained out. One rainy day may ruin your entire location schedule. Therefore, make every effort to have an alternate interior location available, but also make certain that you will be charged for it only if you actually film at the alternate location.

How to Bring in a Motion Picture on Budget and on Time

The Director Has Done His or Her Homework   After the director has, together with the writer, restructured the script and written the shooting script, the script supervisor will join them. Now is the time to start on the various breakdowns. (I am not referring to nervous breakdowns; those will probably loom on the horizon as the shooting date approaches and so many things still need to be done.)

By now locations have been consolidated, omitted, or changed, and the shooting script has been marked with take numbers. You are ready to write:

Location list
Scene breakdown
Story board
Setup list/shot list

It is beneficial for the script supervisor and the director to work closely together. If you, the director, involve yourself with the breakdown *now,* you will have a much better handle on the film once shooting starts.

Location List   First you will consolidate all scenes taking place in a specific location. Determine which of the scenes will be *day* shots and which *night* shots.

Scene Breakdown   (Continuity List) The continuity breakdown lists all information necessary for a scene to be shot. Below is an example of a breakdown sheet.

SCRIPT SUPERVISOR'S BREAKDOWN SHEET (Continuity)

TITLE: *Alms for the Past*

SHOOTING DATES: August 18, 1990

SCENE NUMBER: 19   DAY: X   NIGHT: PAGES: 35   TIME: 4 hrs

SET: INTERIOR/EXTERIOR: INTERIOR/Chris kitchen

SYNOPSIS:

Chris, unpacking, hears some strange sounds outside the house. There is a supernatural happening, a cup flies off the counter and crashes against the kitchen wall.

Ellen arrives, she introduces herself as Seymor's wife and invites Chris to a party. Chris tries to find out about the owner of the house — Inez — and the strange happenings she encountered the day before.

CAST	WARDROBE	PROPS
Ellen	Cotton dress	Bags and groceries,
Chris	Robe	teakettle, tea-bags, etc., tea-cups Duplicate cups for special effect

VEHICLES AND ANIMALS	EFFECTS	
	Cup crashing against kitchen wall (camera: slow motion) Have duplicate cups handy	

SOUND	BITS AND EXTRAS	CONTINUITY
Knock on door Sound as cup crashes against wall Rustling sound from outside Footsteps		

SCRIPT SUPERVISOR: ⎯⎯⎯⎯⎯⎯⎯⎯⎯⎯

SCRIPT SUPERVISOR'S BREAKDOWN SHEET (Continuity)

TITLE: *Jungle Trap*

SHOOTING DATES: August, 1990

SCENE NUMBER: 19   DAY: NIGHT: X   PAGES: 56, 57   TIME: 4 hrs

SET: INTERIOR/EXTERIOR: INTERIOR/Hotel, Chris's room

SYNOPSIS:

Oby shows Chris to her room in the hotel. This scene gives the first indication of the "otherworldliness" of the place.

CAST	WARDROBE	PROPS
Chris	Khaki outfit	Chris shoulder bag
Oby	Tropical helmet	Duffel bag
	Bellman's outfit	Toilet articles on dressing table
		Shirts, slacks
		Dollar bill
VEHICLES	**EFFECTS**	
None	Shrunken head	
	Chair that rocks by itself	
SOUND	**BITS AND EXTRAS**	**CONTINUITY**
Laughter	None	

SCRIPT SUPERVISOR: _____

Shot List and Camera Setup List   The continuity list leads to the creation of the shot and setup lists. Depending on the situation, you may be able to write both lists during the preproduction period. At times, unfortunately, you will be forced to write these important lists on the evening prior to shooting. Make certain that you discuss these lists with your cinematographer. Don't try to do without these lists. During shooting you will be under severe pressure, and without the lists you will be prone to forget one or more takes. Moreover, it is according to your setup lists that the cinematographer and gaffer will arrive at a correct light plot.

As you take another look at the shooting script, you will notice that each take has been numbered. Writing your shooting list, you will assemble all numbers that take place at one certain place in the scene, regardless of whether these segments will be shown in sequence.

For example, referring back to the shot list for *Jungle Trap* (see page 28), you will find four camera setups.

- Camera setup I: Facing door, left from Chris and Oby
- Camera setup II: At the dressing table
- Camera setup III: Hand-held on Oby
- Camera setup IV: At the bed

Story Board   For complicated scenes you may wish to use a *story board,* a series of small drawings that show the way your actors move and the way each segment leads into the next.

Do not confuse a story board with a *breakdown board.* The breakdown board is for the producer's use only. The information in the continuity breakdown has been transferred to a board via individually colored cardboard strips. Fortunately, the breakdown board is not your responsibility.

Production Report   Every evening your production manager (or your script supervisor) will hand in a production report. This report lists the entire activity of each shooting day. Make certain that the production report has been kept meticulously, as it contains some important information about added or deleted lines.

Raw Stock   Carefully estimate how much raw stock you will require for every scene.

Cover Shots   Don't forget to cover yourself with a number of CUs.

Actors   Use skilled motion picture actors only.

Crew   Use skilled key personnel only.

Equipment

- Check your equipment thoroughly before shooting.
- Discuss all equipment needs with the cinematographer. Too much equipment requires more crew and prolongs your setup time; too little equipment may cause delays.
- Take advantage of weekend rental rates.

Setup Time

- Do not waste time by setting up a scene requiring an intricate light plot first thing in the morning. If possible, have this scene set up the day before.
- Try to set up less complicated scenes while you are shooting at a different part of your location.
- Schedule setup time wisely.
- Use unavoidable setup delays to rehearse with your actors.

Locations

- Consolidate locations if possible.
- Minimize travel time between locations.
- Rent an expensive location for one or two days only.
- Set up a reasonable shooting schedule and *stick with it.*

Actors   Use *skilled motion picture actors* only. (These actors do not have to be members of the Screen Actors Guild but they have to be *camera trained.*)

The Director's Homework

Last but not least, a short, comprehensive look at the director's homework that—if done properly—will bring in your motion picture on time and on budget:

- Agree with your writer on the final script. Structure the final script, and if possible participate in any rewrites.
- Write the shooting script.
- Familiarize yourself with those areas of the budget that are your direct responsibility.
- Together with the cinematographer and art director, look for locations. Procure the producer's approval for the selected locations.
- Make certain that the producer has arranged for sufficient liability and equipment insurance.
- Rehearse with actors.
- Together with the script supervisor write the continuity breakdown.
- Work on the shot and setup lists. Discuss these lists with your cinematographer.
- Keep track of setup times and use these wisely.
- Each evening, check the production report and review next day's shooting schedule.
- Each day, view dailies.
- *Always expect the unexpected.* Face every problem that arises with a smile and say, "No problem at all."

Part Two

3.

Motion Pictures:

A

Visual Art

You, the motion picture director, are going to tell a story. You decide how you will relate your story to the audience, and how the audience will *see* it—that is, you'll utilize the powers of the camera to tell your story. But beware; do not decide on a certain camera move or an interesting shot because of its creative value. You have a story to tell, remember? The audience, as disappointing as this sounds, should never be aware of your creative prowess. It is your responsibility to grip the audience, to make them participate in the story you tell. Think about this for a moment: as you read a novel, do you want to admire the writer's elegant use of words, or do you want to know what is going on now and what will happen next? The same applies to a motion picture. Neither do you expect—or desire—to be awed by great acting techniques or incredible camera moves; you go to the theater to see a story unfold.

The Audience's Point of View

First you'll have to decide: from what *emotional point of view* should the audience see what is happening on the screen? As we have discussed previously, a writer is concerned mostly with creating a story via dialog and characters' actions, while you as director will bring it to life via effective camera setups and movements. (Needless to say, effective camera work, which makes *the story interesting* to the audience, won't increase your budget one penny if you have decided on camera setups *before* shooting begins.)

The term *point of view* refers not to the story's theme but to the *position* you want the audience to take while watching the story. This may be either the *omnipotent* position (a viewer who knows everything and sees everything) or the *character's* position. For the audience to be in the omnipotent position, the director will give equal importance to all incidents and to all characters, and will show actions from the hero's as well as the villain's point of view. If the audience is to be in the character's position, then it will see what the character observes and will participate in that character's emotions.

SCENE USING OMNIPOTENT POSITION

Interior Kathy's House. Hallway. Night.

302 *(On the door. We hear a slight scratching noise; it seems a passkey has been inserted. Slowly, ever so slowly, the door opens, and a* BURGLAR *slips in. He seems to be familiar with the place. Quickly he opens the hallway closet and hides.)*

303 Interior Hallway Closet. Night.

*(*BURGLAR *slips out a knife, waits; we hear the front door opening.)*

304 Hallway. Night.

*(*KATHY *enters. She takes off her coat and is ready to open the hallway closet, when a spot on the coat sleeve catches her attention.)*

KATHY: Got to go to the dry cleaner's.

*(*KATHY *throws the coat into a corner, then proceeds to the living room.)*

305 Interior Hallway Closet. Night.

*(*BURGLAR *waits for a beat, then, knife poised, he exits the closet.)*

So far, so good—assuming that Kathy, the karate expert, saves herself. Now we will proceed by placing the audience in the character's (hero's) position.

SCENE USING CHARACTER'S POSITION

Exterior Kathy's House. Night.

302 *(KATHY approaches. Nervously she opens her purse, hunts for her keys.*

303 *CU on her hands searching for the key. She cannot find it.*

304 *Back on KATHY. She looks over her shoulder to see if someone has followed her.*

305 *KATHY's POV. The deserted street.*

306 *Back on KATHY. She hunts through her coat pockets, finds the key, and opens the front door.)*

Interior Kathy's House. Night.

307 **Interior Hallway. Night.**

(On KATHY entering. She slams the door shut.

308 *CU hands shaking as she locks and bolts the door.*

309 *On KATHY. She turns on the light switch, looks around, sighs a sigh of relief. She takes off her coat. Pan with KATHY as she walks to the hallway closet, is ready to open it, but notices a spot on the coat sleeve.)*

KATHY: Got to go to the dry cleaner's.

(She throws the coat into a corner. Pan with KATHY as she proceeds to the living room.)

Interior Living Room. Night.

310 *(Pan with KATHY as she walks to her desk and lights a lamp. Pull In as she leans down to pick up some files.*

322 *Reverse on KATHY, Pull In more to Tight Medium as a hand clamps her mouth shut and a knife touches her neck.)*

VO* BURGLAR: They told me you had the file.

Looking at the two scenes (telling the same story in a different way), you can see why you should decide on the audience's point of view *before* you start shooting. Your decision has to be made while you write your shooting script.

---

*Voice-over.

CREATING EXPECTATION

Second, you will have to be concerned about planting certain expectations in your audience's mind. Take the following scene, for instance:

504 **Exterior Elementary School. Day.**
(KATHY enters the building.)
505 **Interior Elementary School. Hallway. Day.**
(KATHY enters the principal's office.)

If you show Kathy entering the buliding and then pan with her as she walks toward the principal's office, the audience expects nothing out of the ordinary to happen. If, however, Kathy has been summoned to a conference (her first job is on the line) and she is apprehensive, you should let the audience *know* about it. In this case the scene should be shot as follows:

404 **Exterior Elementary School. Day.**
(KATHY enters the building.)
405 **Interior Elementary School. Hallway. Day.**
(Pan with KATHY as she approaches the principal's office. At the door she hesitates.)
406 **Interior Elementary School. Day.**
(Medium Shot on the glass-paneled door. On KATHY looking in. After hesitating for a beat, she opens the door.)

Granted, the second interpretation of the scene is the more interesting one, but *only* if you want to show Kathy's apprehension.

Easy, isn't it? All you have to do is decide what you want the audience to experience. Alfred Hitchcock, the master of suspense, employed the character position point of view to the apex in his film *Rear Window,* when a wheelchair-bound James Stewart watches Grace Kelly searching the suspected murderer's apartment. The camera *never* takes in Grace Kelly's point of view; it shows only what James Stewart observes through his binoculars. Immediately the audience, experiencing the search through James Stewart's eyes as he sees the killer approaching, gets caught in the terror of his helplessness.

EDITING IN THE CAMERA

Your last, equally important, concern is "editing in the camera." As discussed previously, the traditional way of shooting a Master Shot, Two-Shot, Reversals, and Closeups is time consuming, expensive, and sometimes pedestrian. You will do much better to edit in the camera. Therefore you must edit as you write your shooting script. Unquestionably the statement "The foundation of film art is editing" holds as much truth today as it did when Pudovkin first stated it in 1933.*

The Eleven Basic Shots

And now we will take a look at the admittedly complicated choices of camera setup and moves you will use to create a film:

1. Establishing Shot
2. Master Shot
3. Full Shot
4. ¾ or Hollywood Shot
5. Medium Shot
    a. Two-Shot
    b. Walking Two-Shot
    c. Standing Two-Shot
    d. Reversal
    e. Over-the-Shoulder Shot
    f. Telephone Conversation
6. Closeup
7. Tilt
8. Pan Shot
9. Tracking Shot
10. Cutaway Shot
11. Pull In/Pull Out

*Pudovkin, Vsevolod, *Film Technique,* Newness, London 1933, p. 170.

I know this looks overwhelming at first glance, but these eleven shots are the *basis of directing.* You, the beginning director, must master them, in the very same way you mastered your multiplication table. There is no easy way out—sorry!

Each shot has been labeled for easy reference on the following pages. As you move on to the more complicated ones, I have added demonstration scenes. You may easily adapt the camera setups and moves given in each example to the film you are directing.

And now, let's get to work!

1. Establishing Shot

(Long Shot)

The Establishing Shot serves two purposes:

- It shows the general environment (city street, seashore, etc.)
- It shows a character in juxtaposition to that environment (lone man walking down a deserted street).

2. Master Shot

The Master Shot, very much like a filmed stage play, shows the entire scene in a Full Shot. There are no camera moves, Medium Shots, or CUs. At times a Master Shot serves to acquaint the audience with the characters participating in a scene (camera moves and various angles will come later), or it simply serves as a blueprint for the editor. Unless you are shooting a large group scene, avoid a Master Shot. It is too time consuming.

3. Full Shot

A Full Shot establishes an actor from head to toe. You may Pull In or cut from an Establishing Shot to a Full Shot in order to establish your characters' positions more clearly.

4. ¾, or Hollywood, Shot

The ¾ Shot shows an actor down to the knees. Used by directors during the 1930s, this shot is less popular today. But if you are forced to shoot within the confines of a small area, you may as well use it to establish the environment before cutting to a Two-Shot.

5. Medium Shot

The actor is the center of attention, seen from either the waist or hip up. In a moving Medium Shot the hipline shot is best, while a static shot should concentrate on the actor from the waist up. The Medium Shot has these six variations:

Two-Shot
Walking Two-Shot
Standing Two-Shot
Reversal
Over-the-Shoulder Shot
Telephone Conversation

TWO-SHOT

In a Two-Shot two actors are sitting, standing, or walking next to each other. Take great care to frame a Two-Shot correctly:

- Do not show too much headroom.
- Conversely, do not frame a Two-Shot too loosely, or you will be faced with unattractively wide sidelines.
- Because TV will cut off some of your sidelines, leave enough space so as not to have your actors partially cut off.

Next to framing, a Two-Shot presents some other problems for the unwary director:

Positioned (seating or standing) next to his partner, actor *A* obviously has to look at actress *B* while *B* is delivering her lines. Most likely both actors will turn *en profile* while engaged in a dialog. Granted that the two beautiful people just paid off their last installment on their respective nose jobs and the profiles seen on the screen are perfect, nevertheless the fact remains: profile shots are ineffective because they *do not show an actor's emotion.* Only eyes and mouth convey emotions, while the static line of forehead-nose-chin does not. In a two-shot an actor's face ought to be seen halfway between profile and *en face* (frontal facial position), at a 45-degree angle. This way the viewer will see at least some eye and mouth movements.

Once a 45-degree angle has been set, watch the eye line. If actor *A* is taller than actress *B*, *A* has to look down and *B* has to look up.

Since any dialog shot in a Two-Shot appears static by nature, actors should be encouraged to *face* the camera every so often. This, of course, should be done in a natural, never forced, way:

- During the actor's lines.
- While listening to a partner.
- During silent (reflective) moments.

I admit, all of the above seems a little complicated. But don't worry, any skilled motion picture actor who is well versed in on-camera techniques won't have any difficulty with Two-Shots.*

WALKING TWO-SHOT

The same on-camera acting techniques apply to the seated or Walking Two-Shot. In addition, actors should be made aware that they have to walk together closely on a straight line, and avoid wobbling or weaving back and forth. Often during a Walking Two-Shot actors are required to stop, continue their dialog, and then move on. Here are some points you may advise your actors about:

*How to Audition for Movies and TV, by Renée Harmon (New York: Walker & Co, 1992), will give you a clear enumeration of motion picture acting techniques.

- Move into your Reversal Shot (see page 65) smoothly by counting how many steps you will have to take to hit your mark.
- Move out of your Reversal smoothly by stepping out on the foot closest to the camera.
- Know where your marks are. Do not omit or add any dialog, since the grips pulling the camera depend on your hitting your mark *precisely* and/or stopping or commencing to walk on a specific *word.*

STANDING TWO-SHOT

Whenever you are faced with a lengthy, possibly boring but necessary exposition through dialog, you'll choose a Walking Two-Shot. Whenever you do not have the space for one, then you may do well to decide upon a Standing Two-Shot and *move your actors around.*

A Standing Two-Shot looks more natural if you place actor A (Archie) facing the camera and actor B (Babs) in a 45-degree profile position.

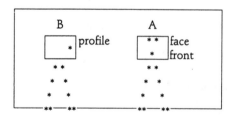

The following scene provides an example of a Standing Two-Shot:

Interior Archie's Living Room. Night.

687 (ARCHIE, *facing camera, waits for* BABS *impatiently.*)

ARCHIE: I have ordered the limo for precisely seven o'clock . . .

(BABS, *in full evening attire, walks into the frame. She stops close to* ARCHIE *positioned at a 45-degree angle.*)

ARCHIE: You know how angry my parents are whenever we're late.

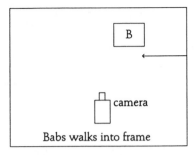

Babs walks into frame

BABS: Too bad. Let them wait.

(Pan with BABS *as she walks to an antique chest of drawers. She picks up her evening bag, and looking into the mirror, she adjusts her hair.)*

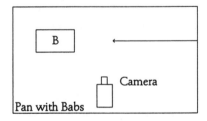

Pan with Babs

BABS: They have nothing else to do. You better be glad that I agreed . . .

(Archie walks into frame.)

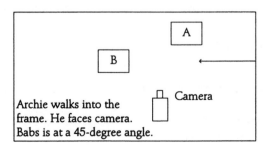

Archie walks into the frame. He faces camera. Babs is at a 45-degree angle.

BABS: . . . to spend a boring evening with those two ancients.

(Now both are in a Two-Shot and the argument begins.)

REVERSAL

In a Reversal Shot two actors are *facing* each other. Reversals should present no difficulties if you have worked them out during your homework session. Just as in the Two-Shot, it is important that actors *do not* look at each other. Have actor A look at actress B's ear that is closest to the camera, and vice versa. You will shoot actor A's lines while actress B delivers her lines off-camera. Then you will go through the same process with actress B. This is not quite as easy as it may sound, but being forewarned about some hurdles, you should have no difficulties:

- Shoot plenty of reaction shots and VOs (voice-overs) of the actors' lines.
- Remind your actors to take two beats (each beat consists of counting "one thousand and one") before answering their partners. Later you will need this time lapse for smooth editing.

In a Reversal Shot you have to keep the direction consistent. If actor A looked to the *right,* he must look to the *left* in the Reversal Shot. Actress B, who looked to the *left,* must look to the *right* in the Reversal. Both actors, though actually looking in opposite directions, will *seem* to look at each other. If you keep this simple rule in mind, you will save yourself much trouble later on during the editing process.

Theoretically, for each of the Reversal Shots the lighting has to be adjusted and the camera has to be moved—as we all know, a time-consuming business. Well, not necessarily: if actor A has been placed in front of a desk and a window, it is obvious that actress B's position is the fourth or open wall, the spot where the camera stands. Leave lights and camera where they are. Do not set up anew, but have your grips bring in a flat and one or two appropriate props (make certain these have *not* been established previously), and shoot actress B in actor A's position.

There are a few things you want to remember as you edit a Reversal:

- Watch the rhythm of the scene. The cuts on each actor should be *unequal* in duration.
- Do not cut: actor A talks, actress B talks, but at times place actor A's reaction shot on actor B's VO for more interesting transitions.

OVER-THE-SHOULDER SHOT

The Over-the-Shoulder Shot is a Reversal Shot taken over the partner's shoulder. If actor A has been established at camera left, he must *remain* camera left in his Over-the-Shoulder Shot.

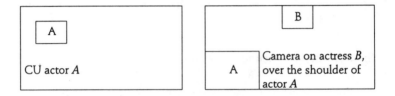

TELEPHONE CONVERSATIONS

Even though a telephone conversation takes place on two different locations, it is imperative that actors are placed in such a way as to *face each other.*

6. Closeup

The Closeup (CU) is your most powerful tool:

- Medium CU is most effective for dialog.
- Head-and-shoulder CU brings the audience closer to the character. Take care that your actor neither stiffens (shows no emotion) nor indicates (expresses emotions too strongly) for CU.

- The critical CU shows the actor's face only. It is perfect for moments requiring the expression of thoughts and feelings, but is less effective for dialog.

Sometimes you may do well to shoot your leading lady's CU first, before shooting Two-Shots and Reversals, as long as she is still fresh and her makeup hasn't caked.

Since you, the beginning director, will have your eyes on rental video distribution (the small screen), you may go more extensively for CU and Medium Shot variations, but do not be tempted to use CUs haphazardly. A CU ought to be used for:

- Reaction shots.
- Highly emotional shots.
- Shots that will give maximum impact to your story.
- Transitional shots from one scene to the next.
- Bridging awkward moments in editing.
- Ambience shots, to add mood to an environment.

7. Tilt

The camera moves in a vertical arch. You may either Tilt Up or Tilt Down. Tilts should be executed with great care. All jerky movements have to be avoided.

8. Pan Shot

The camera moves in a horizontal arc. Lead, don't follow, when panning— that is, the camera moves *ahead* of the actor. Avoid Swish Pans—the rapid movement from one subject to another—unless the Swish Pan makes an *emotional statement*.

9. Tracking Shot

The camera moves either forward or backward. As discussed previously, building track for a moving shot (Tracking Shot) is time consuming and expensive. So why not rent a wheelchair, knowing that your camera director has a steady hand, and trust your grip to push the wheelchair? Your Tracking Shots will be just as effective. Tracking Shots are commonly used for Walking Two-Shots, when actors have to explain some background information. Your audience will take more kindly to such exposition if it takes place at an interesting spot such as a park, shopping mall, or art gallery.

10. Cutaway Shot

Cutaway Shots cutting from one subject to the next are important for matching of shots and transitions.

11. Pull In/Pull Out

These shots pull in or out on an actor or an object, and follow in *continuity with what has happened previously in a scene.*

Now let's move on to the following on-screen directions, which also have much to do with continuity of movement.

Center line
Screen directions
Matching of shots (Overlap)
Transitions
Framing

Center Line

Much has been written, and many have worried, about this nemesis called the center line (or gray line or imaginary line). But if you keep in mind that the center line determines screen direction, and therefore all camera setups have to be placed on the *same side* of the center line, the concept becomes less intimidating.

Let me explain:

Actors A and B move into frame in a ¾ Shot. From there they have a dialog in a Medium Shot, followed by CUs. If the camera has been placed *in front* of the actors for the ¾ Shot, it has to be placed *in front* of the actors for the Medium Shot and CUs. If you decide to place the camera behind the actors or on either side of them for the Medium Shot, then *a new center line has been established,* and you'll have to shoot the ¾ Shot as well as the CUs from this newly established position. In other words, during the editing process you cannot cut from a ¾ Shot, where the camera has been set up in front of the actors, to a Medium Shot, where the camera has been set up to the right of actor A. Whenever you reposition your camera, a new center line has been established.

This does not, however, imply that the camera should never cross the center line. In a scene featuring a group of actors the camera will have to cross the center line every so often. The transit from one center line to the next is achieved by a *Cutaway CU.*

You won't have any difficulties with center lines if you stick to two simple formulas:

- Consecutive takes (¾ to Medium, Medium to CU) have to be shot from the *same* camera setup.
- If, because of the composition of a scene, you'll have to cross the center line, and thus establish a new center line, you'll have to use a CU to *bridge* the transition.

Correct center lines (will work for editing)

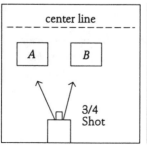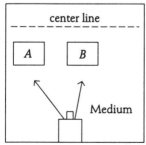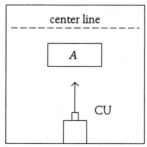

All shots are taken from the same *camera position.*

Unless you use a bridging CU, do *not* cross the center line:

Incorrect center lines (will not work for editing)

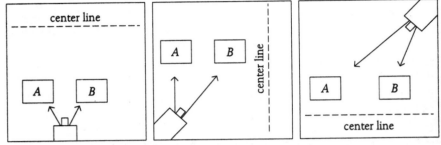

Different camera setups create new *center lines.*

Screen Directions

Screen directions apply to the correlation of camera setup and actor move-ment. You'll have to observe the center line, but you should face no diffi-culties if you keep in mind that *regardless of change of location,* camera setups always have to be on the already established side of the actor. That is, if you start a scene with the camera positioned to the right of the actor, all subsequent camera setups must be to the actor's right. If you desire to change screen direction, make a transition with a neutral shot, and show your subject frontal.

No problem, right? For the purpose of illustration, let's look at a scene that takes Jack from the office building's hallway to Mr. Marvin's office.*

CAMERA SETUP	SCENE NUMBER	ACTION
1. (To JACK's *right at foot of stairs.* *Pan with* JACK.*)*	204	**Office Building. Hallway.** (JACK *descends the stairs. He worries about seeing his boss.)*

*From *Red Satchel* (Ciara Productions, 1990).

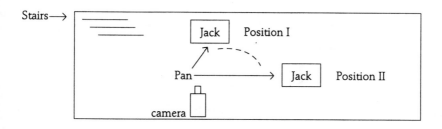

2. *(Frontal setup. Neutral. Tracking Shot.)*   205   **Different Area Hallway. Day.**
(On JACK *walking.)*

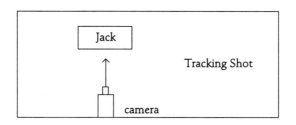

3. *(To* JACK's *left. Pan with* JACK, *as he walks to door. Hold on* JACK. *Change of screen direction. Change of center line.)*   206   **In Front of Mr. Marvin's Office. Day.**
*(*JACK *approaches the door, takes a deep breath, and enters.)*

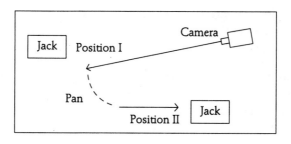

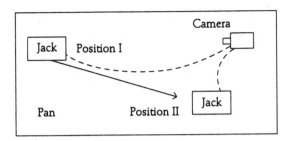

4. *(To* JACK's *left. Over* MR. MARVIN's *shoulder on* JACK *entering. Same center line.)*

207

Mr. Marvin's Office. Day.

(Head held high, a smile on lips, JACK *enters and approaches* MR. MARVIN's *desk.)*

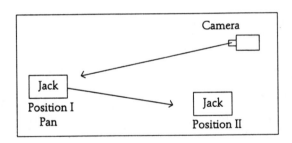

Directional shots that involve a number of different locations, and consequently different camera setups, can become confusing unless you have set up your shots (and directionals) ahead of the shooting.

Now let's assume that half hidden behind a door, Samantha—the villain—is watching our hero. Her looks have to follow screen direction, too:

205 **Office Building. Hallway. Day.**
(On JACK *walking.*
206 *A door opens a little and* SAMANTHA *peeks out. She looks over her left shoulder.*

207 *On* JACK *walking. Without noticing* SAMANTHA, *he passes by her office.*
208 *On* SAMANTHA. *She opens the door a little wider. Looking over her* right *shoulder, she smiles her evil smile.)*

Matching of Shots

(Overlap)

Considering the fact that you are editing in the camera, don't ever forget to *overlap* from one camera angle to the next. In other words, an overlap (match) is the transition between shots that depict the same action. Two simple rules are:

1. Always *cut on motion.*
2. Always *overlap* action as much as possible.

In an overlap (match) it is important to shoot the action *past* the point where it will be cut in the editing process, and *begin* the second angle with part of the action executed before the cut. This way the editor will have no difficulty matching the two angles, and the movement will flow smoothly and naturally. Great care should be exercised so that everything—facial expression; placement of props, hands, and head—will be *identical* in both angles. Take a good look at the following:

¾ Shot	745	**Country Road. Day.**
		(JONATHAN *approaches. Suddenly something catches his attention. He bends down.*
Medium Shot	746	*He bends down more.*
CU	747	JONATHAN's *POV: a glittering object.*
Tight Medium	748	*He picks up the object and begins to rise.*
¾ Shot	749	*His eyes on the object,* JONATHAN *straightens.)*

Take 746 cuts back to some of the bending movement of 745. Take 749 must be started with Jonathan's hand in the same position as in take 748.

Overlap is important in a pickup. At times a scene works fine up to a certain point only, and the director decides to pick up from there. Remember that you have to begin your second take before the point where you had to cut.

Regardless of how diligently you work on matching your takes, the danger lurks that an overlap may not work. The wise director makes certain to have enough Cutaway Shots (CU of faces, objects, etc.) to bridge any awkward moments.

Transitions

The basic purpose of a transitional shot is to:

- Transit from one camera position to the next (crossing the center line).
- Transit from one picture size to the next (never cut from a Full Shot to a CU, but always transit with a Medium Shot).
- To bridge action from one location to another.

To bridge from one location to the next is probably the most cumbersome of all transitions. Don't ever try to follow one picture size with an *identical* one, unless you *show action in motion* (Pull In/Pull Out). For instance, do not follow Tracy's CU as she sighs longingly with the CU of a beach ball in someone's hands. But consider these shots:

8 *(Medium Shot on* TRACY *sighing longingly. Pull In to CU on* TRACY.
9 *CU on beach ball being tossed into the air. Tilt Up with movement.*
10 *Pull Back to ¾ Shot as ball descends.)*

Even though the CU on the beach ball does follow Tracy's CU, both takes will cut, since—because of the Pull In and Pull Out—the transition is not static but shows action in motion.

In the next example we are again faced with two Establishing Shots featuring the same picture size. Here is the kind of transition you *want to avoid:*

Airport Terminal. Day.
674 *(Establishing Shot of terminal.* LAURA *walks into the frame. Pan with her as she walks to a window and looks out.)*
675 **Airport Tarmac. Day.**
*(*LAURA's *POV, the tarmac, Establishing Shot.)*

Boring, right? So why not work a little harder, and come up with this:

Airport Terminal. Day.
674 *(¾ Shot on* LAURA *walking. Pull In to Medium Shot.*
675 *Medium Shot [frontal] on* LAURA *walking [shot used to change directions].*
676 *Pull Back to a ¾ Shot and Pan with* LAURA *as she approaches a window. Hold on her as she looks out.)*
Airport Tarmac. Day.
677 *(*LAURA's *POV, Establishing Shot of tarmac.)*

If you're in a pinch, just changing the picture size should provide you with a satisfactory transition.

305 **Downtown Los Angeles. Day.**
(Establishing Shot of busy downtown street.)
306 **Golf Course. Day.**
(¾ Shot of RALPH *happily swinging his golf club.)*

I'm certain you've got the picture. Effective transitions are not difficult to achieve if you consider the *logical flow* of your motion picture. Here are some basic suggestions:

- Either: begin each scene with a static camera, and have your subjects move.
  Or: begin each scene with a moving camera, and have your subjects static.
- Use CU to bridge from one scene to the next.
- Vary picture size from one scene to the next.
- Pull In on one scene, Pull Out on the following scene (action in motion).

- In addition use sound effects, natural sound, and music for transitional purposes.

Framing

When we speak about framing, we speak about the composition of a frame. In other words, we speak about the pictorial aspects of a motion picture— lines that are pleasing to the audience's eyes without disturbing the story to be told. Clearly, a movie's visual composition should *strengthen* whatever the director wants the audience to observe. All of the above, I agree, sounds rather theoretical, but it is easy to achieve if you remember the following:

BOUNDARIES

Each frame (picture) has four boundaries and is divided into thirds. Let's take, for instance, the Establishing Shot of a suburban street. The pavement and a group of skateboarding children (they provide the necessary movement to the scene) occupy one third, and trees and horizon round off your composition. A tree trunk situated to the far right of your frame provides the focal point that pulls the picture together.

FRAMING PROPS

(Smaller Objects)

Framing props are important for the composition of a Medium Shot. These are used to draw the audience's attention to the *middle of the frame*. Framing props and/or objects should neither *distract* the audience nor *overpower* the actor. Do not position them in such a way that—unexpectedly—a vase seems to grow on your leading lady's head.

PLACING ACTORS

To place your actress *in the middle* of the frame is a poor choice. Always position her *slightly* to either side. Also, do not place your actor *too close to the boundary* of your frame, unless something happens behind him.

SIDELINES

Always be aware of the safe action area, also called the "television cutoff" —the part of the frame that will have to be cut off as the 35mm film is transferred to videotape. For this reason be sure to leave enough open space on either side of the frame. Be especially aware of the necessary open space when working on moving camera shots.

You, the beginning director, should never take framing lightly. Proper framing, as each shot moves into the next, is the basis for the effective sequencing of a motion picture.

Difficult Setups Made a Little Easier

We all have seen movies that unexpectedly begin to drag. This static quality often happens, one has to conclude, as soon as the director is faced with group scenes:

Table scene
Three-character scene
Large group scene
Four-character scene
Fight scene

Now let's find ways to make these admittedly difficult scenes a little easier to shoot.

Generally you ought to avoid a Master Shot, but a group scene does require one. Fortunately, the Master Shot does *not* have to be perfect. Never mind if an actor fluffs a line, or the sound of a lawn mower disrupts a tender love scene. Let the camera roll, go on shooting. The Master Shot serves only as a *road map* for you, the director. It informs the audience as to the characters involved, and it reminds you, the director, of your characters' physical position in the scene, information you will need later on as you edit the respective Two-Shots, CUs, and Reversals. Always remember, the Master Shot as filmed will *never* be seen on the screen.

For all group scenes keep the following in mind:

- Disregard the center line.
- Watch eye lines and opposing looks.
- Compose your picture *asymmetrically* rather then symmetrically.
- If possible, move your actors *and* your camera.
- Shoot plenty of cover CU to bridge as you cross center lines.
- Have lively interchanges among all characters. This may require some revision of your shooting script.

TABLE SCENE

This diagram shows a static four-character scene. All characters are seated in a restaurant booth. This suggests built-in difficulties, as there is no other way to position the actors than symmetrically.

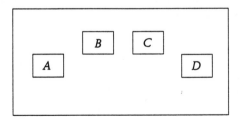

Limiting the dialog between *B* and *C, A* and *D,* or *A* and *B* will only add boredom to a static scene. If, however, you strive for a lively interchange:

A and *C*
D and *B*

C and A
B and A
C and D

and vary your picture sizes between Medium Shots and CUs, you will come up with a visually enjoyable scene.

THREE-CHARACTER SCENE

A three-character scene is most effective if both camera and actors keep moving.

315 **Interior Casino, Las Vegas.**
   (On roulette wheel CU, we hear music, laughter, and the click of the roulette ball.)
316 **Interior Claudia's Dressing Room. Night.**
   (CLAUDIA, a gorgeous show girl, sits at her dressing table. Medium Shot.)

CLAUDIA: I know my career is on the skids.

(Pull Back to include RALPH, her boyfriend. AL, her manager, a wiry, nervous man, enters the frame.)

AL: You have not one offer. Once your Las .Vegas stint . . .

(AL begins pacing. Pan with him.)

AL: . . . is over. We have to do . . .

(Pan with AL as he approaches RALPH. Hold on RALPH and AL.)

AL: . . . something about Claudia's career.

Take a good look at the *Red Satchel* scene, and you will discover:

315 *(Commences with the CU of the roulette wheel.*
316 *Changes picture size from CU to Medium Shot. It uses sound as transitory device. Pull-Back and Pull-In as well as Pan Shots give movement to the scene.)*

If for any reason—such as time or space limitations—this scene had to be kept static, and since there is no good reason to intercut CUs, you'd have to concentrate your efforts on positioning your actors in interesting ways. Diagrammed, the scene might look like this (the arrow indicates the direction of looks):

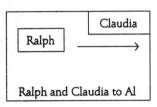

Ralph and Claudia to Al

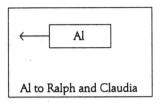

Al to Ralph and Claudia

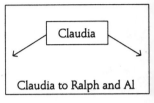

Claudia to Ralph and Al

However, if you wish to show the trio's frustration about Claudia's failing career, bring more *movement* to the scene, such as in the example following.

(Pull Out.	AL: Your name has to become a household word again.
Pan with AL *as he walks toward* CLAUDIA *and* RALPH.	AL: Your name has to be in print . . .
On AL, CLAUDIA, RALPH.	RALPH: . . . on TV.
	AL: Right, so how about my . . .
Pan with CLAUDIA. *She turns, faces* RALPH.	CLAUDIA: . . . insane suggestion?
On RALPH *and* AL.	RALPH: How about it?
	CLAUDIA *(VO):* Why should I become the victim . . .
On CLAUDIA.	CLAUDIA: . . . of a dumb, no . . .
Pan with CLAUDIA *as she walks to her dressing table.*	CLAUDIA: . . . outrageously stupid—and dangerous—jewelry heist.
AL *enters frame, he leans across her dressing table. Medium Shot.*	AL: I'll arrange everything . . .

RALPH *enters frame from the opposite side.*	RALPH: ... reporters ...
On CLAUDIA. *Suddenly beaming, she looks up.*	CLAUDIA: Paparazzi.
CU *on her radiant smile.)*	

LARGE GROUP SCENES

If you shoot large group scenes, you will do well to divide your group into segments of two, three, and four characters, and permit the scene to develop in an ever-shifting, kaleidoscopic manner. Whether you choose the three-camera setup or the traditional setup (Full Shot, Medium Shot, CU) is immaterial, so long as you arrive at a lively visual pattern and have plenty of CUs for bridging. Like the fight scene, the group scene cannot be edited in the camera. Here is an example from our "satchel throwing" scene.

(Full Shot.

Hotel Lobby. Day.
(On everyone. Three satchels are thrown and tossed, caught and thrown again.)

DR. MEEK *(screams):* A bomb ...

Medium Shot, various angles.

(On everyone, vary between designated groups.

CU.

On satchel.

Medium.

On hands.

Pull Back.

On LIL. *Frightened, she holds on to the satchel. Finally, screaming, she tosses it.*

Swish Pan.

On hands and arms, catching and tossing three satchels.)

CU.

BILLY BOB: Run ... run ...

Medium Shot.

SHEIK: The bomb explodes at midnight.

Medium Shot, different angle.	OLD LADY: That's better than bingo.
	(She tosses the satchel.)
Medium, different angle.	BARBIE: I'm going to faint.
	(Sound: The clock strikes one.
CU. .	*On clock, it is almost midnight. The clock strikes two.*
Flashes, all different angles:	
CU	*Red satchel.*
CU	MEEK's *face.*
Medium	SHEIK *tosses satchel. Sound of clock, strikes three, four.*
CU	*On clock, strikes five.*
CU	BARBIE.
CU	OLD LADY.
CU.	*The clock strikes five, six, seven.*
Medium.	*On hands tossing satchel. The clock strikes eight.*
Various angles.	*On satchels being tossed. The clock strikes nine.*
CU.	*The satchel lands in someone's hands.*
Pull Back to Medium.	*A minister, smiling calmly, holds one of the red satchels.)*
	MINISTER: Good evening, I hope I'm not interrupting anything. *(The clock strikes ten, eleven.*
¾ Shot.	*On the group, catatonic. They stare at the minister.* BARBIE *holds a satchel; so does the* SHEIK. *The clock strikes twelve. Sound of explosion.*

Cut to SHEIK, *Medium.*
Face blackened but otherwise alive, the
SHEIK *shakes his head sadly.)*

FOUR-CHARACTER SCENE

And now we will look at another scene (the arrest scene from *Red Satchel*) that proved tricky because it had to be shot within a limited area. This scene adhered to the center line, and there was *no* possibility for the actors to move. Consequently we depended on rather short takes and Pull In/Pull Out. Here is the setup of the scene:

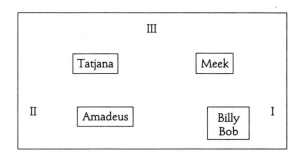

¾ Shot.

Park. Exterior. Day.
(On DR. MEEK, *looking around.*
Apparently he is waiting for someone.

BILLY BOB *rushes up to him [enters frame left]. He flashes his badge.*

AMADEUS, *entering frame right, grabs* MEEK's *arm.)*

AMADEUS: You are under arrest.

*(*TATJANA *approaches from upstage.)*

TATJANA: Shut up, that's my line.

BILLY BOB: You may remain silent,

or everything you say may be held against you.

(LIL runs in, frame left.)

LIL: Forget it, let's not waste any time ...

Pull In to Tight Medium on LIL.

LIL *(turns to camera):* We'll have only ten more minutes on this movie ... Hurry up ...

Pan with LIL as she runs out of the frame.

Cut to MEEK and TATJANA. Medium Shot.

MEEK: What are you arresting me for?

TATJANA: You are wanted for jewel theft.

Cut to AMADEUS, Medium.

AMADEUS: Open your satchel.

Cut to BILLY BOB.

BILLY BOB *(threateningly):* Please.

On MEEK and TATJANA.

MEEK: I can't.

TATJANA: Why not?

(MEEK looks at TATJANA. He knows he has been caught. There is no way out. He looks at his satchel.

CU.

TATJANA, *waiting.*

CU.

BILLY BOB, *waiting.*

CU.

AMADEUS, *waiting.*

Tight Medium on MEEK.

He sighs. He looks at the satchel again.

Tilt Down to CU satchel.

On MEEK's hands and the satchel, as he opens the satchel slowly—ever so slowly.

Tilt Up.

He opens the satchel slightly.

Pull Back to Medium.

On MEEK, opening the satchel more. He

turns his head away, he does not dare to look at the jewelry in his satchel. But TATJANA, BILLY BOB, and AMADEUS — all eager anticipation — lean over the satchel.

CU TATJANA.

Her expression changes, she is puzzled.

CU BILLY BOB.

Furious.

CU AMADEUS.

Amused.

Tight Medium on MEEK.

MEEK dares to look into the satchel. His eyes widen . . .)

Medium Shot on MEEK.

MEEK (smiling): All right. I give up.

Pull Back to include TATJANA, BILLY BOB, and AMADEUS.

MEEK: Go ahead, arrest me.

¾ Shot.

TATJANA: What happened?

BILLY BOB: Crook.

Pan with MEEK as he leaves.

MEEK: Have a nice day.

Cut Back to AMADEUS, Medium.

(AMADEUS shakes his head, then he sighs admiringly.)

Pull In on AMADEUS.

AMADEUS: Magician . . .

This particular scene illustrates the following:

• A static group scene works if it has inherent suspense.
• A static group scene requires quick cuts and constant variation of picture size.
• A static group scene demands close attention to *detail*.
• A static scene has to be built on *motive* and *reaction*.

FIGHT SCENE

Fight scenes, like large group scenes, may be shot by using either three cameras or one camera. But regardless of the method you choose, make certain that you'll have a great number of CU bridging shots of faces, fists, guns, knives, etc.

Once the characters participating in a fight have been established, it is a *poor* choice to continue in Full Shots and ¾ Shots while intercutting with a few Medium Shots and CUs. Restrict yourself to about two or three ¾ Shots *at the most*. All other angles have to be CUs and Tight Medium Shots.

To make difficult fight scenes easier to set up and shoot, it is imperative that—regardless of how fast the fight moves—you follow the logical sequence of Motive, Reaction, and Action:

A punches *B* (motive)
B sees punch coming (reaction)
B punches back (action)

It is always better to shoot a fight scene *without* interruption. Also, shoot a fight scene several times from different angles, remembering that since you will *bridge,* you do not have to concern yourself about the center line. Don't forget that a fight scene *cannot* be edited in the camera but has to be worked on in the editing room. Once you are ready to cut your fight scene, go for *short* takes that move quickly in the sequence of Motive, Reaction, Action.

The following sample fight scene is from *Four Blind Mice* (Ciara Productions, 1992).

Establishing Shot.	**Benji's Bar. Day.** *(A small, run-down place in East Los Angeles.* BENJI, *a huge man, looms behind the bar.* JOE *and* ALEX, *perched on bar stools, nurse their beers.)* BENJI: What is it you two guys want?
Pull In to Medium Shot.	ALEX: Actually . . . we are interested in a friend of yours . . . Jeff Biles. JOE: He has taken a powder. ALEX: Rather suddenly. BENJI *(laughs):* So he has flown the coop.

Cut to BENJI. *He is busy stacking some beer glasses.*

BENJI: I never squeal on my friends.

Pull In tighter on BENJI.

BENJI: You two guys better get out before I feel funny.

Low angle on BENJI.

BENJI: Real funny.

Tight Medium on ALEX *and* JOE.

JOE: Take it easy . . .

On BENJI. *Tight Medium. Quickly* BENJI *grabs the detectives' beer glasses.*

(VO) JOE: . . . you are talking to police.

On JOE *and* ALEX, *their POV.*

(Their distorted view of BENJI *as the beer hits their faces.*

On BENJI. *He grabs a bottle, smashes it against the bar.*

CU.

On the bottle's broken edge.

Tight Medium on BENJI. *Pan with* BENJI.

Lifting the bottle, he rushes out from behind the bar.

Flash: CU.

Reaction shot ALEX.

Tight Medium.

JOE *lunging at* BENJI.

Medium.

BENJI *lunging at* JOE.

CU.

The raised bottle.

Medium. On JOE *and* BENJI.

JOE *countering the blow.*

CU.

Edge of bottle hits JOE's *face.*

Medium JOE, BENJI, ALEX.

ALEX *grabs* BENJI.

JOE *gets hold of the bottle.*

CU.

JOE *punches bottle out of* BENJI's *hand.*

CU.

On BENJI *breathing hard.*

Medium on BENJI, ALEX.

ALEX *slams his fist into* BENJI's *stomach.*

Medium on BENJI.

BENJI *doubles over.*

Medium, BENJI *and* JOE.

JOE *pulls* BENJI's *head back.*

CU BENJI.	BENJI *screams.*
Tight Medium.	JOE *grabs* BENJI *by his throat.*
CU on BENJI.	*Reaction.*
CU on JOE.	*Reaction.*
Medium on BENJI, ALEX, *and* JOE.	*With one quick move* BENJI *gets loose. He grabs* JOE.
Tilt Down.	ALEX *throws* BENJI *on the ground.*
Tight Medium.	BENJI's *fist punches into* ALEX's *face.*
Pull Back.	JOE *jumps on* BENJI's *back.*
Tilt Up.	BENJI *and* JOE *roll on the floor.* JOE *jumps up.*
	ALEX *pulls his gun, points it at* BENJI.)
Cut to BENJI.	*(VO)* ALEX: Sing.
	BENJI: You ain't got the guts to use your gun.
Tight CU on ALEX.	*(Silent, he stares at* BENJI.
Tight CU on BENJI.	BENJI *stares back.*
Tight Medium on ALEX.	*His gun is pointed at* BENJI.
Tight Medium (flash).	JOE.
CU BENJI.	*He looks from* ALEX *to* JOE.
Medium on JOE.	*Silent.*
Medium on ALEX.	*Silent. He lifts the gun.*
CU.	ALEX's *finger moves to the trigger.*
CU.	BENJI *looks at* ALEX.
Tight Medium.	JOE *looks at* ALEX's *hand.*
CU on the gun.	ALEX's *finger moves closer.*
CU on BENJI.	*He hardly dares to breathe.*

CU *on* JOE.

JOE *shakes his head, he looks at* ALEX.

Medium Shot on ALEX.

Reluctantly ALEX *puts the gun down.*

Medium on BENJI.

He lifts his head.)

Pull Out to include ALEX *and* JOE.
BENJI, *hurt all over, gets up.*

BENJI: One of these days I'll get you. You know what they say about police brutality.

Finally, here are a few Dos and Don'ts that will make camera setups and movements a little easier for you. Here we go:

DOs

- If you *begin* a scene with an actor walking into a shot, Pan with the actor. Do *not* have your actor walk into a frame.
- Use Tilts as your actor either gets up or sits down. If you change picture size (¾ to Medium, for instance), do *not* forget to *overlap*.
- Light all CUs carefully. Use backlighting, and if your leading lady is past her first youth, or if she has skin problems, put silks over the lights and position umbrellas close to the lights.
- Pull In and Pull Out gives movement to the beginning of a scene.
- Unless you need an Establishing Shot, considering your film's rental video market, a ¾ Shot is preferable to a Full Shot.
- If you shoot a lengthy dialog scene that for some reason cannot be accommodated by a tracking camera, or if you film a seated dialog scene, acquire movement by having extras move either behind or in front of your actors.
- If possible, move your camera *and* your actors.
- In a seated Two-Shot, have actors *do* something—have them drink a cup of coffee, or let them doodle on a notepad, etc.—but make them *move*.
- Watch screen direction, and use CU bridge shots to change directions.
- In a large group scene, first establish the group in a full shot, then cut to individual groups. Depend on reaction shots, CUs, and Reversals. Every so often cut back to a Full Shot of the group.
- Tight Medium is best for dialog scenes.
- CU is best for reaction shots and short verbal responses. It is less effective for any lengthy dialog.

- *Always* edit in your camera as you write your shooting script.
- Fight scenes and action scenes, however, are the exception. These need to be edited in the editing room. For such scenes use either a three-camera setup or shoot the traditional way (Full Shot, Medium Shot, CU). Don't concern yourself about screen direction but have plenty of CU Bridge Shots. As you edit concentrate on short, quickly moving segments. Once the participants have been established, *avoid* lengthy ¾ or Full Shots, and concentrate on CUs, flash cuts, Tight Medium, and Medium Shots.
- In Reversals watch eye lines and the setup of each actor.
- In a Reversal have the actor *on* camera and the actor *off* camera wait *one beat* (the count of "one thousand and one") before speaking his or her lines. If there is no space between lines, you will have difficulties editing the scene.
- Always *cut* on movement, and *overlap.*

DON'Ts

- Do *not* cut from a Full Shot to a CU. Either Pull In or cut to a Medium Shot and then cut to a CU.
- In a Reversal, picture sizes should be identical. Do not cut from a Medium Shot on actor *A* to a CU on actor *B.*
- Background should not interfere with actors. Do not place your actor in such a way that a picture or vase grows out of his head.
- Avoid placing your actor:
    In the middle of the frame
    Too far to the side
- Changing from location to location, *do not:*
    Begin each scene with a static shot.
    Have an identical picture size ending one scene
        and beginning the next.
- Actors' hand and body movements should not be too fast.
- Don't fail to shoot a sufficient number of CUs for bridge shots.
- Failure to "match" might force you to substitute a bland Full or ¾ Shot for the more interesting combination of Medium Shots and CUs.
- Failure to write a detailed shooting script *will* extend your shooting schedule and *will* make your film more expensive.

4.

The

Fluid Camera

Much of a film's emotional statement depends on camera angles and movements. But keep in mind that none of these should be chosen arbitrarily. Therefore, make certain that you and your camera director are on the same wavelength, that you envision the motion picture going in front of the camera in the same way. Holding detailed talks during the preproduction period, as well as making an effort to understand, consider, and respect each other's point of view, are invaluable.

Confer again and again and again, *before* your film goes on the floor. At times the decision whether to pan or cut is the cause for distressing—and time-consuming—arguments. To arrive at a solution, consider:

• If you wish to put the viewer into the character's shoes, so to speak, I suggest you pan with the actor. In this instance the viewer moves with the character emotionally.

• If you decide that the viewer should be omnipresent, the one who observes but does not participate in the events, then a cut is more logical.

In any event the audience should never become aware of camera angles or movements. If that happens, you have defeated your purpose. The following scene illustrates the omnipresent viewer's position.

Establishing Shot. Ben's House. Night.*
215 *(A party is in progress. At one end of the pool a bar is set up. At the other end a combo plays, couples are dancing.*
216 *Pull In on* BEN *and* TED. *Holding drinks, they observe the proceedings.)*

TED: I don't think your hobnobbing with the upper crust serves your purpose.

BEN *(shrugs):* I have to. It's business, that's how I make my contacts.

*(*BEN *moves out of the frame. Hold on* TED.
212 TED's *POV.* BEN *approaches the bar.)*

BEN: Scotch on the rocks.

(On BARTENDER *fixing the drink.*
218 *Cut to* TED *observing* BEN. *Medium Shot.*
219 *Cut to* BEN, *gulping his drink. Medium Shot.*
220 *Cut back to* TED, *observing.* MARGE *[*BEN's *wife] enters the frame. Pull Back.)*

MARGE *(slightly drunk):* Hey Ted ... good to see you, haven't been around for a while.

(She looks around.)

MARGE: Take a look at all this glitz, look at all those diamonds ... Well, excuse me, I'll have to keep circulating ...

(Pan with her as she joins BEN *at the bar.)*

MARGE: I ... I ... feel like poor Cinderella ...

BEN: Spare me your comments ... please.

221 *(Medium on* MARGE, *feeling sorry for herself. Gesturing to the dancing couples, she mumbles.)*

*Four Blind Mice (Ciara Productions, 1992).

MARGE: This crowd is poison for us.

222   *(Cut to* TED, *smiling to himself.)*

And now a different scene, where the fluid camera establishes the character's apprehension, and puts the viewer into her shoes.

Abandoned Tenement. Staircase. Night.

456   *(Long Shot. Camera framing through the banister.* AHNA *enters shot. Her flashlight casts eerie shadows.*
      Pull In to ¾ Shot as AHNA *walks up the stairs. Pan with her.*
      Hold on AHNA. *Her flashlight explores the wall.*
457   AHNA's *POV. The wall. Paint peels off. Graffiti covers the wall.*
458   *Back on* AHNA. *Pull Back as* AHNA *ascends the stairs and Pan. Pan with* AHNA *as she enters the hallway. Again she stops, looks around. Tight Medium Shot.*
459   AHNA's *POV. A door leading to one of the apartments.*
460   *Back on* AHNA, *Pan with her as she approaches the door.*
      Over the shoulder, AHNA. *We notice that the door stands slightly ajar. Pull In to Tight Medium.*
462   AHNA's *POV. Shock Zoom: the door is thrown open and a shadow looms over her.)*

Editing for Logic

When we speak about the fluid camera, we also have to concern ourselves with editing. It is editing that pulls all the bits and pieces of angles and camera movements into a logical unit. The beginning director does not have the luxury of shooting every scene from various angles, and consequently has to decide on editing methods *before* the first shooting day. The beginning director has to decide on the editing method to be employed while *writing* the shooting script. There are four basic types of editing:

Subjective editing
Point-of-view editing

Invisible editing
Empathic editing

Keep in mind, both camera work and editing have to further the dramatic purpose of your film.

SUBJECTIVE EDITING

Depending on the power of the CU, subjective editing lets the viewer observe events through the character's eyes. Most likely you will use subjective editing if you want your audience to expect something to happen.

276 **Urban Street. Day.**
(Establishing Shot of a dilapidated urban street bordered by a row of run-down tenements. BOB's *car stops in front of one of the buildings.)*
277 **Interior Bob's Car. Day.**
(Medium Shot on BOB. *Leaning out of the car window, he looks up at the tenement.*
278 *CU on the tenement looming in front of him [Tilt Shot].*
279 *Back on* BOB, *Medium Shot. He hesitates for a beat, then reaches for his gun.*
280 *CU.* BOB's *POV, the gun.)*

Urban Street. Day.
281 *(Pull Back to ¾ Shot.* BOB *gets out of the car; Pan with him as he approaches the tenement.)*
Interior Tenement. Hallway.
282 *(*BOB, *pointing his gun, enters. He stops, looks around.)*

This is subjective editing—the audience has been put into a character's shoes.

POINT-OF-VIEW EDITING

Point-of-view editing stresses the *facts* in a scene. It does not attempt to interpret the characters' reaction to a given situation; neither does it put the viewer into the characters' shoes. The viewer remains omnipresent, knows everything, sees everything, and remains emotionally uninvolved.

Now let's take a look at the previous scene employing point-of-view editing.

276 **Urban Street. Day.**
(*Establishing Shot of a dilapidated urban street bordered by a row of run-down tenements.* BOB's *car stops in front of one of the buildings.*
Pull In as BOB *gets out of the car. Pan with him as he walks toward the tenement.*)

As you can tell, since the CUs (Bob's POV) have been omitted, we *see* Bob's action, but we have no clue as to his *reaction* to the event.

INVISIBLE EDITING

Invisible editing is keyed to *movements*. Each take begins with movement and ends with movement. Invisible editing is important for scenes that are static by nature, as it keeps such scenes moving.

276 **Urban Street. Day.**
(*Full Shot on* BOB's *car driving.*)
277 **Interior Bob's Car. Day.**
(*On* BOB *driving.*
He reaches for his gun.
278 *CU his hand on the gun.*
279 *Back on* BOB, *driving. He lifts the gun.*)
280 **Exterior Urban Street. Day.**
(BOB's *car stops.*
281 *Different angle.* ¾ *Shot,* BOB *gets out of the car.*)
282 **Tenement Interior. Hallway. Day.**
(*On* TED, *walking to the door. He stops. Pulls out a knife.*)
283 **Urban Street. Day.**
(*On* BOB, *walking to the tenement's front door. Pan with him, his hand reaches for the door handle.*)
284 **Interior Tenement. Day.**
(*On* TED. *Slowly he lifts his knife.*)
285 **Exterior Tenement. Day.**
(BOB *kicks the door open.*)

In this example, the audience is in the omnipresent position. Looking at the scene location directions, you will notice that the entire scene has been based on the actors' movements.

EMPATHIC EDITING

Empathic editing relies on the contrast of rhythm and *visual pattern*. This method, pioneered by famous silent movie director D. W. Griffith, uses *crosscutting* (interweaving bits of two or more scenes), *pacing,* and *emotional juxtaposition.* Here is an example:

Ted's House. Pool Area. Day.
275 *(¾ Shot on dancing couples.*
276 *Different angle on dancing couples. Pull In on a dancing couple, Pan to* BEN *watching the dancing, Pull In on* BEN *to Tight Medium. He lifts his champagne glass and takes a sip.)*
277 **Exterior Urban Street. Day.**
     (On car driving, headlights move — CU — to camera.)
278 **Interior Tenement. Hallway.**
     (CU feet descending stairs. Tilt Up to Tight Medium on TED *and hold.)*
279 **Interior Ted's House. Pool Area. Day.**
     (On dancing couples reflected in pool.
280 *Various angles on dancing couples.*
281 *Various angles on dancing couples.*
282 *Various angles on dancing couples.)*
283 **Exterior Tenement. Day.**
     (¾ Shot, BOB *gets out of his car. Pan with him as he walks toward the tenement. Hold as he stops in front of the door.)*
284 **Interior Tenement. Hallway. Day.**
     (Medium Shot on TED, *standing and waiting.)*
285 **Exterior Tenement. Night.**
     (On BOB. *He pulls out his gun.*
286 *On gun.*
287 *Flash cuts: Tight Medium on dancing couples*
     BEN *waiting*
     CU gun
     TED *waiting*

> *Dancing couples*
> *CU gun*
288   *Tight Medium,* BOB *lifts his gun.)*
289   **Interior Tenement. Hallway. Day.**
    (On TED. *He lifts his knife.)*

In this example of empathic editing, the audience is in the omnipresent position.

The sample scenes show clearly the importance of deciding on editing methods *before* going in front of the camera; they show how the same basic scene, depending on the manner of editing, can have an entirely different scenic logic. My advice is that you choose your editing methods while writing the shooting script.

It is true, the director with a substantial budget can shoot more extensive coverage by filming a scene from various angles. This allows the luxury of deciding on editing methods during the editing process. But I seriously doubt that such creative freedom will actually make for a better film. To have an extensive amount of material at one's disposal raises the danger of placing more emphasis on creative editing than on the film's narrative. I feel it is easier (and far less expensive) to check a film's pace, logical flow, emotional content, and narrative clarity via a detailed shooting script than via your Moviola. (Using a Moviola will be further discussed in chapter 7.)

Pacing

Take a good look at the previous scene, and you'll know that pacing is the inherent *rhythm* of a scene. This rhythm might be visual (seascape *vs.* hectic downtown traffic) or emotional (lonely old woman *vs.* children at a birthday party); it might be inherent in the sound accompanying a scene or in your actors' dialog. However it is achieved, pacing indicates the rate of movement, progress, and/or emotional juxtaposition. If you are working with a sufficiently structured script, and if you have worked out a detailed shooting script, chances are you needn't worry. If, however, you came up with some "creative" ideas during shooting, you may be well advised to look closely at pacing and at the logical development of your film.

It is also possible that the middle of your film, regardless of a tightly written shooting script, drags here and there. The fault might be that the scenes are pictorially too *uniform* (too many Medium Shots). If this is the case, look through your cover shots and insert a *logical* CU here and there. On the other hand, some scenes, even though well varied pictorially, seem to be static. This often happens in a scene based on a verbal confrontation. Unfortunately once the film is in the editing room, there is little you can do about it. Even inserting CUs won't help the visual flow. Maybe, just maybe, you will be able to add some variation by employing background sounds. (We will discuss sound in the concluding portion of this chapter.) If sound doesn't help, all you can do—short of reshooting, which I advise against— is admit that you have made a mistake, have learned a valuable lesson, and will remember to use Pan and Track Shots wherever logically appropriate.

If a scene seems to go on forever, check the dialog for:

Repetitions
Irrelevancies
Long, involved sentences

Needless to say, all these flaws should have been corrected in writing the shooting script, but if a "guppy" does slip through now and then, you should have no difficulty editing out the bothersome little mistake if you have had the foresight to shoot plenty of reaction and environmental ambience shots:

- If you are unable to edit repetitions and irrelevancies, show a reaction shot of a character reacting to them and VO the other character's dialog.
- If you are unable to edit out segments of long, involved sentences, show environmental ambience shots and VO dialog.

Here is an example:

The Van Burens' Living Room. Day.

134 (MRS. VAN BUREN *explains to* BUFFY, *her daughter, why she should marry elderly Richard Galen.)*

MRS. VAN BUREN: Buffy, my angel, you know that I had always—and have now—only your best at heart. Your future has been on my mind . . .

135 (*On* BUFFY, *sitting erect, sipping tea demurely. Smiling bitterly, she keeps herself from erupting with anger.*)

(VO) MRS. VAN BUREN: . . . husband, your dear father, had the audacity to leave his wife, and you, his daughter, to find happiness with a manicurist . . .

136 (*CU of desk with family pictures.*)

(VO) MRS. VAN BUREN: . . . a circus trapeze artist . . .

137 (*Cut to Mr. Van Buren's stern-looking oil portrait hanging over the mantel*).

(VO) MRS. VAN BUREN: . . . and last, but not least, I suppose . . . with the lady taxidermist. Darling Richard Galen would never . . .

138 (*Cut to stuffed moose head on the wall.*)

(VO) MRS. VAN BUREN: . . . ever show such inconsistency.

(*Back on* MRS. VAN BUREN.)

MRS. VAN BUREN: He is the man you should entrust your future to.

Strange as it may seem, even the most exciting car chase, shoot-out, or fight scene becomes tiresome if dragged out too long. I know such scenes are expensive to shoot, and no director wants to see one foot of precious film land on the cutting floor. But contain yourself; realize that the audience's attention span is much shorter than the director's. If, however, a relatively short car chase or fight scene seems too long, you can bet your last production dollar that this particular scene lacks *detail*. All action scenes must *involve* the viewer, and it is detail that does the trick. For an example, turn back to the fight scene shooting script in the previous chapter under "Difficult Setups Made à Little Easier" and look at all the detail shown in this scene.

Probably the least obvious, and therefore often overlooked, reason for drag is that the director has disregarded *time expansion* and *time compression*.

These two qualities are most likely to be forgotten in the script rewrite, and are easily overlooked in the shooting script.

TIME EXPANSION

Let's say your script states: "Adam aims and fires. Frank, hit, topples back and falls off the roof." That sounds simple, but believe me, you are faced with a difficult shot. Remember, you want your audience to cheer brave Adam, but you also want them to participate in the shock of Frank's fall. You want to make this scene exciting.

So you have rented an expensive western town location, obtained huge air bags to soften Frank's fall, have set up three cameras, and paid a sizable stuntman's fee. You are all set to get your money's worth. On the screen, unfortunately, the fall is less than impressive. It looks something like this:

101 *(Full Shot of* ADAM *hitting* FRANK. FRANK, *clutching his chest, begins to topple.*
102 FRANK *falling.*
103 *Full Shot as the townspeople gather around* FRANK's *body.)*

You are at a loss and ask yourself why the fall didn't work. The answer will be found in the fact that the fall seen on the screen took exactly as long as it took the stuntman to fall. Time expansion—stringing visual detail on visual detail—encompasses more time than it takes for the fall to be completed, and therefore makes the fall visually impressive.

Now take another look at Frank's fall:

101 *(¾ Shot. Tilt Up to* FRANK *as he clutches his chest.*
102 *On* ADAM *watching.*
103 *Medium.* FRANK *topples backward.*
104 FRANK's *POV, the townspeople looking up to him. [Camera angle from roof down.]*
105 *Medium shot [against the sky].* FRANK *begins to fall over the edge of the roof.*
106 FRANK's *POV: camera Tilt Down to the side of the building,* CU.
107 *Tilt Up:* FRANK *falls, Medium Shot.*
108 *On townspeople, Medium.*

109 *Other angle on* FRANK *falling,* ¾ *Shot.*
110 *Medium on townspeople, a girl screams.*
111 *Other angle on* FRANK *falling, Tight Medium.*
112 *CU* FRANK *screams.*
113 *Camera on rooftop down, Medium Shot on* FRANK *falling.*
114 *Full Shot, the townspeople gather around* FRANK. *[You cannot show your stuntman landing on the air bag.]*
115 ¾ *Shot, townspeople's POV,* FRANK *lying on the ground.)*

This scene has visual logic:

- Several successively closer shots make the action become larger and larger on the screen.
- The insertion (crosscutting) of the townspeople's reactions, the Tilt Up to the sky, and the Tilt Down to the wall, make the viewer participate in Frank's fall.

Remember the importance of overlapping (matching) for this and any other action scene, and cover yourself by shooting plenty of reaction shots to have on hand to bridge the action.

TIME COMPRESSION

Time compression comes in handy if unnecessary screen time has to be omitted, or if an important part of a segment is missing. Your script calls for Becky to get out of her car, walk up to her parents' house, and enter. The scene looked fine when you shot it, but looking at Becky's walk once you are in the editing room, you know it is too long. You will edit this way:

(Full Shot, BECKY *gets out of her car.*
Cut to Medium Shot, BECKY *rings the doorbell.)*

You will use the same method if for some reason Becky's walk from the car to her parents' house is fine timewise, but has been marred by a technical flaw. If (this happens rarely) you are unable to cut from Becky's car to her parents' door, then use an insert of Becky's mother watching from the window. True, reshooting should usually be avoided. If, however, you need a few inserts or reaction shots (easily done in Tight Medium or CU against a neutral background), then adding a few hours of pickups won't break your budget.

Here is another time compression sequence, which will be effective for a comedy:

408 *(On* HERCULES, *a diminutive man, carrying a huge suitcase. He stops for a moment, looks at his watch, then increases his pace.*

409 *Tight Medium on* HERCULES's *feet running. The suitcase bounces up and down.*

410 *Flash cuts: plane
                    train
                    bus
                    feet pedaling bicycle*

411 *CU on suitcase, Pull Out and Tilt Up, on* HERCULES *standing, waiting. It is hot. He takes out a handkerchief and wipes his face. He looks at his watch.*

412 *CU watch.*

413 *On* HERCULES, *covered with snow.)*

Lighting

A properly (not necessarily artistically) lit scene needs three components:

1. *Key lights* (main light source)
2. *Fill lights* to balance the shadows created by the key lights.
3. *Back lights* to make the actors stand out from the background and give actresses a softer and more beautiful facial appearance.

Excessive Lighting   Often there is the tendency to overlight a film. True, one has to take into consideration that sooner or later the film will play the home video screen. Since the TV screen does not handle shadows well, it is understandable that director and camera director alike shot with one eye (if not both) focused on the requirements of home video distribution. Yet it is the *balance* between light and shadow that creates mood, not the dimness or brightness of the entire picture.

Light Plot   The placement of lights is the camera director's responsibility, using artistic knowledge to convey mood on the screen.

Backlighting   As you and the producer peruse the many demo tapes camera directors will send in, keep your eyes open; make certain that the prospective camera directors know how to create pictures with lights. Also, they should be familiar with the fact that a man needs to be lit different from a woman. Regardless of her age, a woman should—as mentioned previously—be backlit; that is, the background should be lighter than the actress. The very best light setup for a CU uses a diffused light source from above (about 45 degrees to the camera) and a bright *kicker* light from the side of the camera. Furthermore, make certain to use a scrim* in front of the kicker, an added light source, when photographing a woman.

A scrim   When filming in natural sunlight a scrim is also useful. Natural sunlight needs either to be diffused by a scrim, or augmented by artificial light. Sunlight, keep in mind, is not easy to handle. Improperly handled sunlight will make a beautiful woman look haggard. The same goes for reflected light from a swimming pool or any other light source.

   If possible, *avoid* panning from sunlight into the artificial light of a cabin, for example. Such a shot demands an intricate and time-consuming light setup. It is much better to show your actor opening the door in an exterior shot, then closing it in an interior shot.

Rim Lighting   Directors and camera directors alike agree that the very best light source comes from above. I hope you remember the disadvantages of scaffold lighting discussed in chapter 2, and will insist on having lights placed on high stands. If your camera director wants scaffold lighting for dark scenes in a dimly lit place or even quasidarkness, don't give in; suggest rim lighting instead. If set against a dark background, rim lighting (the actor is lit from right and left) leaves an actor's face in shadows. If your actor is supposed to look for something, give him a flashlight to handle, then light the spot where the beam of the flashlight hits. This method needs close coordination between actor and gaffer, as the flashlight and the light have to hit a prop or a person *simultaneously*.

*A length of sheer silk placed in front of a light source.

Likewise, don't ever use scaffolding when filming a hallway scene, or you will remain on your hallway location forever and three days. When lighting a hallway, simply place a light source behind each door leading to the hallway. Keep the doors ajar and you have plenty of light.

If you wish to emphasize some details on a mantel or a door, place light sources at the foot of the architectural detail to beam along the edges of it.

Basic and Secondary Light Plots   As I have mentioned a number of times, changing your lighting plot is time consuming and, therefore, expensive. You will save precious production hours by establishing a basic light plot and a secondary light plot. The basic light plot illuminates the entire area where action takes place; the secondary light plot, necessitating the move of only a few lights, is used to light specific areas as needed. To simplify matters use 500-watt photo floods for these quick light plot changes. Yet the art of lighting encompasses more than lighting actors sufficiently and attractively. Lighting creates space and moods. The right lighting makes a room cheerful or, if you so desire, dismal; it makes an area seem large or claustrophobic; it can trap your characters in shadow or pave their road with gold. It all depends how lights are set up.

Using Locations

At best motion pictures reflect life experiences and show the filmmaker's conclusions about these experiences. Such experiences move either in the realm of the abstract, where the trappings of everyday life turn into metaphors, or they become the background that underscores the reality seen on the screen. In both cases, you the director will have to decide on two basic conceptions:

- Character is in conflict with environment.
- Character is in harmony with environment.

Environmental conflict should never be expressed in dialog ("To look at skyscrapers makes me so dizzy I could scream") but should be expressed *visually.* Only then will the audience have empathy with what is going on in the character's mind. With a little imagination, you won't have difficulties finding appropriate visual metaphors. Two examples follow.

CHARACTER IN CONFLICT WITH ENVIRONMENT

(MARK *has been looking for a job, unsuccessfully. By now he has given up all hope of ever working again, and he is close to a nervous breakdown.*)
Interior Office Building. Hallway. Day.
312 (*Extreme Long Shot on* MARK *walking down the hallway.*
313 MARK's *POV, hand-held camera: the hallway begins to sway,* ¾ *Shot.*
314 *On* MARK, *looking up. Medium Shot.*
315 MARK's *POV. On door, camera Tilt: the door begins to sway.* ¾ *Shot. Quick Tilt Down: the door shuts.* ¾ *Shot.*
316 *Hand-held camera, Medium Shot,* MARK *running down the hallway.*
317 *Track Shot, hand-held camera, frontal on* MARK.
318 MARK's *POV, hand-held camera, Tracking Shot, on the doors, insanely swinging to and fro.*
319 *CU on* MARK.
320 MARK's *POV: In rapid succession, one after the other, the doors close. Hand-held camera, quick Tracking Shot. Crashing sound as each door closes.*
320 *On* MARK, *Medium. High, piercing sound. He stands for a beat, then runs again.*
321 *CU on* MARK's *feet running, piercing sound increases.*
322 *Tight Medium on doors closing, crashing sound. Pull In on last door— explosionlike sound, then silence.*)
Exterior Office Building. Day.
323 *([Please note the time compression from 322 to 323. We do not see* MARK *exiting the building.]* MARK, *exhausted, leans against the front door. The silence continues for a beat, then the piercing sound begins again.* MARK *looks up, the piercing sound increases.*
324 MARK's *POV, extreme Long Shot, on a high-rise building insanely swinging to and fro. Slow Tilt as the building, threatening to crush him, leans toward* MARK.
325 *On* MARK. *Fast Tilt, up to CU.*)

CHARACTER IN HARMONY WITH ENVIRONMENT

(Today is a little girl's first day of vacation.
104 *Extreme Long Shot on* AMY *dancing in a meadow. The telephoto lens, creating a hazy background, gives an impressionistic effect. Pull In to a ¾ Shot on* AMY. *She continues to dance, as she slowly elevates and begins to float. [We will discuss the special effect of floating in chapter 9.]*
105 AMY's *POV. Extreme Long Shot on the blue, cloud-laced sky.*
106 *Back on* AMY *floating.)*
107 **Exterior Amy's House. Day.**
(On AMY, *her parents, and her dog* POOCHY, *happily loading camping gear into the family car.)*

Visual metaphors are far stronger than any verbally expressed emotion or opinion. This holds especially true as you show your characters within the *reality* of an environment. Here, you and your art director will have to work diligently to make the depicted reality conform to the reality of the characters on the screen.

Take a kitchen, for instance. Every prop—furniture, appliances, kitchen gadgets, even the calendar on the wall—has to conform to the place, time period, and socioeconomic status you wish to portray. A farm kitchen of the 1880s was different from a farm kitchen of today. And a farm kitchen in Iowa is different from a condo kitchen in, say, Los Angeles or Chicago. But a condo kitchen for a young family has a different feel from the one of a single career woman. The gadgets seen in the kitchen of a middle-class suburban home are a far cry from the ones cluttering the kitchenette of a downtown welfare hotel.

Besides furniture and props, you should take walls and window treatments into consideration. Peeling paint *vs.* bright wallpaper, subdued patterns *vs.* flashy ones, a tidy room *vs.* a disorderly one, antique furnishings *vs.* Danish modern: all are silent signals that give powerful clues about the characters occupying a specific location. Since the information given is never verbally stated, the audience will absorb it by osmosis, which is a highly effective way of dispensing information.

Use the look of your location to make an emotional statement about the characters in your film:

• A once-grand mansion, now stripped of all possessions and furnished with only the barest necessities, makes a strong statement about your leading character Lillian's financial and (probably) emotional state.

• A bedroom lovingly decorated with a chintz bedspread and matching draperies, Currier & Ives prints, and country furniture—but also cluttered with overflowing ashtrays, boots, and nail-studded leather outfits—makes a strong statement about Frances as she lolls, smoking a cigarette, on her unmade bed.

• Greg's living room, with its stacks of neatly arranged scientific magazines, extensive computer system, and graphics adorning the wall, tells the viewer immediately that his friendship with Jennifer—a free spirit—will encounter some difficulties.

You, the beginning director, rarely have the luxury of shooting in a pristine studio environment; you'll have to rent actual locations. Seldom do these locations come even close to what you need. Work hard with your art director to create your envisioned environment as nearly as possible.

Production design is one of the most powerful aspects of your film. I cannot stress enough the importance of discussing every detail with your art director. Consider a variety of design approaches, play around with them, try them out, so to speak, on the characters occupying specific locations; after all, it is the preproduction period that gives you the chance to discover and create. Don't ever give in to the temptation of disregarding the importance of environment. You may rationalize, "The actors are terrific, the script is well written, the producer has hired a skilled and creative camera director, so even if my locations are kind of humdrum, the statement I wish to make and the mood I wish to create will come through"—don't fool yourself. The audience will not pick up on mood or statement unless the environment (location) gives them the proper visual clues.

Using Sound

Sound, like locations, is an integral and very important part of your movie. We classify sounds into:

Dialog
Natural sound and sound effects
Music

Don't try to save on either sound equipment or operator. Your sound equipment must be of excellent quality (I recommend the Nagra system and Sennheiser directional microphones), and your operator has to be highly skilled, if you want clear-sounding sync dialog.

RECORDING DIALOG

Microphone placement is important. A closely placed microphone minimizes any background noises (important for exterior locations) and gives "pressure" to the actor's voice—that is, the actor's voice seems close to the audience.

Sync Sound A Nagra recorder is equipped with an oscillator identical to the sync pulse generator that controls the camera speed. In this way sound and picture are shot synchronously, or in movie terms, *sync.* During the editing process each of the camera takes is lined up sync with its corresponding sound track.

When using sync sound for dialogue, always use a *noiseless* camera. Unfortunately no camera is completely noiseless. Besides *blimping* (putting a cover over your camera), you may employ a telephoto lens and place the camera at a distance from your actors.

And then, of course, you can always hide some unwanted noise with natural sound and sound effects.

NATURAL SOUND AND SOUND EFFECTS

Sound reveals and strengthens the reality of the moment. We see the plane taking off as we hear the roar of the engines; we see the door of the abandoned house open as we hear the screech of the unoiled hinges. In other words, a distinctive sound is particular to a distinct action. Sound continuously supplies your audience with information. Even sound without action can turn into a source of information, and at times is more expressive than the combination of action and sound. This is a blessing for the beginning director, who should consider substituting sound for an action shot or special effect. For instance, the audience does not have to see Bobby throwing a football through the plate glass window. It is equally effective to hear the shattering of glass while we see Bobby's reaction.

Natural sound is an effective device to express a location's atmosphere and a scene's mood. Bells tolling, a faucet dripping, add considerably to a scene's anguish, while a fire crackling in a fireplace and the soft sound of rain on trees set a tranquil mood.

The *distortion* of sound and voices helps to express a character's emotion in a symbolic way (as we saw in the example illustrating character in conflict with environment). Amplification is an excellent device to make a sound even more disturbing. A finger stabbing on a wooden surface, voices attacking from all directions, a telephone ringing incessantly—amplified, these make a powerful statement.

Natural sound is also effective if used as *counterpoint*—that is, in contrast to the visual image on the screen. For instance, on the screen we see an old, frail lady lovingly placing a doll in a box, while we hear the happy squeals of a children's birthday party and the song "Happy Birthday to You."

Within the confines of a scene, natural sound should match from take to take (or angle to angle). Granted, this is sometimes impossible to achieve. For this reason you should *always* make it a habit to record some natural sound (ambience, also called room sound), to add where needed during the editing process.

MUSIC

Either composed especially for your film, or canned (prerecorded), music pulls your film together. Even though the audience is unaware of it, background music does add considerably to the visual power of the pictures seen on the screen. Background music:

- Conveys information.
- Serves to establish continuity as it carries over from one scene to the next, or from one location to the next.
- Serves to establish the mood of a scene or location.
- Expresses the *actor's* emotion.

At times background music is used in a less than effective way, especially if it provides just any sound, instead of giving *specific* information about a place or a situation. After all, we do expect to hear a string quartet playing some old-fashioned tunes as we view the exterior of an elegant turn-of-the-century hotel, not some insignificant elevator music.

Even worse, music can give false information. Take, for instance, Little Red Riding Hood, happily skipping through the forest on her way to Grandmother's house. Yes, *we* know that the Big Bad Wolf is hiding behind the trees. But does Little Red know? Of course not. So, if we hear ominous music accompanying her scampering, *we* the audience (who ought to be in Little Red's shoes) are misled. The music *must always match* the character's emotion. The tune we hear should be happy and lighthearted, but *change* the moment the Big Bad Wolf reveals himself.

Continuing music as well as continuing sound should be used to carry the audience from one scene to the next. Imagine, if you will, a scene taking place at a carnival. We cut from the merry-go-round to the children crowding around a booth that sells cotton candy, to a barker announcing his nerve-shattering attractions, to the glittering wheel of fortune, all pulled together by snatches of music, voices, and laughter. Now all these sounds will continue, diminished of course, as we cut to the tender scene of Sally and Tim kissing in back of the magician's trailer.

Part Three

5.

The Director

and

Actors

You, the director, know that actors make or break your film. Once you have selected an exciting script, labored over your shooting script, found perfect locations, and—in concert with the producer—hired a skilled camera director, you need actors to make your vision come alive. The right actors, who look the part and act the part, as the old saying goes, will make your motion picture sparkle, while mediocre ones may make your picture mundane. Agreed, a poorly written script cannot be revived by excellent acting, while a solid script cannot be ruined by uninspired acting (after all, many a crafty editor has turned a questionable performance into an acceptable one), but such motion pictures lack vitality and consequently fail to grip the audience.

So, how do you go about finding these scintillating actors who, through their skill and personality, succeed in drawing the viewer into the world on the screen?

Let's admit it: the kind of actor you need is not necessarily brilliant and/ or good looking, but is the one who has a solid acting background, is skilled in on-camera acting techniques, and, most important, has screen personality, or charisma.

Now, what is screen personality? It is not a God-given, intangible, and therefore exciting talent; stated very simply, it is an actor's ability to communicate with the audience by expressing believable emotions that in turn arouse the viewers' emotions.

Believable emotions are simple. They are expressed in a straightforward manner. Believable emotions never try to impress an audience with the depth of the actor's feelings or the brilliance of the acting technique displayed. The actor makes the audience see a *person,* not an actor playing a part. And this brings us to the subject of communication.

The actor who has screen personality connects with the audience in a subtle way. It is the actor-audience communication that draws the viewer into the events on the screen, and not, as many producers contend, million-dollar production values such as special effects, car chases, and exotic locations. The actor communicates with the viewer in two ways that are continuously interchangeable:

- The viewer becomes the character's partner.
- By the process of osmosis the viewer feels addressed, threatened, or embraced by the character on the screen.
- The viewer becomes the character on the screen and participates in his or her adventures.

In short, the most effective motion picture acting permits the viewer to participate in the events on the screen. You should assemble your cast with utmost attention to the visual power of every one of your actors. Think about your cast as a tapestry whose colors (your actors) have to complement one another, contrast effectively, yet blend harmoniously. In other words, their looks and demeanor should contrast sufficiently to make each *character* stand out in his or her own right, yet blend in with the rest of the cast.

This is the moment when the threatening concept of typecasting rears its ugly head. Agreed, a hood is supposed to look like a hood, a nun like a nun, a college professor like a college professor, and a socialite like a socialite, but do not present your audience with types they have seen over and over ad nauseam. Types that one recognizes immediately tend to become boring. Only types that, while recognizable, still manage to challenge the audience will add the necessary spice to your film. For this reason never insist that a character has to have a certain look; in the search for just the right type you may overlook another and better actor. For my motion picture *Frozen Scream*

I was looking for an Irish priest. I had found the ideal type, but instead I cast an Italian-looking actor for the role. Why? Simple: the second actor had screen personality, whereas the first one had only the look.

The Casting Process

In case you have to contend with a rather bland "star" (an actor whose name value your distributor insists upon), you ought to surround your star with effective and impressive actors. And this brings us to casting your picture. Most likely the distributor—if you are in the fortunate position of working for a producer who has a distribution contract—will suggest a few recognizable names, and it is the producer's responsibility to contact the respective actors. First the producer will contact the actor's agency to find out about the star's availability. The producer will negotiate with the agent; you as director are more or less out of the picture. The same holds true for the rest of the cast.

A production company that is able to attract a recognizable star will most definitely hire a casting director. The casting director lists the roles to be cast with the Breakdown Service, and the agents in turn submit their clients' names. For each part to be cast the casting director will present you with three or four choices. You, at times in concert with the producer, will have the final decision. Here a word of warning: the casting director might not supply you with the most exciting or talented actors. He or she will, however, bring in actors who have experience—that is to say, actors who are on time, have learned their lines, and know how to hit a mark.

USING UNION ACTORS

Admittedly SAG (Screen Actors Guild) actors are not necessarily better trained or more talented than nonunion actors. Let me explain: unless an actor has been hired by either a TV show, feature film, or commercial production company that is signatory with SAG, he or she cannot join the Screen Actors Guild.

There are many members of SAG who are not trained actors but were able to join via a TV commercial. Conversely, there are many—yes, thousands—of well-trained and highly talented actors who never had the opportunity to work for a commercial, TV show, or feature film shot by a production company signatory with SAG, and for this reason they are ineligible to join SAG. Many of these actors join AFTRA (American Federation of Radio and Television Artists). This union, covering radio and live TV (soaps, some game shows, and situation comedies), does not require—as SAG does—*proof of work.* Anyone, actor or nonactor, is permitted to join. Once a member of AFTRA works as a *principal* (a role with more than five speaking lines), he or she is eligible to join SAG, one year after the date the AFTRA contract was signed. An actor who worked as an extra (nonspeaking) for an AFTRA show is not eligible to join SAG.

Things look quite different if you are working on a low-budget feature where you, in concert with the producer, are faced with the entire casting process from A to Z.

Let's assume the production company that hired you is signatory with SAG, and adheres to the union's rules and regulations. This means you will be able to cast *SAG actors only,* and are prohibited from hiring a mix of union and nonunion actors. You have, of course, the opportunity to have a non-SAG actor admitted to SAG via your feature film. All your producer has to do is write a letter to SAG, requesting that the actor be admitted to the union. Again, your roster of roles to be cast will be listed with the Breakdown Service, and agents will submit their clients.

And now let's speak about the situation you will find yourself in if you work for a production company that has not signed with SAG. Obviously no agency will submit any of their clients to a nonsignatory company. You and, most likely, the producer are responsible for the entire casting process. Since the Breakdown Service will not accept your casting list, you should send your casting requirements to *Hollywood Drama-logue* and *Casting Call* if you live in Los Angeles, and *Back Stage* if you live close to New York. In places not featuring *trades* (trade magazines), you might get in contact with your local college's cinema or telecommunication department or drama department and ask for permission to post a casting notice on the bulletin board. If you do not have access to a college, pursue your local community theater and any drama schools that teach acting for the camera.

Have your financing all arranged before you start casting. Sending out casting notices before you are positive that your project will go in front of the camera is unfair to you and the actors involved. But take your time casting. Do not rush. About three months prior to your shooting date, when you are in preproduction, is a good time to begin your casting process.

HEADSHOTS AND RESUMES

My advice is to look at the actors' submitted headshots (8 × 10 photos) *before* you read resumes. An impressive resume might easily lead you to consider an actor who has extensive credits but turns out to be wrong as far as age and type are concerned. (This, I admit, should not keep you from casting "against type" if you find an outstanding actor.) It is a good idea to sort submissions into groups:

Suitable age and type
Unsuitable age and type, but interesting
Hopeless

Refrain from making any decision as yet. Do not call in actors for auditions, but permit your creative forces to simmer a little before you go through the photos again. At this point pay special attention to your "unsuitable but interesting" file; you may find just the right actor in this particular group. True, the actor might not be exactly the right type for the part you have in mind, but there might be something special about him or her. If you have a gut feeling about an actor go with it, and call the actor in for a reading.

As soon as you have identified several possible actors for each part, it is time to take a good look at resumes. But here a word of warning: the most impressive resume might not indicate the most qualified actor; in other words, the resume might not reflect the actor's true qualifications. I am not speaking about a fictitious resume—in twelve years of producing I have rarely come upon one. Actors are honest people, but at times they are prone to *glorify* the work they have done. The beginning director may rather easily fall into their innocently set traps.

Take actress *A*, for instance. She lists a number of recent box office hits, but since she doesn't list SAG membership, you know she worked as an extra (providing atmosphere) on these movies. Extra work, unfortunately, does not give you any information about her acting ability. It is true that many excellent actors, in order to make a living, *do* extra work, but they refrain from listing it on a resume. If you see extra work listed, you know you are dealing with an actor of limited experience.

Actor *B* lists a number of stage credits, but mentions no theater where the plays were performed. There is no doubt that *B* performed these roles in acting class, not onstage.

Actor *C* has a solid stage background but lacks film credits. Since he has not attended an on-camera class, it is unlikely that *C* will perform adequately in front of your camera.

Actress *D*'s resume, at first glance, does not look impressive. But she has attended on-camera classes as well as a number of acting courses conducted by respected coaches. Actress *D* has participated in a number of student films (she mentions that a demo tape is available), and gained stage experience via college and community theaters. Here you're faced with an actress who has prepared herself quite well. At least you know *D* is familiar with basic acting techniques, is able to hit marks, and knows how to perform in front of a camera. Confidently you may call in actress *D*.

An actor's resume should list:

- *Actor's name* and (if not represented by an agency) telephone number.
- *Union affiliation* (SAG, AFTRA).
- *Film and TV credits.* The actor should list such credits *only* if he or she had speaking lines, regardless of whether the film mentioned was a SAG production, nonunion film, or student production.
- *Stage credits.* All stage credits for legitimate theater, college, and community theater should be given.
- *Workshops.* This segment of an actor's resume is important for you, the director, as it tells that the actor, by attending workshops, keeps his or her skills sharpened.
- *Training.* Another important segment that shows how well the actors have prepared themselves for their chosen profession.
- *Sports.* Needless to say, this segment lists the sports an actor can do.
- *Special abilities.* If the actor is an accomplished athlete, singer, dancer, etc., it will be mentioned here.

INTERVIEWS

I would recommend that you *not* lock yourself into a mental image of how a character in your film should look and act. Keep an open mind as you interview your actors. Maybe you had pictured a wiry, almost spidery man, given to sarcastic smiles, for your villain, when a heavyset, jovial actor may be a better choice. At times, look for *acting ability,* and forget about *type.*

As you interview actors, observe:

- Do they look like the headshot they submitted?
- Do they show the same vitality displayed in the headshot?
- Are there any signs of nervousness, such as tension about mouth and eyes? Are their shoulders tense or hunched? Do they fiddle with jewelry, fingers, or flick off an imaginary fleck of dust from their clothes?
- Do they try to impress you by assuming a phony personality?
- Are they exceedingly timid?

Always look for actors who are relaxed, friendly, and positive about their personal background and achievements. Only the relaxed actors who feel comfortable in an interview situation will be secure in front of the camera. This is an important consideration, since inner tension will make the actor's performance bland or, even worse, "acty." Only *relaxed* actors, who are able to concentrate fully on the task at hand, will give natural and therefore effective on-camera performances.

Have the courtesy to give all the actors you called in the opportunity to read for you. Don't forget, actors are spending their time and money to audition for you, and you never know—one seemingly hopeless actor might surprise you with his or her acting ability. Excerpt short scenes from your script, all applicable to the various parts to be cast. Make plenty of photocopies. Give each auditioning actor the appropriate sides* and plenty of time to study them.

It is best to have your assistant read opposite the actors. This gives you a better opportunity to observe an actor's performance. At the initial reading *do not* expect a polished performance. Even more important, *do not* confuse actors by supplying any suggestions, such as, "At the beginning of this scene Millie is kind of apprehensive, but then she gains confidence." Permit actors to let their own creativity soar. By the same token, if the interviewing actress asks how you want her to play this scene, refrain from guiding her, and suggest that she present the scene in any way she sees fit.

The best initial reading is easy, natural, free of any phony theatricality, yet gives an indication of the character to be portrayed. Such a reading communicates the character's opinion and feeling. It has *immediacy;* that is,

*Pages of a script used for auditioning.

it gives the impression that the actor has something to say and demands an answer. Don't be disappointed if only a few readings come up to par. It takes a skilled and experienced actor to give an "easy" reading.

You should expect that some readings will be nothing but a dull mouthing of lines. Others will sound "acty," and quite a few will look and sound more like a stage than a screen performance. And this brings us to the question, "What is considered an effective screen performance?"

To answer this question, let's look at the difference between stage and screen performance. The stage actor reaches the audience *audially* by the spoken text. The screen actor communicates *visually;* words mean relatively little. Thoughts and emotions count on the screen. Both have to be executed simply and honestly. The camera catches the phony emotion as well as the bland excuse for one.

Most actors auditioning for you undoubtedly will have an extensive stage background. For this reason they might either seem "acty" or, trying to be natural, come across as bland and one-dimensional. On the other hand, the actor who is *only* camera trained is innocent of the most rudimentary acting techniques. You may venture to cast such an actor if you have sufficient off-set rehearsal time. Lacking rehearsal time, this actor might require too much of your personal attention during the shoot and will slow down the production.

CALLBACKS

You will call back actors who:

Have been relaxed during the initial interview.
Have given a *fairly* satisfying reading, even if it was a
   little bland or acty.
Do look *somewhat* the part.

Permit *all* actors to take their audition sides home, and call the ones whom you wish to see again for a callback. These actors hopefully will have worked on their scene. A number of the readings will have improved; others may turn out bland. You never know.

Once you have settled on three to five actors to be considered for the more important roles, you are ready to videotape. This session is the most telling part of your interview sequence, and definitely the most rewarding. Only the camera reveals a person's true personality, or charisma. And as we know, it is charismatic actors who pull the audience into their spell.

At times an actor whose reading was acceptable but not exciting will blossom in front of the camera. The actor who is most effective in front of the camera realizes that the camera is not a piece of equipment, it does not stand in the place of a person, it *is* a person.

The effective motion picture actor:

Communicates with the camera.
Knows how to move in front of a camera.
Has a facial expression (in CU) that is neither dull nor
    overly animated.
Above all, has the *personality* that fills the screen.

After some trial and error you will have assembled your cast. It is a grand day when you finally look at the tapestry of your cast in which each actor complements the rest of your cast, yet still stands out individually. (This holds true for the leading characters as well as for the small parts.)

The Director Creates the Character

The desire to be moved emotionally is your audience's main, if subconscious, reason for attending a movie. Always be aware of the significance of character delineation and development. Remember, you do not tell your audience whether a character is good, bad, or indifferent; you *show* them so they can judge for themselves.

The audience's emotion toward a character is created step by step, as the result of thoughtful and deliberate characterization. Character traits, whether admirable or despicable, are messages that call forth the viewer's emotion, and for this reason they must be shown in action (what characters *do* is more important than what they *say*).

Before you begin rehearsing your actors I recommend that you give close consideration to the characterization of each role. True, you should incorporate whatever your cast has brought in during interviews and call-backs. But do not leave the task of characterization entirely up to your actors.

The individual actor, naturally, is primarily concerned about his or her role, while you, the director, have to consider the tapestry of your entire motion picture.

It is through your own understanding of life that you will create characters who move your audience emotionally. Characterization based on this understanding will keep you from falling into the trap of creating cliché characters. This does not mean that you will bring truly living human beings on the screen. The people we meet in everyday life have so many unrelated traits that, if a director were to try to bring them all to the screen, he or she would succeed only in confusing the audience. In this respect you present to your audience the illusion of life.

Characters are divided into three types:

Simple character
Complex character
Flat character

Simple Character   This character has *one* dominant character trait. Other character traits have to be in accordance with the main character trait, and as such must complement it. You will use the simple character in a *film of purpose,* such as action or adventure films. The *dominant character trait* drives the character to achieve his or her purpose. Do not attempt to give this character a contradictory character trait, or you will weaken the narrative purpose. The simple character is *always* one of your lead actors.

For example, Bill's wife was killed by a gang, and he sets out to avenge her:

Dominant character trait: Loyalty
Secondary character traits: Humor and perseverance

Complex Character   This character has *two contradictory character traits.* Like the simple character, the complex character has some other traits in the background. The complex character has to decide between courses of action, as the contradictory traits pull him or her in two different directions. Both traits have to be developed with equal strength. The complex character is always *the* lead character of a motion picture based on psychological drama.

For instance: Bill has been married to Mary for a number of years; they have two children. They had married very young and now have grown apart, while their marriage has become a marriage of convenience. Bill's professional life is equally stagnant. Even though he has worked hard on his MBA degree, he doesn't get anywhere in the firm he works for. He changes jobs, and meets Belinda, a beautiful young girl. Immediately Bill falls in love. Belinda's father, who owns the company, promises Bill a vice-presidency if he will divorce Mary and marry Belinda. (Yes, I agree, the story sounds as corny as a soap opera, but it serves to make my point:)

Dominant character trait I: Loyalty
Secondary character trait: Honesty
Dominant character trait II: Ambition
Secondary character trait: Pride and sensuality

Flat Character   This is always a secondary character. Featured players fall into this category. Most likely it is the flat character who starts the ball rolling. The flat character has only *one* dominant character trait and no secondary character traits. Belinda's father, in our example above, should fall into this category.

Don't forget that secondary character traits make your characters interesting and make them come alive. The character tapestry of our little Bill-Mary-Belinda "soap" might look like this:

Bill: Complex character. Dominant character trait I, Loyalty. Secondary character trait, Honesty. His first dominant character trait keeps him in his marriage. His honesty makes him confess about his love for Belinda. His second dominant character trait makes him consider Belinda's father's proposal. His pride and sensuality make Belinda a prized possession.

Mary: Simple character. Dominant character trait, Love of home and family. Secondary character trait, Courage.

Belinda: Simple character. Dominant character trait, Willfulness. Secondary character traits, Narcissism and sensuality.

Belinda's father: Flat character. Dominant character trait, Love of power.

Looking at this list, you will agree that only one character, the star, should have contradictory character traits.

My advice to you, the beginning director, is that you have a firm grip on the characterization of your various characters *before* you go into rehearsal. Nothing, and I mean nothing, makes an actor more uneasy than a director's vague concept of the characters in a film. Unfortunately, some directors only pay lip service to characterization. They may explain a character this way:

Millie, age 53
Occupation: cashier
Married to a fireman
Two children
She is overworked.
She worries about her children and her husband.

A sketchy characterization like that is a waste of time, and of no help to either you or your actors. So let's consider ways to make characterization work.

Characterization is divided into:

Static characterization
Dynamic characterization
Emotional characterization

STATIC CHARACTERIZATION

The elements making up this type of characterization are:

Lineament (habitual posture, habitual expression)
Occupation/Education
Clothing
Environment
Voice
Health

Lineament Consider the actors' lines of face and body. Of course, once you have cast an actress to portray one of your film's characters, Millie, these features cannot be changed. But you'll work on the actress's facial expression and her body posture.

Millie forces herself to appear younger than her years.
She works hard on her perpetual sunny smile, erect

posture, and quick, young movements. Her job is important to her, and she has to compete with a number of young, perky girls. Once at home she turns into a middle-aged woman. Her smile is gone, the corners of her mouth turn down, her shoulders sag. She puts on slippers and drags herself from one never-ending household chore to the next. We can tell she is frustrated by the way she bangs her pots and pans around. Her eyes have a far-away look. She worries about her husband, who works too hard, about her married daughter, who is expecting another child, and her son, who never seems able to finish college.

Occupation/Education   Millie works as a cashier in a supermarket. She enjoys the hustle and bustle of the store, but is afraid that she may be replaced by a younger girl.

Occupation is an excellent way to come closer to a character's *core*. A college professor will not only have different characteristics from, say, an army officer, truck driver, or musician, but will solve problems by different means, and will react to situations in different ways.

Millie, who has been a cashier from the time she graduated from high school, reacts quickly to any given situation. She is not, however, accustomed to thinking things out, nor does she look for the hidden reason behind someone's action. Moreover, she takes everything at face value.

Clothing   Audiences deduce a great deal about a person by what the person wears (approximate cost of clothing, style or lack of style, color, cleanliness, suitability for the person and/or the occasion).

Unfortunately, Millie is given to wearing garments that are more suitable for a younger woman. She is fond of showy jewelry. Her hair is dyed bright blond, and she spends a small fortune on sculptured, brightly painted nails.

Environment   Since we already discussed the importance of environment in chapter 4, suffice it to say that a character is in either harmony or conflict with his or her environment and reacts accordingly.

> Millie liked the excitement and ever-changing display of her workplace. Home is another story. She and Sam, her husband, have lived in the same house amidst the same furniture and bric-a-brac for years. At times Millie "hankered to get something new," but now she has forgotten about "redoing the place." In fact, she is hardly aware of anything in her house. Her home has utilitarian value only.

Voice   A character's voice and way of speaking is another excellent tool for characterization. Granted, your actors have to speak *naturally,* but they have to speak as characters of their age, educational level, and socioeconomic background should speak.

> Millie's voice is rather harsh. There is even a nasal twang to it.

Health   Don't skip health, as it may give you some clues to dynamic characterization.

> Millie's general health is good, even though she has reached an age where her feet and her back hurt as she stands at her cash register.

DYNAMIC CHARACTERIZATION

The way a character moves and gestures, the way he or she handles props, establishes dynamic characterization. In other words, characters express themselves by physical action. For instance Alex, whom you wish to portray as a meticulous young man, will pack his suitcase very differently from Nancy, the scatterbrain.

Dynamic characterization applies as well to a character's behavior and attitude when faced with different situations. Brad, the young executive, behaves differently when taking lunch with Mrs. Murdock, his boss, than the way he acts when bowling with his buddies.

EMOTIONAL CHARACTERIZATION

Here, I suggest you characterize sharply. No fuzzy attitudes or phony feelings should crop up on the screen as you show a character's outlook on life. Emotional characterization gives you, the director, the opportunity to manipulate by stressing the character's *dominant emotion*. The dominant emotion refers to the combination of mental and emotional attitudes. Here are but a few examples:

> Mental: intelligence, attitudes, and opinions about life
> and people.
> Emotional: desires, moods, displays of affection or
> dislikes, aggressiveness, submissiveness.
> Millie is an outgoing but rather humdrum person.
> She is of average intelligence, and her philosophy of
> life is "live and let live." She never held book learning
> in high esteem, and she does not understand her son's
> quest for knowledge. She is aggressive with her
> children but submissive with her husband. She is given
> to quick mood swings. No burning desires guide her
> life.

Rehearsals

Compared to the stage director, you the motion picture director have only a limited time available for rehearsals. At times you'll have the luxury to rehearse a few days before shooting; at other times, because of budget restrictions or the availability of key actors, you'll have to rehearse on the set. The time spent on rehearsals varies with each production.

Some actors favor rehearsals; others abhor the idea. The ones who favor rehearsals like to have the entire script "down" on the first shooting day. Those who oppose rehearsals claim that first impulses and intuitions, both creating a gripping performance, tend to get lost during the rehearsal period. Both opinions have their pros and cons. What it boils down to is the fact that you, the director, must be able to *understand, motivate,* and *control* your actors, regardless of whether you rehearse off or on the set.

A delicate combination of control and sensitivity on the part of the director is needed when dealing with actors. Primarily, you'll have to give your actors *security.* Some actors are subconsciously afraid that the director will not be able to control their performances sufficiently. Some, considering the director nothing but a traffic cop who determines camera moves and setups, will call in a lackluster performance or, even worse, ham it up. A few, rejoicing about the director's insecurity, will try to take over.

Know *precisely* what you want; have a clear idea about your motion picture's concept. Have enough sensitivity to listen to your actors' suggestions. If possible, refrain from giving your actors line readings such as, "Please, Janice, read that line this way," or "Do me a favor, Ben, and emphasize this word." Don't forget, actors are professionals; they know what to do, and any amateurish attempt at coaching will meet with strong resistance on their part. Yes, control your actors' goals, motives, and reactions, but never direct their lines. If you do, you may lose their respect.*

The rehearsal period should be used by the director to introduce the actors to their respective characters:

- Decide what makes a character function (goal).
- Decide *why* a character behaves in a certain way during a certain situation (action).
- Define relationships between characters.

Granted, there are some actors who are set against any psychological probing. There is not much you can do about it; either replace the actors in question, or make clear to them that a good motion picture is more than mere words and gestures.

On the other hand, never overdo your rehearsal. Don't freeze your actors into line deliveries or emotions. Most important, do not try to block any scene during off-set rehearsals. Wait until you are on the set or location to make your actors move in front of the camera.

*Consult *How to Audition for Movies and TV,* by Renée Harmon (New York: Walker & Co., 1992).

When rehearsing with actors, always remind yourself of Stanislavsky's statement, "The material of the director's creativity is the creativity of the actor."* This does not necessarily imply that you should not *guide* your actors. After all, Stanislavsky also said, "Acting is neither fixed nor static. Acting is a process, and process implies change."† Therefore you, the director, should demand that the actors understand their roles in terms of the content of your motion picture. Firmly remaining within the narrative boundaries of the film, you should help your actors to reach for their own explanations and observations. Try not to force your own ideas upon them, but compare your ideas with theirs. Be sensitive to your actors' needs. This means you should never expect a specific emotion to be delivered in a specific way.

As far as rehearsals are concerned, do not expect to see a finished performance in the first rehearsal. Give your actors time to explore and to experiment. (This, unfortunately, does not hold true for on-set rehearsals, where you should expect and demand a polished performance. And this is why, if possible, you should opt for an off-set rehearsal period.) Emotions, honestly expressed, require the process of a chain of motives and reactions— that is, a specific circumstance (motive) causing a specific action leads to a specific emotion.

MOTIVE: A CAR CUTS IN FRONT OF YOU

leads to	Physical sensation:	a knot in your stomach
leads to	Physical action:	you step on the brakes
leads to	Thought:	(unprintable)
leads to	Speech:	"Idiot!"

The logical chain of action and emotion often cannot be established because of the obstacle of disconnected scenes (we will discuss a solution to this particular problem later on), and therefore should be dealt with sufficiently during rehearsals, regardless of whether the rehearsal takes place off the set or on. Without the basis of this motive-action-emotion chain, even a skilled actor might be tempted to substitute a cliché emotion for an honest one.

*†Stanislavsky, Konstantin. *Creating a Role*. New York: Theatre Arts Books, 1968.

FUSION OF ACTOR AND CHARACTER

The director has to deal with two identities, the *actor's* and the *character's;* the camera captures the *fusion* of the actor's own personality (experiences, behavior, action, and reaction) and the *character as written* (goals, traits) in the script.

Let me explain: Actor Adam Adams has been cast to portray Jeremiah, a stern Puritan elder. If Adam insists on playing *Adam Adams,* who just incidentally wears a seventeenth-century outfit and carries the name of *Jeremiah,* he will be as wrong as if he were to obliterate his own personality in order to portray Jeremiah.

I said "portray," not "become," Jeremiah on purpose. The widespread misconception that an actor loses himself in the part and becomes the character falsely assumes the actor loses control while going into a trancelike state. To be honest, I have never seen an actor go into a trancelike state. I don't believe it exists, except in poorly written novels and screenplays. Yes, the skilled and effective actor will "forget" about himself while working in front of the camera. But this "forgetting" refers to the actor's complete disregard of personal concern and personal prejudices. The actor who forgets himself concentrates to the fullest on the takes at hand. He doesn't want to impress either the director or audience, he doesn't worry about showing emotions or looking great; no, he is fully absorbed with *doing the scene* in front of the camera.

So please don't ever ask an actor to *become the character.*

DIRECTOR-ACTOR RELATIONSHIP

During a rehearsal, regardless of whether off the set or on, the following should occur:

- The actor fulfills the director's demands.
- The director respects the actor's creativity and sensitivity.
- Both director and actor work to achieve the fusion of actor and character as written.

In this sense a true director-actor relationship will be established. Keeping this relationship in mind, *never* permit your actors:

• To *force* an emotion that they don't feel, and cannot justify. When a particular emotion takes place during a particular scene, never ask your actor "What would you feel in this situation?"; ask instead, "What would you *do?*" At times an appropriate physical action will call forth the appropriate emotion. If no emotion should surface, accept the actor's physical action in lieu of it.

• To *inflate* an emotion (fear, joy, anger) by disregarding the motive that causes the emotion. (For instance, the fear a character experiences when sighting a mouse is different from the fear of being chased by a wild bull.)

• To *stereotype* a character by executing gestures and mannerisms that lack logic and/or consistency. In this way the actor presents only a cardboard imitation of a living, breathing character.

• To work on the *effect* of a line instead of the reality of the scene. If this should happen, advise your actor: "Forget about the emotion expressed by the line you speak, but look at various items in your environment and point them out to me, such as: This is a table, this is a chair, this is a carpet. Now go back to the line you had a problem with. Without any emotion, simply stating a fact (as you had done previously while you pointed out the items in this room) speak your lines."

• To bring in a *polished* but *shallow* performance. Such a performance is easily recognized: The actor reads lines in a skilled but lifeless way, does not react to the given situation sufficiently, or does not think and react while the partners speak. You may help by suggesting your actor get off the lines, to paraphrase the text and improvise the situation.

And now to you, the director:

• Do not try to make your actors carbon copies of yourself—how you would speak a line, how you would react to a given situation.

• Do not demonstrate how you would play a scene. (Granted, this is a temptation for the actor-director.) Don't forget, you are different in temperament, facial expression, and vocal quality from the actor performing the part.

• Respect and develop your actors' creativity; only then will you be able to control them.

• Be prepared for an emotional spiral during your rehearsals. Don't worry if scenes that looked so well in the beginning suddenly seem to go down the drain. If you keep your calm and sense of humor, things will pick up again. The great Russian director Vakhtangov put it so well as he wrote to one of his actors: "You got frightened, then gathered your forces and improved. Then, pleased at how well things were going, you wanted to be still better, and began to overact . . ."*

Always remind your actors that *simplicity* is the key to the effective on-screen performance. If the viewer feels that the actor is not acting at all, since everything seems so easy and natural, you the director have done your job well.

IMPROVISATION

If you are faced with continuous rehearsal difficulties, you may try to get your actors back on track by improvising the scenes or segments of scenes that cause uneasiness. But don't permit an improvisation to turn into an empty rehashing of lines and gestures. Instead encourage your actors to search for the inner meaning of situations or relationships. The helpful improvisation permits actors to make contact with one another, and to discover the various characters' open and hidden goals.

Any improvisation intended to lead to an effective screen performance is based on the *authenticity* of feeling.

Actors must talk to each other and gauge their interaction not on the basis of the lines to be memorized, but on the basis of relationships between characters. This means *thoughts* and *opinions* have to run through the listening character's mind. Any response must come as a result of these thoughts. (We will be dealing more thoroughly with the concept of thoughts later on.)

In exploring the effect of each other's presence, actors should ask themselves:

Handbook of the Stanislavsky Method. New York: Crown Publishers, 1955. "Preparing for a Role" from the diary of E. Vakhtangov.

How does the opposite character appear?
How do characters change?
How do characters influence each other?

Do not permit actors to "act feelings." In fact, ask them to forget about emotions altogether and to concentrate on *goals* (again, we will look more closely at goals a bit later). Let them discover the *open* as well as the *hidden* goals each character deals with.

Ask actors to invent obstacles that will keep their characters from reaching the desired goal.

Give each actor specific tasks that must be accomplished in specific ways. Establish:

Action	*What* I am doing.
Volition	*Why* I am doing it.
Adjustment	*How* I am doing it.

As actors work on their tasks, ask them to concentrate on the *what* of the tasks, never on the *how*. For instance: *Ann smiles at Elmer*. Her goal: I think Elmer is a neat guy. I would like to get to know him.

Action	Ann smiles.
Volition	I want to show Elmer that I like him.
Adjustment	I smile sweetly.

Now, if the actress portraying Ann smiles at her partner because of her goal, she executes the important What in an easy—and therefore effective—way. If, however, she smiles to show off her radiant smile and beautiful white teeth, then she executes the detrimental How, and her performance lacks honesty.

If, even after improvisations, you are unable to break a deadlocked rehearsal, ask yourself:

• Are my expectations too high?
• Am I theorizing too much?
• Have I prepared myself sufficiently as far as characterizations are concerned?

- Am I temperamentally opposed to any actor, and—unknowingly—tormenting him or her?
- Am I restricting the actors' creativity?

At times I have found that seemingly insurmountable rehearsal obstacles were based on an actor's unrecognized body tension. Such body tension manifests itself most likely in stumbling or forgetting lines and actions. The usual remedy of rolling one's head and shoulders does not help; in fact, as it brings tension to the surface, it makes matters worse. My suggestion is: have the actor stop *immediately*. Ask him or her to *forget* about the lines or task, and then *concentrate* on a straight line somewhere in the room, such as a table top, the outline of the camera, or the line where ceiling and wall meet. I have found this exercise—even during shooting—immensely helpful.

There are times when it will be impossible to schedule off-set rehearsals. Even worse, if you were not involved in the casting of the smaller roles, you will meet your "day players" on the day of the shoot. At this point assuredly you are at the mercy of your actors, who (hopefully) are skilled and experienced.

Even if you won't be able to schedule off-set rehearsals, make every effort to meet with your lead actors at least once prior to the shooting date, to discuss story line and characterization of the respective characters.

Regardless of whether you had off-set rehearsals, use the time while lights are being set up to rehearse with your actors:

- Ask the AD (assistant director) to "run lines" with the actors.
- Take a look at the scene and adjust to appropriate levels:
  Reactions
  Emotions
  Interaction between characters
- Block the scene and let your actors walk through it, giving them plenty of opportunity to familiarize themselves with their physical movements and the locations of floor and peripheral marks.*
- Do not ask the actors to act out the scene during the camera

---

*Marks: Floor marks (line, ⊤, and x marks) are taped on the floor. Peripheral marks are points the actor can see out of the corner of his/her eyes.

rehearsal. Acting out again and again results in a stilted scene on-camera.

• Ask your actors to keep their performance fresh for the camera.

It is true, time is money. Still, many beginning directors make the mistake of cutting on-set rehearsals too short. Determine *before* you go on the set how much time you should allocate for each camera rehearsal, and incorporate the time into your shooting schedule.

Overcoming the Problem of Disconnected Scenes

Unlike a stage play, a motion picture is not filmed in a straight and logical line from point A to point Z, but is shot as a hodgepodge of unrelated scenes. The stage director, as well as the stage actor, take the development of an *emotional arch* for granted. You, the motion picture director, cannot. You'll have to work with disconnected bits and pieces. For instance:

> Johnny and his bride, Lisa, arrive at their new home in scene one (location: the Smiths' living room). In scene one hundred fifty the marriage has failed, and they are getting a divorce. Lisa, after another bitter argument with Johnny, storms out of the house. On the threshold she meets Bambi, Johnny's new lady-love.

It stands to reason that both scenes will be shot the very same morning. Performing onstage, actors have the opportunity to build their relationship and reactions to each other (the *emotional arch*); on a film production, they don't. Appropriate emotions and behavior have to happen right then and there.

Even worse, the beginning and the end of a highly emotional scene might be shot directly following each other:

> Betty, ready to discuss her decision to leave college, enters her father's office. After a long encounter she

leaves—exhausted and furious, but determined never
to see her father again.

Betty's entrance and exit will be filmed using the same camera setup, at the door. Since her exit and entrance will be shot back-to-back*, the actress portraying Betty has no opportunity to react to any event that took place in the interim.

Without any doubt, it is your responsibility as the director to discuss with your actors in detail what has gone on before the segment of the scene to be shot, and what will happen next. This is particularly important if your actors have to deal with props: Larry will handle his paperwork one way if he is worried about a forthcoming meeting with his boss, another way if he is looking forward to a pleasant weekend. Mary Ellen will enter her apartment tired after a hard day's work, or elated after a successful shopping trip. Always discuss with your actors:

- Where has the character been at the end of the previous scene (or segment of a scene)?
- Why was the character there?
- What did the character do there?
- Where will the character be in the following scene?
- What will the character do in the following scene?
- What was the character's relationship to other characters in the previous scene? Have any of the relationships changed?
- Discuss how thoughts, feelings, opinions, and attitudes of previous scenes will influence the scene to be shot presently.

You, the director who is responsible for the tapestry of your film, should be fully aware of the *reality* of each scene, and the way each scene, each event, and each emotion should build on the previous one.

The Scenic Blueprint

Regardless of where you are rehearsing, a scenic blueprint is a must. Your scenic blueprint is as important as your shooting script. You, the beginning

---

*"Back-to-back" refers to takes or scenes that follow each other immediately.

director, are especially in need of one, as the numerous pressures and distractions you will encounter on the set—the decisions to be made, the tempers to be calmed—make on-the-spot creativity impossible. The workable scenic blueprint deals with the following:

Goals
Motive
Relationships
Physical actions
Conditioning forces

GOALS

Emotions, opinions, and relationships are built on goals. In simple terms, a goal is *what a character wants to achieve*. There is one overall goal that determines all of a character's actions throughout the script (*Snow White:* the Queen wants to get rid of Snow White), and subgoals within each scene that lead to the achievement of the overall goal. (First subgoal: the Queen hires the Hunter to kill Snow White. Second subgoal: she dresses as a peddler and presents Snow White with a deadly comb. Third subgoal: she hands Snow White a poisoned apple.)

Each goal should be stated specifically, never generally. As an example, let's take another look at the little dressing room scene (page 79) and the individual goals it contains:

Claudia wants to *revive* her career.
Ralph wants to *help* Claudia.
Al wants to *orchestrate* Claudia's career.

As you can see, each goal is stated clearly and therefore understandably for the audience. One knows what each character *wants*. None of the goals has been stated in a general way, such as, "Claudia is angry because she's worried about her career," "Ralph feels sorry for Claudia," or "Al is enthusiastic about getting Claudia's career back on the right track." You can tell, stating a goal in a general way tells about the respective characters' emotions, *not* about their actions. *Physical* (what a character does) and *mental* (what a character desires) *actions* are the foundation of simple and honest acting. The keys to arriving at clearly stated—and therefore actable—goals are:

> Keep your goal sentence short.
> State "I want to"—followed by a verb.
> Claudia: I want to *revive* my career.
> Ralph: I want to *help* Claudia.
> Al: I want to *orchestrate* Claudia's career.

In developing a goal, make certain that the goal is based on each character's *desire* as well as the *motive* that caused the desire. And this brings us to *open* and *hidden* goals.

Take another look at the dressing room scene. You will agree with me that, even though the given goals are actable, they will not make for a captivating scene. Too bad; after all, this scene sets the film's events in motion. So, what happens in this scene? Claudia, Ralph, and Al all decide to revive Claudia's career. *To revive* is the scene's open goal, which—unfortunately—does not carry much creative power. The director's and the actors' artistic opportunity lies in each character's hidden goal.

The open goal states *what a character does,* and the hidden goal reveals *why a character acts in a certain way.*

It is the *hidden goal* that is the true reason behind a character's open goal and his or her resulting actions. The hidden goal adds color and depth to the actor's performance. Hidden goals will make the bland dressing room scene interesting. So, here we go:

Claudia What is she doing? She wants to establish her power over Al and Ralph. How is she doing it? She uses her wiles. Hidden goal: I want to enjoy the power I hold over Ralph and Al.

Ralph What is he doing? He wants to remain in Claudia's good graces. Why is he doing it? He is afraid of losing Claudia to Al. Hidden goal: I want to show Claudia that I am caring and reliable.

Al What is he doing? He wants to show Claudia that he is her boss. Why is he doing it? He needs to revive Claudia's career, because she is his meal ticket. Hidden goal: I want to show Claudia that she is nothing without me.

MOTIVE

In order to arrive at a goal, a character must have a motive. Webster defines *motive* as "to supply with a reason to move." Your script gives your characters basic problems and the ways they try to solve them. You and your actors are responsible for the motivational interplay, which, to be sure, must be based on reasonable motives.

The motive is the springboard for mental and physical goals and physical action. All motives are based on human urges:

The life urge	Self-preservation, preservation of others, fear, hunger.
The sex urge	Love, loyalty, sexual drive.
The power urge	Construction and destruction, the desire to better self or others, control.
The creative urge	Creativity in all its forms.

Motives form relationships, or in case a relationship has been established, a motive may change the relationship. And from here, quite naturally, we will concern ourselves with relationship.

RELATIONSHIPS

If you want to bring electrifying relationships to the screen, you must set characters against one another. This does not indicate that you have to pit one character against another, that characters must fight or become involved in biting discussions, but it means that you, the director, have to be very much aware of *changes* in relationship. Relationships are never static. Characters come together or they move apart:

COMING TOGETHER

Initiating	Characters show their interest in each other. Putting his best foot forward, a character will initiate a relationship: "Hi, how are you?"

Experimenting	Characters begin to search for common interests, opinions, and beliefs. "You like the beach?" "I adore the beach, do you like to visit museums?"
Intensifying	Now characters know each other, and a desire for commitment arises. "I am so happy we met." "Nothing better ever happened to me."
Bonding	Characters become partners. They get married, move in together, or—on an unemotional level—form a business or political partnership.

COMING APART

Differentiating	After characters have bonded, they will establish their individuality. This, basically, is a healthy process that may either deepen a relationship or be the cause for an eventual breakup.
Stagnating	Characters treat each other without much feeling. They are bored. "How are things at the office?" "Fine, when will dinner be ready?"
Avoiding	When a relationship becomes unpleasant, characters tend to avoid each other.
Terminating	The relationship dissolves.

The relationship stages in your film, of course, are never as cut-and-dried as the above list suggests. Your script's dialog may not even touch on them, but the *feeling* is beneath the lines. Search for it, dig it out, and let your actors express it in thoughts and physical actions.

As far as relationships in all stages are concerned, one partner leads, the other follows. Positions in relationships are characterized by the way characters *communicate* with each other. Generally we find two basic communication patterns:

- One partner consistently overpowers the other.
- Power is fairly evenly distributed between partners, or tends to shift according to different situations.

The way characters communicate with each other is not necessarily spelled out in the written dialog of your script, and therefore it ought to be shown in each character's tone of voice, attention or inattention to the partner, and physical actions.

Once a basic relationship has been established, search for the telling details. Isolate moments in the relationship that will challenge, surprise, elate, or worry your characters, and find the appropriate expression for them.

PHYSICAL ACTIONS

Physical actions *must* arise from a goal, based on a motive—not the vague feeling, "It's time that I move my actors around." Communication established via physical action is one of the most powerful acting tools if—and only if—the actor believes fully in, and concentrates on, the physical action as he executes it. The actress ironing a pleated shirt should not *act* ironing but concern herself with doing the very best ironing job she can, carefully first straightening, then dampening, and finally ironing each pleat.

Decisions about physical actions (not to be confused with blocking) should be made when you write your shooting script. If you wait until you are on the set, the physical actions might turn into a general rehash of things you have done or seen before, instead of the character-revealing signals they are supposed to be. Therefore it will serve you and your actors well if you write a list of physical actions.

For purposes of illustration we will go again (for the last time, I promise) to our friends Claudia, Ralph, and Al, to find out how physical actions are based on each character's hidden goal.

LIST OF PHYSICAL ACTIONS—CLAUDIA

Claudia, seated at her dressing table, checks her perfect makeup. She brushes off a speck of powder, dabs on a little more rouge, and all the time admires herself. Completely absorbed in her task, she seems oblivious of both Al and Ralph.

She brushes Ralph's attention off. She is used to him. Maybe she is even getting a little bored by his considerate behavior.

When she finally stoops to give Al's suggestions a

fleeting thought and word, she gazes at him with looks that could freeze a polar bear. Immediately dismissing Ralph and Al, she walks to the costume rack.
Examining her costumes, she indicates that these are more important than either Ralph or Al.

Having chosen an appropriate outfit, Claudia takes it off the rack and moves back to her dressing table.

Finally, wielding the power of her charm and beauty, she rewards her vassals with one of her radiant, and famous, smiles.

LIST OF PHYSICAL ACTIONS — RALPH

Whenever possible Ralph sidles up to Claudia. Like a barnacle he attaches himself to her. His sweet, subservient smile seems to be glued on his face. If he is unable to follow Claudia physically, he follows her with the trusting, begging eyes of a Saint Bernard rescue dog.

Whenever Al speaks to him, Ralph's head twitches to the side, and his shoulders pull forward protectively.

As soon as Al moves close to Claudia, Ralph takes up his guard post next to her.

LIST OF PHYSICAL ACTIONS — AL

Al is constantly on the move. His posture is erect. He makes certain that whenever he makes a point, he towers over Claudia. As far as Ralph is concerned, Al could not disregard him less. He hardly ever looks at him.

CONDITIONING FORCES

Inherent in any story are the conditions of time, place, and climate, as well as any obstacles that may be associated with them.

Time   Elements that are not directly stated in the script can be established through references to time. Many beginning directors, unfortunately, disregard the implications of time, or consider only the obvious aspects of it. Yet in many ways time influences the opinion, behavior, and ethics of the characters you have to create for the screen.

For example, let's say that the subplot of your film deals with the relationship between Lucy, a young woman, and Homer, a married man. It is 1798. The French Revolution has swept away all social and religious restrictions. Personal freedom is the buzzword of the time. Lucy and Homer are seen together everywhere. They flaunt their affair as they attend the opera together and patronize the most fashionable Paris restaurants. Everyone invites them, no one cares about their illegitimate relationship—even Homer's wife (she has a lover of her own) couldn't care less. She and Lucy are dear friends.

If the story is set fifty years later, things have changed considerably. Queen Victoria graces the British throne, and her own rigid moral behavior has become society's measuring tape. Yet behind this facade of stern respectability hovers a shackled and therefore morbid sexuality. Homer, the respected citizen, rules wife, children, and servants with an iron hand. His sweetly submissive wife suspects he has a mistress but never dares to mention her. Homer visits Lucy, his "Lady Love," on the sly. They are never seen together, and only Homer's closest, most discreet friends know about Lucy's existence.

Then we rewrite to 1970. Free love reigns. Lucy, a professional woman, can afford an expensive foreign car. She lives in a penthouse and prefers to buy designer outfits. She also can afford to have one affair after the other. She discards lovers as casually as her clothes that are out of style. Homer is just one of her lovers. He knows it and expects that one of these days Lucy will leave him, as he has left the hat-check girl he had seen for a while.

And then, without anyone noticing, it is 1990. People are afraid of casual encounters. Relationships that depend on emotional involvement have become important again. Lucy and Homer are deeply in love, and for this very reason complications arise. Lucy wants a home and a family of her own, but Homer is reluctant to ask his wife for a divorce. He doesn't love her anymore, but he is attached to her, and loves his two children. A divorce would tear his family and comfortable surburban life apart. And anyway, who wants to pay child support and alimony?

Not only does time apply to the ethical and moral atmosphere of a period, it also very specifically defines part of the day. In this respect time governs the way characters move and behave.

Mark, getting up early in the morning, will lumber slowly to the coffeepot to pour the first reviving cup of the day. Yet he will move quickly and efficiently as he waits on the customers in his father's hardware store. In the evening, with the TV remote control in hand, he stretches comfortably on the couch.

Ella, the intern, moves more efficiently during the afternoon. At night, after she has been on duty for hours, her movements are sluggish.

Consider, too, the amount of time it takes characters to accomplish a given task. For example, Betty will spend far less time combing her hair and applying makeup when she gets ready to go to work than when she is preparing for an important date.

Place   As we have discussed in the previous chapter, characters are either in harmony or in conflict with their environment (place) and must react to it accordingly.

Climate   Make your actors aware of the climate of particular scenes. (It never fails; by some quirk of fate beach scenes are shot in freezing cold weather. And in August, I bet, you will be shooting a scene that takes place on an icy mountaintop in the middle of winter. Moreover, the set has been constructed on a stage that of course lacks air-conditioning.)

Climate affects the rhythm of characters' movement and speech. It changes body posture and at times is responsible for mood swings and variations.

I know you'll agree with me about the influence that the various conditioning forces exert. Conditioning forces give the actors the impetus to move, speak, act, and react in certain ways; they add to the reality of a scene; but they do *not* constitute the scene per se. For this reason, don't permit conditioning forces to overpower a scene or confuse your audience with unnecessary details.

The Director's Creative Safeguard

It might happen to you: you started out with a solid script, wrote a thorough shooting script, worked diligently on camera setups and moves, found terrific locations, cast skilled and talented actors and rehearsed with them, supervised postproduction—in short, you did everything according to plan, and yet finally you were forced to watch a movie that was not really *satisfactory*.

Yes, it can happen. It happened to me.

So, what went wrong?

In the excitement of creating the characters on the screen you, and to a lesser degree your actors, have moved too far from the characters as written in the script. Remember, the character seen on the screen must be a fusion of the character as written and the actor's own personality. It's likely that the two most vital components of your film—*script* and *acting*—do not quite fit. Note that I said, do not *quite* fit, and this makes a difference. Your movie is all right, but not quite as exciting as you had envisioned it, because its *narrative logic* is slightly off balance. You strayed too far from the characters as depicted in the script; in other words, the goals and ensuing actions of the characters on the screen do not quite fit the motives given in the script. Yes, your actors' responsibility is to breathe life into the characters, but neither you nor your actors should change them.

Unfortunately, in the heat of creation subtle changes—which turn out to be monsters later on—remain undetected. To prevent such mistakes, it might be a good idea to employ, prior to rehearsal, the device of "facts and conclusions," a technique actors have used for a long time. It works like this: Perusing your entire script, you make a list for each of the leading characters:

What the character says about himself or herself.
Appropriate stage directions.
What other characters say about him or her.

You list all the facts you have found, and next to them you write your conclusions. But be careful (and this is where creativity often goes astray): stick with the *given* facts first, then tack on your conclusions. Granted, the fact and assumption search is a tedious job, but it pays off in the end with motivated characters who follow a clear goal, since the totality of facts and conclusions gives an excellent picture of the character as written.

We'll use one of the beginning scenes from my film *Four Blind Mice* as an example:

Exterior Park. Day. Early Morning.

(It is a seemingly cold, slightly foggy fall morning. The camera [various angles] takes in the group of homeless people having taken shelter in the park. Most of them are still asleep.

Cut to AHNA's *car, a dilapidated old vehicle overflowing with her poor possessions. There are bags and cardboard boxes. Some old clothing has been spread on the hood of the car. There are pots and pans, an old calendar has been taped to one of the windows. The car doors are open.* AHNA *is busy with her "household chores."* ART, *an elderly homeless man, leans against one of the doors.)*

ART: You should go with me to the mission—nice people, and the food is good. Well, you'll have to listen to a preacher, but who cares . . .

AHNA: Maybe . . .

ART: Come on . . . why not.

(AHNA, afraid to hurt his feelings, hesitates.)

ART: 'Cause it's a handout. Woman, you have much to learn. We all have to accept . . . what you call it?

AHNA: Charity.

ART: Yeah, charity . . . how long have you been on the streets?

(AHNA tries to remember. She has difficulty stringing one thought on the next.)

AHNA: They let me go at the hospital . . .

ART: The nuthouse?

(AHNA nods. She counts on her fingers.)

AHNA: Mhm . . . I guess that was in May . . . the sun was shining, and the flowers on the matron's windowsill were in bloom . . . I went back home . . . I can't remember when. I was in this apartment . . . but then my money ran out and they evicted me . . . I have been on the streets for about three months . . . *(now positive)* . . . yes, three months.

ART: You are still green, but you'll learn, you'll get with it.

FACTS	CONCLUSIONS
1. Ahna lives in a park in an old car.	1. Ahna is homeless.
2. Her car is overflowing with her possessions.	2. Compared with the other homeless who sleep in cardboard boxes, she is still "well off."
3. She hesitates to hurt Art.	3. She is sensitive.
4. She refuses to go to the mission for a handout.	4. She has pride, and possibly some money to buy her food.
5. She was in a mental institution.	5. She is either mentally or emotionally ill.
6. She lived in an apartment after her release.	6. There was some money she lived on.
7. She was evicted.	7. She has no one who takes care of her.
8. She is still new on the streets.	8. She has much to learn, and much to adjust to. Life on the streets is still new, and probably frightening for her.

THE DIRECTOR'S REHEARSAL BLUEPRINTS

For you, the beginning director, it might be a good practice to write out characterization and scenic blueprints, to serve you as creative springboards during rehearsal and shooting.

The characterization blueprint (for leading characters only) should contain the following information:

COMPLEX OR SIMPLE CHARACTER:

Dominant character trait(s)
Secondary character trait(s)
(Both traits cannot clash with the motive given in the script).

Static characterization:
    Lineament (habitual posture, facial expression)
    Occupation
    Clothing
    Environment
    Voice
    Health

Dynamic Characterization:
    Emotional characterization
    Mental attitudes
    Emotional attitudes

The scenic blueprint should contain the following:

Motives
Goals
State of relationships
Conditioning forces:
    Time
    Place
    Climate
    Obstacles

6.

Dialog

We have already discussed the problems of dialog in the motion picture, and the fact that clearly expressed emotions arouse the audience. The audience reacts more to what it *sees* than what it *hears*. Consequently, important information and character detail may be unclear to the viewers unless you, the director, are able to draw their attention to what characters *say* as well as what they *do*. This, I warn you, will happen only if the spoken word is carried by honest and simply expressed emotions. All of us—you and I, the audience and the characters on the screen—exist most vitally in the world of emotions. Therefore no fuzzy dialog is allowable if you wish to create a full emotional effect. Always consider, the emotions felt by the protagonists on the screen are the emotions that ought to be felt simultaneously by the viewer. For this reason, remind your actors:

- Dialog shows character.
- Dialog shows the emotional state of the characters.
- Dialog not only gives information; by the way the actors deliver their lines, it has to build suspense.

Be careful that no two of your characters speak alike. For instance, in a discussion between two corporate lawyers, the dialog as written in your script sounds pretty much alike, the facts they are discussing are rather humdrum, yet are important for the picture's story line.

You will make Roger McGowan and Charlie Reynolds, his partner, much more palatable by characterizing their dialog. Make Roger a stickler for detail..Give him a pointed and precise speech pattern, let him emphasize his contentions by pointing a pencil whenever he hits a mental obstacle. Add to all of this his quick head and hand movements, and you'll show a truly stinging man.

In contrast, make Charles a jovial kind of person. Permit him to loll in his chair, smile, shrug his shoulders as he accentuates his slowly delivered but well-thought-out arguments with rounded hand movements.

Even the way a character delivers as bland a line as "I guess it will rain tomorrow" identifies that character as kind, angry, bitchy, shy, phony, elated, compassionate. In short, effective line delivery encompasses the entire spectrum of human emotions. Therefore don't ever permit actors to "read lines," which refers to a stilted dialog delivery. Likewise, do not condone any bland or lackluster line interpretation. Dialog has to show color as it conveys a character's opinions and emotions.

When it comes time to rehearse both off the set and on, be cognizant that all of us have different *vocabularies*. We speak differently to a teenager, the plumber who fixes our leaking kitchen faucet, the boss who calls us in for a conference, a friend we share a leisurely lunch with. While writers and directors are well aware of the vocabulary differences among different socioeconomic groups, they often disregard *tonal shift* that determines dialog between characters. These delicate shifts are impossible to discern in the script, and only rehearsal will open everyone's ears to them.

Tonal shift also applies to the meaning behind the spoken lines. Elinor's line, "Are you planning to play tennis next Saturday?" will sound different if she:

Suspects John of having an affair with Linda.
Wants to go to a movie if John plans to play tennis.
Wants to make small talk.

Furthermore, be aware of sentence structures that *read* well but do not *speak* well. The following line does not read too poorly, but try to speak it, and immediately your speech sounds phony: "It was a lovely morning. I played a round of golf and then went for a swim in the lake." Now try this: "Great morning. Chased a few balls around the course and took a dip in the lake."

At times you may not become aware of stilted sentences until rehearsal. If a skilled actor delivers a line in a theatrical way, don't blame it on the actor, but rewrite the line.

The *speed* at which a character talks, the *spacing* and *physical actions* that separate words or sentences, are sound indicators of a character's personality:

> Kathy keeps on ironing as she says briskly:
>
> "No, I have not seen Robert for some time. It has been about a year since I met him at a teacher's convention. Any reason why you ask?"
>
> or:
>
> "No."
>
> Carefully Kathy spreads a pillowcase over the ironing board. She looks up:
>
> "... It has been about a year ..."
>
> Kathy begins to iron.
>
> "... since I met him at a teachers' convention."
>
> Kathy continues to iron. She inspects a rip in the pillowcase before she — unexpectedly — explodes:
>
> "Any reason why you ask?"

Watch carefully, or you will have every character on the screen talking alike. Your audience wants contrast in everything, including the dialog on the screen.

All of the above means that you should do thorough characterization work *before* you start rehearsals (but after you have cast your actors), in which you'll have to consider a character's age, emotional state, cultural and socio-economic background, as well as his or her basic personality.

During rehearsals listen to your actors. Watch their facial expressions and bodily movements, for it is the way in which a character operates that characterizes him or her. And don't forget to concentrate your attention on the way your actors express their thoughts.

The skillful application of thoughts greatly enhances any screen performance. This is yet another reason why you, the director, should choose experienced motion picture actors over stage actors. Whereas stage actors are concerned primarily with words, the screen actor is fully aware of the importance of thought expression:

Always have your characters think under stress.
If at all possible, get conflict into a character's thinking
    process.

Technically, thoughts may be expressed:

Before a line.
In the middle of a line.
After a line.

A thought leads into a line and as such causes a character's emotion:

Thought: Finally I can take a few days off. What a relief.
Line: "Tomorrow we're going on vacation."

A thought might oppose the spoken line:

Thought: What a waste of time and money.
Line: "Tomorrow we're going on vacation."

A thought might be stronger in emotional content than the spoken line:

Thought: If I don't get away, I'll collapse.

Actors must think dynamic thoughts while their partner speaks. The listening actor's thoughts are the springboard (motive) for any spoken or physically expressed answer.

Thoughts, like dialog, must be in character. Cedric, who weighs his words carefully, will think differently from Ralph, whose opinions tumble out in unrelated sentences.

Always ask your actors to *think real thoughts;* do not permit them to stare soulfully into empty space.

Part Four

7.

Postproduction

The film has been shot, it is "in the can," but your responsibility has not yet ended. Some directors even contend that the most crucial work begins *in the editing room*. Fortunate is the director who possesses a solid editing background, but every director—whether from the writing, acting, or producing side—should have at least some basic knowledge of the editing process. No matter how experienced your editor is, do not turn over your film to him or her indiscriminately, or you may find its rhythm has been changed, its style has been distorted. On the other hand, do not expect a film editor to save a hopeless movie. (The miracle of *High Noon*, wherein the editor literally saved the motion picture from destruction, happens only once in a blue moon.) You should, of course, expect that minor flaws will be taken care of:

- A faulty line can be corrected by substituting the same track from a different take (one of the reasons that even though the first take is perfect, you should shoot another one for security).
- If an actor's performance is not quite up to your standards, you can substitute another actor's reaction over this actor's lines.

- A "wild line" (a line recorded after the movie has been finished) can be added wherever deemed necessary.

To put it simply, editing is the process of cutting a film from one shot to the next in such a way as to give the audience the illusion of continuous action. Like camera movement, every cut should follow the *narrative logic* of your film.

Editing the Picture

During the production time, each day's output of exposed film, the "dailies" or "rushes," will be developed by the lab. You'll receive a "1 light" print, which, while the original footage is stored in the lab's vault serves as a work print, the print your editor edits.

The following are the stages a film moves through from the dailies to the answer print:

- *Dailies:* Each day's footage should be spliced together. Some directors omit this step, but I feel that splicing dailies together helps to keep the avalanche of exposed film in some kind of order.
- *Rough cut:* Scenes are strung together in appropriate order. The film is still uneven, in some parts too long, others too short or illogical. In this way you can evaluate strong and weak points.
- *First assembly:* The film's weak points need to be corrected, and its final length has to be established.
- *Three-quarter cut:* The film is now fairly smooth in appearance, and the sound editing has been completed.
- *Final cut:* Even though the "final cut" shows the supposedly final version of your film, some minor changes are still possible. By now picture and sound tracks can be run in interlock—that is, film and sound will be projected from different sources.
- *Negative cut:* Once your final cut has been struck, the original footage will be edited based on it.
- *Answer print:* This print is struck from the negative cut. If you so desire, you still can change a thing here or there. I would,

however, strongly advise against this money-wasting practice. Decide on changes while cutting your final cut.

And now let's take a look at the equipment your editor needs to cut the picture.

- *Moviola:* The Moviola is the standard editing machine. It consists of a motorized viewer and sound system. Sound head and viewer head are interlocked so they run together.
- *Splicers:* Mylar splice, perforated
  Mylar splice, unperforated (guillotine)
  Cement splice

Mylar Splice The Mylar splice requires a far less skilled editor than the cement splice, and it can be made much faster. It is the preferred method for cutting dailies and the rough cut. A Mylar tape very much like an ordinary type of tape is placed across the cut on both sides. It can be removed easily, but will—since it is thicker than the film—throw the image somewhat out of focus as the film moves through the projector gate.

Guillotine Splice This is an excellent method for the skilled editor, who works quickly and efficiently with the unperforated guillotine tape. Guillotine splicing is most effectively used for sound editing.

Cement Splice A cement splice should be used for the negative cut. A cement splice is made by overlapping two sections of film. The base of one cut is dissolved into the base of the next, so the two sections become one. If the editor is not skilled in this splicing technique, the overlap becomes thicker than the film and will be seen as a distracting flash on the screen. When using a cement splice you'll lose a frame at the point of cutting and joining. (For sound editing cement splices should be avoided, since they cause a drop in the sound level.)

No matter what type of splicing technique the editor employs, he or she needs storage reels and storage bins, leaders, and—most important—white gloves. Make certain that your editor handles your film with utmost care. Dust, scratches, or fingerprints will ruin your film. No film should ever be wound so tightly as to cause cinch marks. Scratches may have been created during the editing process, by the camera when the film was shot, or, even more likely, during development. Base scratches can usually be buffed, but if they are on the emulsion side, obviously there is little anyone can do about them.

Leaders are made of yellowish-white undeveloped film. Leaders are used to mark the *head* (beginning) and *tail* (end) of every roll. Your editor uses a non-water-based marking pen to mark the leader. Leaders are useful for slugging (the replacement of damaged footage).

EDITING AND SPLICING

Even though it is unlikely that you will get hands-on experience, as director you ought to know about editing and splicing techniques.

EDITING

- Rewind the film so that the beginning of the footage is on the outside of the reel.
- Thread the footage and view it.
- Make notes on the intended editing sequence.
- View the film again and start cutting.
- After making cuts, label the individual "clips" with white tape and clamp them on the editing table.
- Keep track of the order of the film clips by listing the scenes on a pad and by marking the clips with corresponding numbers.
- Splice all of the unused takes, the *outtakes,* together. At times during the editing process these outtakes may turn out to be lifesavers.
- Put the film clips together in the order in which they are to be cut.

Splicing needs practice and practice and practice again. Here is how it works:

SPLICING

- Lift the left side of your splicer, and lock your film clip into the right-hand side. The emulsion side of the film must be placed face up.
- Bring down the left side of the splicer and cut the clip.
- Raise the right side of the splicer and lock the other clip into the left side (the emulsion side must face up).

- Bring down the right side and cut the film. Raise the right side again.
- Scrape the emulsion (cement splice technique) and scrape the film.
- Apply cement on the scraped side, bring down the right side, and lock.
- Wait about seven seconds for the cement to dry (a hot splicer will cut down the drying time to about three seconds), then lift the upper half of both sides of the splicer. Wipe off excess cement.
- Remove the film and tug slightly to check whether or not the splice will hold.

CREATIVE EDITING

Now that you have some idea about the mechanical side of cutting (splicing), let's move on and take a look at the more creative side of the process. Let's say you are cutting a dialog between two people, actor *A* and actor *B*, as they walk down a busy downtown street. We will have to concern ourselves with:

- Picture
- Sound: Dialog, sound effects, and possibly music.

Run this scene on the Moviola until you get to the point where you want to cut from the Two-Shot into a Reversal of actor *A*, and mark the spot with a grease pencil on both the picture frame and the sound frame. Lift the material out of the Moviola and cut with scissors. You repeat the same process with actor *B*'s lines, then splice the two cuts together. If picture and sound track have been marked correctly and locked into the Moviola in sync, you will be rewarded with a synchronized scene.

Matters are a little more complicated if you wish to show actor *B*'s reaction over actor *A*'s lines. Let's say you have decided to show forty frames of actor *B*'s reaction while actor *A* speaks; then you must take forty frames out of the picture shot of *A* talking. Choose the part of the shot you wish to "over" with *B*'s reaction, cut the picture and corresponding sound track out, replace the forty frames with *B*'s reaction, and place the sound track of actor *A*'s lines "over" *B*'s reaction.

Once the picture and dialog tracks have been cut, you set them aside and put the sound effects and music into place. (We will discuss sound editing in detail next.) On the sound effect and music tracks, the places between effects (where dialog belongs) will be filled in with blank tape. Picture, dialog, sound effects, and music tracks have to be combined later on in a procedure called a *mix*.

SOUND EDITING

Just as you send each day's film footage to the lab for dailies, you will send your recorded sound to a sound lab. The lab transfers the recorded sound (mostly dialog) to 35mm magnetic film (MAG). MAG looks exactly like the raw stock used in your camera, except that the light-sensitive emulsion used on camera film has been stripped and replaced by oxide. There is prestripped film—raw stock with the magnetic stripe already applied—on the market, but I advise against using it. If the magnetic stripe is of inferior quality, it will cause unnecessary wear on your camera.

Ask your producer to use the very best sound lab the budget can afford. At times a poor sound track has ruined an otherwise excellent movie.

The magnetic sound tracks will be returned to your sound editor, who works with at least three sound tracks:

- *Dialog* (Make certain that the dialog track can be removed from your finished film. Foreign buyers will replace it with a sound track of their own.)
- *Sound effects* (these may be on one track, or several)
- *Music*

Your sound editor first cuts the dialog track, then sets music and sound effects in place. You have to watch the continuity of sound effects. For instance, at times sound is more continuous than picture: Mary and Sam attend a lively party, greet their friends Billy and Jo, then move on to meet with their host, Ralph. Every so often we cut back to the waiter Jo, watching what is going on. As we cut from group to group, the entire scene is pulled together by the continuous sound of laughter and talk.

The editor cuts the sound to match the picture. At times he or she *plugs* the picture with leader for a "wild sound," stretches where sound has to be added later.

The sound editor lays the corresponding sound and picture tracks together and places a start mark (X) on the head leader at the point of synchronization. Once your work print has been synchronized, it is a good idea to send it back to the lab for *machine edge numbering*. When picture and sound have corresponding edge numbers, making your negative cut will be easier (and therefore less expensive).

As soon as picture and sound editing has been completed, your film goes back to the sound lab for a mix.

Working with magnetic tape can cause your equipment to become magnetized. Scissors, splicers, recorder heads, and reels may all become magnetized. When scissors and splicers become magnetized, they will add a clicking sound wherever your track has been cut. Magnetized equipment must be *degaussed*. A small pencillike degausser will do the trick.

MIXING

The mixing session is an exciting period. It is now that you view your film with all its component parts together. Mixing sessions, unfortunately, are expensive. Ten minutes of film to be seen on the screen may take from thirty minutes to two hours to mix. For this reason, edit sound and picture meticulously before attempting the mix. Here are some hints that will make mixing a little less intimidating:

- Practice the mix several times before you record one.
- With masking tape make a label next to each volume control: dialog, music, sound effects.
- If you have to choose between clarity of dialog or music (sound effects), choose the former.
- If you are short on tracks, you should use a "tape loop" for a continuous effect such as surf, wind, party, or traffic sounds. A section about three feet long is spliced to its own beginning, forming a loop.

Most dialog is put on either one or two tracks. Separate tracks are used for sound effects, room and/or environmental ambience, and music. A mixer adjusts the levels of each track and equalizes them to get the best results. Whenever one sound melts into another, both sounds must be placed on separate tracks, with one foot *overlap* at least.

Most mixing studios feature a footage counter, and you should supply the person responsible for the mix with a cue sheet indicating at which point the picture track has dialog, sound effects, or music. Make a log that has a column for the picture track and separate columns for each sound track.

Once the mixing session has been completed, the lab will supply you with a ¼" tape of the mix.

OPTICAL TRACK

Next you'll take your ¼" tape to an optical lab to have an optical track made. This lab manufactures a separate film that has no picture image but has the photographic image of your sound along its edge.

You need to know whether you need a negative or positive track:

Black and white negative film—negative optical track
Black and white reversal film—positive optical track
Color negative film—negative optical track
Color reversal stock—negative optical track

The optical track, let me warn you, is expensive, as are all other opticals. The term *opticals* covers:

Optical effects
Many special effects
Titles

Optical Effects   Most optical effects are used for transitions between scenes. Since optical effects are expensive, you may well reconsider whether you really need all those effects indicated in the original script. My advice is that while working on your shooting script you eliminate as many optical effects as possible.

- *Fade:* A shot gradually disappears or appears.
- *Dissolve:* Two shots are superimposed. The second shot appears out of the first shot.
- *Wipe:* The second shot pushes the first shot off the screen.
- *Flipover:* The image turns over, revealing what seems to be its other side.

- *Optical zoom:* An area is enlarged progressively. (Since there is always the danger that the picture may appear grainy, it is better—and less expensive—to use a zoom lens whenever a zoom is desired.)
- *Skip framing:* By printing only some of the frames of the original, action is speeded up. Skip framing can be used for comical effects, or—very effectively—for all car chases. If you are doing an action film, skip framing will make a mediocre car chase exciting.
- *Double framing:* Each frame can be printed twice or more to slow the action down. It is, however, less expensive to shoot at higher speed to achieve the same effect.
- *Freeze:* Action is stopped. Freezes are often used at the end of a film to "over" credits. I feel money spent on freeze for end titles is wasted.

Special Effects   Most special effects requiring the services of a lab are too expensive for you, the beginning director. That does not mean that you should stay away from special effects—after all, what is a horror movie without them—but it indicates that you should be aware of ways to bring inexpensive but highly effective special effects to the screen. Chapter 9 will deal with this highly creative part of your work.

Titles   Especially if superimposed over action, titles can be very expensive. To keep costs down to a minimum, you must give your optical house detailed instructions. Do not leave any decisions about titles up to them. Your first trip will be to the title house to have title cards made. Check the spelling of all names carefully, for you do not wish to redo titles. My advice is to stay away from complicated titles. White lettering on a black background always serves well. I like to begin my films with a short action sequence and from there go into simple titles, followed by another sequence of action and the remainder of the titles.

NEGATIVE CUTTING

The negative cutter (I suggest that you employ the most skillful cutter your budget can afford) will match each of the cuts in the work print with the corresponding cuts in the original footage. (Remember, you had corresponding edge numbers printed on both the original footage and the work print.) The negative cutter finds the edge numbers and places the shots into the synchronizer with the edge numbers aligned side by side. Once the frames are lined up correctly, the editor will cut the original footage. The negative cut should be cement spliced.

ANSWER PRINT

When the negative cut has been completed, the *original* footage goes back to the lab for printing. At this point the footage will be "timed" — that is, a scene that looks too dark can be lightened or vice versa; one can even change skin tones somewhat. The lab makes a composite print, with picture and sound on a single strip of film, and all opticals such as titles and special effects included. The first print is usually called the "answer print" or "first trial print." If there are any changes or corrections to be made (preferably only minor ones), they should be taken care of now.

Once the answer print has been completed to your satisfaction, you are ready to have your "release prints" (the ones to be shown on theater screens) made. I suggest that you have a *"dupe"* made, leave the original safely tucked away in the vault, and have the release prints cut from the dupe.

8.

Equipment

Choosing the best (most effective) camera, lenses, raw stock, lights, and sound equipment is your camera director's privilege and responsibility. But you, the beginning director, should have at least some basic knowledge about the equipment to be used on your film. (I will never forget how embarrassed I was when during the shooting of my very first film, I confused a "Sennheiser" with a catering company.) So here we go. These are the areas we will discuss (hopefully in a short and painless way):

Cameras
Miscellaneous lenses
Sound equipment
Lights
Grip equipment

CAMERAS

The standard camera has been—and still is—the 35mm camera. You may choose among the Mitchell 35mm camera, the Mitchell Mark II S35R

HardFront camera, the Arriflex 35 BL camera (my choice), and the Arriflex Model II C/B camera. Generally these cameras should be rented with these accessories:

- *Mitchell 35mm:* Comes with 25mm, 35mm, 50mm, 75mm SuperLenses, two 1000' or four (better choice) 400' magazines, compact matte box, viewfinder, variable-speed or sync motor.
- *Mitchell Mark II S35R HardFront:* This camera is adapted for high speed and includes a 110-volt universal high-speed motor. It does not have support rods, required for zoom lenses, but has BNCT lens mounts and comes with 25mm, 50mm, and 75mm lenses, plus two 1000' magazines.
- *Arriflex 35 BL:* Self-blimped (camera noise does not interfere with sync sound), lightweight, can be hand-held. Includes 16mm, 24mm, 32mm, 50mm, 85mm Ziess F2 lenses, two 400' magazines, and crystal motor 24/25fps. Has dual-pin registration, matte box that accepts two 4" square filters plus one 3" square filter. Though expensive to rent, this is the very best if you are shooting sync sound.
- *Arriflex Model II C/B:* Has interchangeable 28mm, 50mm, 75mm Schneider lenses, two 400' or two 200' magazines, 16-volt variable-speed or constant speed motor, nicad battery. This camera will work well if you are on exterior location and do not have to shoot dialog.

There is a wide variety of excellent 16mm cameras on the market, but if you are shooting a feature film, I'd like to suggest that you choose a 35mm camera. Here is a list of the 16mm cameras:

- *Arriflex 16mm BL:* Comes with 12mm to 120mm zoom lens, matte box, universal motor or sync motor, one 400' magazine, and standard accessories, Eclair.
- *NPR or ACL 16mm:* Crystal universal motor, 16mm, 25mm, 50mm lenses, matte box, two 200' or one 400' magazine, nicad battery, and standard accessories.
- *Mitchell 16mm:* 17mm, 25mm, 35mm Baltar lenses, variable-speed motor, three 400' magazines, matte box, viewfinder and support bracket.
- *Frezzi Cordless Sound:* Crystal sync motor (for sync shooting), two

batteries (for dialog on location), charger, magnetic pickup head, two 400' magazines, 12 to 120mm zoom lens with finder. May be rented with sound equipment: MA-11 amplifier, microphone, and headset.
- *Bell & Howell 70R:* With 16mm, 25mm, 50mm lenses, one 400' magazine.
- *Bolex Rex:* With 16mm, 25mm, 75mm lenses. One 100' magazine.

If you are shooting on tape you need, of course, a video camera. During the past few years video cameras have come and gone, and you should consult a reliable rental outfit to decide which camera should be used. The cameras that have been used during the past few years are:

- *Ikegami HL-77, Ikegami HL-35:* Comes supplied with 10/100 Canon zoom lens, AC power supply, two batteries, battery charger, quick-release plate, output cables.
- *Hitachi FP-3030:* Comes supplied with zoom lens, battery, microphone, power supply/charger, output cables.
- *Sony DXC-1600 Trinicon:* Comes supplied with C.C.U. zoom lens, battery, power supply/charger, cables.

It is obvious that your choice of motion picture camera and accessories depends on the particular shots and/or scenes you have planned to film. (Note that whereas different motion picture cameras should be used for different parts of your motion picture, you will use the *same* video camera throughout your video project.) A dialog scene requires the expensive sync camera; an action scene calls for a hand-held camera that takes small (100' to 400') loads; if you wish to shoot the interior of a historical building that does not permit floodlights, you should select a camera that allows the shutter to be held open long enough for adequate exposure.

MISCELLANEOUS LENSES

Not all lenses adapt to all cameras. (Some 16mm cameras have permanently mounted lenses that are not interchangeable.) The interchangeable lenses are attached by a mechanism called the lens mount. As many as three lenses can be accommodated by the lens turret.

A variety of lenses unquestionably helps to make your footage exciting, since by using lenses of different focal length the camera director will produce various effects. There is such a variety of lenses on the market that we will discuss only the most commonly used ones. The focal length of a normal lens is 35mm to 50mm. A telephoto lens has twice the focal length of the normal lens, and therefore the on-screen image will be twice the size of that obtained with a normal lens. Do not use a telephoto lens if you use a hand-held camera, as the image will jiggle. The telephoto lens will give you a shallow depth of field (the zone of sharp focus).

If you wish to give your audience a sense of perspective, your camera director chooses a wide-angle lens (lenses of different focal length do not have different perspectives). A wide-angle lens has a much greater depth of field than a normal lens, an important fact to consider when you shoot action, because with a wide-angle lens the camera director can shoot without having to follow focus during a shot. For instance, if you wish to create a dynamic impression of a fist coming toward the screen, use a wide-angle lens. The fist punching toward the audience will double in size.

The zoom lens can focus down to ⅜ of an inch in front of the subject. Shock zooms have been a standby (now already cliché) in horror pictures.

Viewfinder The camera director views what the camera sees through the viewfinder. The best system is a through-the-lens reflex viewfinder, in which the image transmitted through the lens is projected onto a ground glass. Always take into consideration the slight (but at times significant) difference between the image seen through the viewfinder and the image projected on the screen. This difference is called the parallax.

Camera Motors Motors are either spring wound or operated by an electric drive. You will find spring-wound motors on 16mm cameras only. Electrically driven motors do require a source of electric power or a battery. You'll find two types of electric motors: wild motors and synchronous motors. Wild motors permit various filming speeds. You are able to film at a faster speed than normal, and when the film is projected at normal speed the action on the screen will be slowed down. Conversely, if you film at a slower speed than normal, then project at normal speed, the action will speed up.

A synchronous motor is used as you shoot sync sound. On location this motor is run by battery power. To avoid unnecessary delays, ask your camera director to check the motor from time to time.

Variable Shutter Each frame is exposed by stopping briefly as it moves through the camera. The shutter blocks the light so that the film is exposed. Most likely your camera director will opt for a variable shutter. It can be shut down gradually, to effect a camera fadeout (you save on the expensive optical fadeout), and it allows the use of fast film for exterior shots, as well as a decreasing and/or increasing depth of field.

Filters Most cameras have a built-in filter for using indoor film outdoors, or they come equipped with a matte box that permits the use of gelatin filters in front of the lens. (Generally, however, if I may advise you, do *not* use outdoor raw stock for an indoor shot, and avoid indoor raw stock for an exterior shot.)

SOUND EQUIPMENT

The most flexible sound recorder is the Nagra. This recorder can be fitted with an oscillator identical to the unit that controls camera speed. The tape's running speed is recorded along the edge of the sound tape, thus giving a *precise* reference when picture and sound go into editing.

The starting point for sound and picture is marked by the *slate,* a board to which a piece of wood *(clapper)* has been hinged. The scene number, take number, production title, and name of director are penciled on the slate. Once the camera is up to speed, the production assistant holding the slate reads aloud the scene and take numbers, then slaps the clapper down on the board. Later on the editor will line up this banging noise with sound and picture tracks. The soundman should always wear earphones that are plugged into the Nagra, so he or she will be able to hear the sound exactly as it is picked up.

The best microphones on the market, as mentioned previously, are Sennheisers. At times you may want to use a *lavalier* mike, which can be attached to your actor's outfit. And, without any doubt, you need a *fishpole* mike, which dangles from a fishpolelike mechanism held above your actors.

The following is a basic sound package:

Nagra 4.2L Synchronous tape recorder, with three speeds,
    two OPSE-200 preamps, self-resolving camera speed

indicator, ATN unit, batteries, headset, soft and hard
case.
Boom stand
Fishpole
Microphone desk stand
Sennheiser microphones
Microphone mixer

LIGHTS

Shooting your motion picture on film requires a fairly extensive light package:

Fresnels: Midget, Baby, Junior, Senior, Tener
Softlights
Arcs
Nooklights
Molettes
Minibrutes
Maxibrutes
  (all these come with silks, barn doors, and stands)
Overhead lights
Strip lights
Daylight source units—200, 400, 575, 2500 watts
  (stands, barn doors, gel frames, scrim net, snoot)
Mole Kit: Teenie mole kit, micky mole kit, mighty
  mole kit.

Needless to say, you do not need all these lights for every scene in your film. The light plot will change from location to location, and some changes may be needed between scenes and camera setups.

GRIP EQUIPMENT

And now, hold on to your seat as you take a look at the grip equipment necessary. I know it sounds like a lot, but please listen to me: it is better to have some equipment in store you'll never use, than to have to send a production assistant to fetch something. Delays are far more costly than a clamp that rents for a few dollars. So, here we go:

GRIP EQUIPMENT

Small sandbag
Large sandbag
⅛ apple box
¼ apple box
½ apple box
Full apple box
Flex arm (gooseneck)
Grip head and arm
C stand
Hi overhead stand w/wheels
Stair blocks (8)
Cup blocks (12)
Wedges (24)
Cribbing (24)
Clip boards (baby, junior, and senior)
12' × 12' butterfly set
6' × 6' butterfly set
4' × 4' silk
4' × 4' single net
4' × 4' double net
24" × 36" open end single
24" x 36" open end double
18" × 24" open end single
18" × 24" open end double
10" × 12" open end single or double
Dots: single, double, solid (set/6)
Fingers: single, double, solid (set/6)
5' × 4' solid flag
24" × 36" flag
18" × 24" flag
10" × 12" flag
24" × 36" open end silk
18" × 24" open end silk
24" × 72" cutter flag
18" × 48" cutter flag
10" × 42" cutter flag
4' × 4' cube

24″ × 36″ cube
18″ × 24″ cube
Alligator clamp
Ladders, 4′, 8′, 10′—each
Ladders, 12″ ext.—each
Umbrella and stand
6′ parallel and tops, w/wheel, post rails, and screen
  jacks
Bear claw
Meat ax
Furniture pad
Block and fall w/rope
Sawed off C-stand
Dolly track (4′ × 8′)
4′ × 4′ reflector (complete)
2′ × 2′ hand reflector (complete)
Ford axle
Auto tow bars
Grip box (complete with contents)
Double suction cups
Riser
Polecats
Bar clamp
12′ × 12′ tarp
20′ × 20′ tarp
20′ × 20′ black backing
20′ × 20′ white silk
20′ × 30′ white silk
Wall spreaders (2)
20′ × 20′ frame

MISCELLANEOUS

Director chair (high)
Director chair (regular)
Gold water cooler

Cooler box
Walkie-talkie set, batteries (5 watt)
Signal horn
Staple gun
Staples (as used)
Gas can w/spout
First-aid kit
Water hose
Nozzle
Broom
Dustpan
Garbage pail
Shovel
Posthole digger
Rake
Rubber mats, 24" × 36"
Battery clip set
Flashlight

HANGERS AND MOUNTING ACCESSORIES

Baby offset arm
Furniture clamp (bar clamp), 12" or 18"
Baby C-clamp ⅝ pin
Baby pipe clamp
Baby wall sled
Baby trombone
Baby nail-on plate (Reg. or 12" Stud)
Baby boom
Gaffers grip
Junior Offset arm
Junior C-clamp
Junior pipe clamp
Junior wall sled
Junior trombone
Junior bazooka
Junior nail-on plate

Junior pigeon
Junior telescoping hanger, 6', 8', and 10'
Junior trapeze
Junior stand bracket
Junior set wall bracket
T-Bone (floor spider)
Senior wall sled

9.

Special Effects

Major production companies spend millions of dollars on breathtaking special effects. To be sure, these are not the ones to be discussed in this chapter. Instead we will cover those special effects that are within your budget and expertise. You will want to use these "homegrown" special effects if you:

Wish to avoid costly opticals.
Wish to avoid paying for expensive locations.
Need fire effects.
Need visually exciting shots that are either too
    expensive or too dangerous to shoot the
    conventional way.

Special Effects Instead of Opticals

"SUPER OVER" EFFECTS

Visually you want to convey your heroine's torn state of mind, so you have decided to superimpose her CU over a broken window. If you "super" the conventional way, that is, you first film the window, then the CU, then have the CU supered via opticals, you are facing a considerable expense.

Fortunately you'll achieve the same effect if you buy an inexpensive piece of glass, glue strips of plastic tape over it to resemble a broken window, place it in front of the camera, position your actress behind it, and—presto—shoot.

If you want a ghost to appear on-screen, you have two choices to avoid a costly optical:

• Coat a mirror slightly with petroleum jelly and film your actor's mirror image.

• Create a transparent ghost (only a little more complicated): choose a fairly dark environment in which (thanks to rim lighting) furniture and architectural details are only barely visible, and place a piece of window-sized glass in front of it. Position your actress (the ghost) some distance away from the glass, direct strong light beams on her, and film. Her image appearing on the screen will be frighteningly transparent.

"Now You See Me, Now You Don't" This great old standby is lots of fun to see on-screen, and easy to do. As you film your environment and actors, you'll have the camera stop at a *specific* moment. Make your ghost appear by positioning your actor in front of the camera. Then run the camera up to the moment when the ghost disappears. Stop the camera, remove the ghost, and complete the shot showing the actors who had been established previously. Easy to do if you keep in mind:

The camera *must* be placed on a tripod. No hand-held camera for this specific effect.

The actors present in the environment must freeze the moment the camera stops running.

They must be in exactly the same positions when the camera starts rolling again.

Avoiding Expensive Locations

Dialog in Front of an Ancient Castle Given your budget, naturally you do not plan to travel to England to shoot the exterior of "Castle Hunsbury" but have to be satisfied with a stock shot of the edifice (many film libraries have a wide variety of magnificent stock shots). Have your art director paint some architectural detail on a piece of glass (glass image). Place the glass image in front of your camera and position your actors for a Medium Shot. The effect—your actors standing in front of a magnificent Renaissance window or within a heavily carved door frame—will be surprisingly real.

On the Train   Your script calls for a holdup on a vintage train. Naturally you won't find an old train that still runs; even if you did, the exorbitant rental fee would preclude filming on it. But you should be able (for some money, proof of insurance, and many, many good words) to film the interior of a nonmoving historical train. There are a number of train museums around, and many a small town has elevated its long-defunct train station to a local museum.

Film your actors boarding the train, making it a night shot if at all possible. Close the windowshades and light the lamps. With the shades closed, your audience won't be able to discern that the train is not moving. The actors must take care to rock to and fro in their seats, and the conductor and the holdup men must sway as they make their way through the aisle. All you need are the sounds of rumbling wheels and the rush of the steam engine, to be added during the editing process, and you have created a believable "on the train" scene.

On the Plane   You need not rent an expensive mockup of a plane interior. Rent only a few authentic plane seats (any motion picture prop house can supply them), have your art director build a mock window area, and every so often let a pretty stewardess walk by.

On the Bus   Shoot all your dialog scenes on a nonmoving bus. Later, place your actor on a moving bus and

> film the actor looking out of a window
> film the actor's POV.

Rain, Snow   You don't have to wait for rain or snow to hit your area before shooting an important exterior scene. Wet your actors' outfits, or sprinkle artificial snow on them. From your favorite supply house rent a rain or snow machine, have a production assistant hold it in front of the camera, and shoot.

Jungle and Forest Scenes Jungle and forest scenes are easy to create. If you have a sufficient number of stock shots on hand for establishing shots, all you'll have to do is add the Medium and ¾ shots of your actors. For this purpose some very believable scenery can be created by covering a relatively small area with greenery. You can get any amount of greenery from a tree-trimming service, or—more expensive—rent it from a nursery.

Fire Effects

First of all, a word of warning: regardless of what your friends tell you, *never* attempt to do any effects requiring the use of flammables or gunpowder in-house. Neither you, the art director, nor any of your assistants is qualified for such tasks. Only a *certified* explosives expert (a motion picture supply house will have names available) should handle explosive and flammable materials.

Fire effects require the attendance of a fire marshal (you can get the names of retired firefighters from the municipal office that handles motion picture location permits), and a water truck and driver must be stationed at the location where the fire effect takes place. All these items run up your budget considerably. (The special effects for my film *Executioner II,* which showed Vietnam scenes including a helicopter, flamethrowers, and many extras, took up one-fourth the entire budget.) Because of the expense, think twice about whether your story really needs fire effects, and if so, whether a substitute effect might work just as well.

In one of my films the hero and heroine had to run through a burning building. The nature of our chosen location, a historical California mission, prevented even the thought of using real fire.

First we filmed a scale model of the mission's exterior with flames shooting out of windows and the roof. (Yes, we had an expert setting our model on fire, and yes, we will discuss scale models later.) In this way we established the burning mission in the audience's mind.

For the interior shot, our gaffer mounted red gels over all production lights. A pan of dry ice in hot water was held in front of the camera. (A smoke machine from a motion picture rental house would have been better, but because of the artifacts in the building, smoke could not be used.) Finally, production assistants waved blankets in front of the lamps as our actors ran "through the fire" to safety.

Extraordinary Visual Effects

(Miniatures)

Miniatures are your answer if you need extraordinary visual effects that are either too dangerous or too expensive to shoot the conventional way. Most art directors are enthusiastic creators of miniatures. They create great-looking stuff from practically nothing. If you desire top-quality miniatures, you may commission a special effects studio. Major production companies use miniatures all the time. The fantastic sea-air battle scenes we admired in the film *Tora! Tora! Tora!* were created using miniatures. The term *miniatures,* agreed, seems to be somewhat misleading when one considers that the battleships used for *Tora! Tora! Tora!* were each about eighteen feet long. Don't worry— the miniatures we are talking about are on a more conservative scale.

A CAR GOES OVER A CLIFF

If you should consider the conventional way of shooting a car going over a cliff, you have to count on a full shooting day on a remote location that features a road and cliffs, a special permit, a fire marshal plus water truck and driver, possibly a motorized police escort, a stunt car rigged for the stunt (expensive), a skilled stunt driver, a tow car and team to pull the totaled car up from the cliff, a junkyard that will take the car, and last but not least a *huge* insurance policy. (Believe me, a shot that lasts a few seconds on the screen takes all of this—I have done it.)

You may, of course, buy a stock shot of a car going over a cliff, which is fine if just any type of car will do. If, as is most likely, the car going over the cliff had been established as an important part of your story, you better have a miniature made. This miniature car going over a miniature cliff must resemble the actual car used in previous scenes in color, shape, and detail as closely as possible, or you'll be in trouble.

The effect works as follows: Your stunt driver drives the actual car to the spot where it is supposed to go over the cliff (the dangerous promontory ought to be comfortably far away), then by way of clever editing you cut to the shot of the miniature car going over the cliff.

In shooting miniatures, remember that the audience should see the miniature for *short* periods of time only. Therefore, *intercut* the miniature's action with a number of shots of the driver's face, her hands on the steering wheel, hands covering her face, etc.

Also, don't forget that you must show the actual time it would take the actual car to go over the cliff, which is another reason why you intercut with the driver's reactions.

A YACHT EXPLODES

Let's assume that part of your film takes place on a yacht that—at the film's climax—explodes. Cleverly you have scheduled the explosion to occur at night. All action and dialog are to be filmed on the "actual location," the yacht you have rented for that purpose. As tempting as it may be, do *not* take the yacht out to the open sea when filming. Leave it safely anchored in the harbor, if you want to avoid unattractive back-and-forth rocking during framing. Take the yacht out for the Establishing and POV shots only.

The climax, after your characters have made their way to a life raft, is indeed the explosion. Remember it is night—a moonless night—so the miniature needs to resemble the actual yacht in outline only. Your art director has built a believable ocean by using nothing more expensive or elaborate than dark green plastic garden bags. Behind the ocean is placed the *cyclorama* (a slightly curved background) of the dark night sky. A dark fishing line is attached to the miniature yacht and slowly, while the camera rolls, a steady-handed production assistant pulls the yacht across the plastic ocean.

For the ensuing explosion (I have to remind you) you have to hire an explosives expert, unless you wish to face the possibility of the studio's going up in flames.

Getting back to the scene as your characters evacuate the yacht: By now, to be realistic, the sinking yacht ought to be in a tilted position, which, because of the sheer weight of the craft, cannot be done safely. A smaller boat has to be substituted for the yacht. Have your production manager look for a small-craft dry dock. Rent a boat that has been placed on a wooden frame for repairs. Shooting at night, fasten a tarpaulin behind the boat and tilt the boat slightly. Do *not* allow your production assistants or grips to do this job, but leave it up to the dry dock's employees—they know how to handle boats safely. Set up for a ¾ Shot, to be intercut with CUs and Medium Shots, and shoot your characters evacuating the craft.

A UFO CRASHES IN THE BACKYARD

Don't despair if your script calls for a UFO crash, but put in a call to your art director. Calmly she will inform you that the special effect requires two easy-to-come-by items: a UFO miniature, and a glass image.

The art director will create the UFO miniature, which has to be placed against a sky background. If you have wisely chosen a night scene, flickering Christmas lights on the UFO will add a feeling of reality. For a daytime shoot you might want to use dry ice to give cloud effects. Two fishing lines have to be attached to the UFO. The rigging of the second is somewhat tricky, as this is the line that directs the UFO's descent.

With the limited resources at your disposal, you cannot film the UFO's actual crash, but will have to find other means to make this scene believable. So, you show the interior of a suburban house (most likely the people living there will play an important part in your story anyway), and have your characters *hear* all the terrifying sounds that accompany the UFO's crash.

Next you show the crashed UFO—no big deal to that. Your art director has painted a glass image of it, which will be mounted in front of the camera in such a way that it seems the UFO barely missed the house.

A Moving Train   A moving train is easy to film. Depending on the kind of train you need, many types of train models, including surrounding environment, will do. To create a truly believable effect, you ought to film the moving train via an *aerial* shot; your camera director, with a hand-held camera, perches on the top rung of a ladder while shooting.

The Burning City   This effect also needs to be shot from an elevated camera position. From cardboard boxes, barrels, some magazine cutouts, and strings of Christmas lights, your art director has created a nighttime (forget about daytime) urban street. Most likely the miniature set is about two feet high and eight to ten feet long. May I remind you that a miniature, in order to look real, can be shown only briefly, so you must intercut with exterior nighttime shots of an actual urban street and interior shots of the cars whose occupants are involved in the story. For the fire effect, let me repeat, you will hire an explosives expert.

I hope these few examples have given you a taste for creating your own homegrown special effects. They are lots of fun to do.

Safety with Guns

Permit me to say a few words about the use of guns on the set. I know, every action film requires at least one good shoot-out. Fine. But guns, even the blanks that are used, are dangerous. Don't forget, *blanks can kill.* Some producers insist on using blanks because a small wisp of smoke escapes the barrel at the moment the gun is fired. If you have to use blanks, please observe the following safety rules:

- Do not permit actors or crew to "horse around" with the guns.
- Assign a responsible "gun handler" to hand out guns before every scene using them, and to collect the guns after the scene finishes.
- Allow only the gun handler to load the guns, and make him or her responsible for the blanks used.
- Do not permit any loaded guns in a scene that does not require a shoot-out. For these scenes, have the gun handler check *each* gun to see whether it is loaded.

On the films I produce, I must admit, I do not permit the use of blanks. I prefer to rent guns that cannot be loaded because the barrel has been blocked. True, no little wisp of smoke escapes while our hero or villain fires the gun, but so far I have not received any complaints. Besides, no matter which type of gun one uses, gunshot sounds have to be added later in the mix, because blanks do not sound quite genuine.

Well, we've come to the end of this book. I hope my advice and suggestions will help you get a project of your own off the ground. Good luck.

Suggested Reading

Bare, Richard L. *The Film Director.* New York: Collier Books, 1971.
Harmon, Renée. *Film Producing: Low-Budget Films That Sell.* Hollywood, Calif.: Samuel French Trade, 1989.
———. *How to Audition for Movies and TV.* New York: Walker and Company, 1992.
Seger, Linda. *Making a Good Script Great.* Hollywood, Calif.: Samuel French Trade, 1987.

Index

The
Beginning Filmmaker's
Business Guide

Contents

Preface

Never before in the motion picture business have practices and guidelines changed as much as they have during recent years. These changes have caused havoc. Many once-solid companies have ceased to exist; others, employing different business methods, have sprung up. Therefore, today more than ever, the producer, director, and/or writer must be knowledgeable about the ins and outs of getting a film off the ground.

The Beginning Filmmaker's Business Guide provides this knowledge, as it guides you through all phases important to your film's successful marketing: the movie's germinal idea (or acquisition of literary property), its sellable "hook" and distribution appeal, design of the effective, hard-hitting package (offering, prospectus), ways and means of financing your project, the nitty-gritty of today's production practices as they exist in studio deals, studio acquisition, and independent and foreign distribution as well as in the auxiliary markets (cable, TV, and home video).

This book is a problem-identifying and problem-solving guide, giving you examples of various budget scenarios, offering/prospectus contracts, and distribution agreements that will help you give your project the professional expertise it deserves.

1.

High concept, hooks,

and

other facts of life

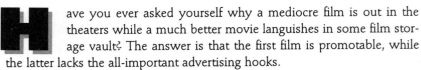ave you ever asked yourself why a mediocre film is out in the theaters while a much better movie languishes in some film storage vault? The answer is that the first film is promotable, while the latter lacks the all-important advertising hooks.

A producer's knowledge about film marketing may make the difference between a movie on the screen and one on the shelves. Unless the producer has worked toward marketing from the conception of the movie's idea through the final production stages, even a thought-provoking screenplay, skilled director, exciting actors, outstanding special effects and/or stunts, as well as professional photography and editing won't get the movie into theaters. Clearly, then, you the producer ought to concern yourself with the promotable—in other words, *marketable*—elements of your film, *prior to financing*.

So let's walk through the various steps required before you can talk about finance. You accomplish this first step by keeping your mind on the audience—that is to say, your film's promotable elements that will draw the ticket-buying audience into theatres. This means you'll have to stress your movie's *high concept*.

Before going on, permit me to correct a misconception: high concept *does not* refer to:

- High budget
- Expensive star

- Well-known director
- Outstanding stunts and/or special effects
- Exotic locations

High concept applies to the fact that a commercially viable picture must provide the distributor with *promotional elements* that touch upon the audience's emotions:

- A gripping story
- Characters the audience either hates or can identify with (if these characters are to be portrayed by—at the moment—popular stars, so much the better)
- And most important, a seemingly intangible ingredient that permits the audience to let go of hidden fears, frustrations, and/or desires

Don't ever forget, "making movies" is big business. (It goes without saying that every distributor, whether major, mini-major, or independent, expects your film is of high professional quality.) But after lip service has been paid to the art and message of a film, a distributor's consideration boils down to one thing only: high concept.

Whether you have written (or intend to write) your own screenplay or are ready to spend a few hundred or many hundred thousands of dollars to option a screenplay (an area we will discuss later) or book, short story, newspaper article, or even the germ of an idea linked to any of these, always keep high concept in mind. Here are six key questions always to ask:

1. Can the basic idea be developed into a clear story line?
2. Does the basic idea feature components (hooks) that make it promotable?
3. What segment of the paying audience will the idea attract? (genre)
4. Will the idea lend itself to the creation of a catchy title?
5. Can this idea by expressed in an interesting visual way?

And since, let's admit it, there are really not any new story ideas and/or plots floating around, you may ask yourself:

6. Can this idea be turned around and/or given a new twist to give a new approach to a frequently used concept?

If none of the above can be answered in the affirmative, you know that the idea is either too vague or too complicated to be turned into a successful (read: promotable) movie. Most likely such material lacks the promotional hook, and therefore will have difficulties in finding distribution and financing.

Here are some answers to these six key questions:

1. *Clear Story Line.* Test your material's soundness and the strength of your idea by reducing it to one sentence that tells the gist of the story. Examples from fairy tales show these one-sentence truths:

Hansel and Gretel
Two children lost in the woods survive life-threatening danger.

Cinderella
Courage saves a princess and a kingdom.

Snow White
An evil queen tries to kill a beautiful girl.

Jack and the Beanstalk
A young boy outsmarts a giant.

As you take a look at the story sentence, you'll discover that each one of the old fairy tales features powerful human emotions (motives) that compel characters to do something to reach a goal based upon:

Survival
Love
Hate
Fear

The emotions "talk" to the viewer until he or she, subconsciously identifying with the character on the screen, taps into his or her own hidden emotions, fears, and/or desires.

In a nutshell, your story sentence should lead the audience to ask: Will the character accomplish his or her goal? Yet, the audience won't ask this question unless the character's goal springs from one of the above-listed emotions. These emotions in turn are the basis for the *promotional hook.*

2. *Promotional Hook*. Back to our fairy tales:

Hansel and Gretel
Hook: Children face death.

Cinderella
Hook: Love conquers all.

Snow White
Hook: Beauty is dangerous.

Jack and the Beanstalk
Hook: Intelligence outwits size.

(Just for fun, apply the above-listed hooks to some of the recently released, successful films, and you'll be surprised to see the correlation.)

Take a good look at the hooks, and you'll notice that each one of them has been designed to express loudly how scary, heartwarming, entertaining, or exciting the story is. The practice of the promotional hook goes way back to the carnival barker bellowing:

"See the bearded lady."
"See the fire eater."
"See the fearless lion tamer."

Simply imagining yourself to be a carnival barker will lead you to your story's hook and from there to its high concept.

You may train yourself in the art of recognizing high concept by taking a good, hard look at this year's five most successful movies, by studying movie ads in your local paper, or simply by perusing the *TV Guide*.

3. *Genre*. Keep a close look at genres, and decide whether your idea or script falls within any of them. In keeping with high concept, it is best to avoid mixing genres within one film. Familiarize yourself with the current selling power of each genre, but keep in mind that by the time your movie is ready for release this particular genre might be out of favor, or the market might be flooded with similar products. For this reason it is a good idea to keep a tight tab on current production schedules by reading the "trades." If you should discover a number of projects that are similar to yours, you better have some second thoughts before forging ahead.

Before beginning your project you ought to get acquainted with the distribution companies specializing in your movie's genre, and—maybe most important—familiarize yourself with the hooks promoting various genres. This information is easy to obtain through the annual new film issues of the trade papers *Variety* and *Hollywood Reporter* advertising the following film markets:

American Film Market
Los Angeles, USA (February issues)

Cannes Film Festival
Cannes, France (April issues)

MIFED
Milan, Italy (October issues)

The following is a list of basic movie genres:

Action has been, and still is, the staple of both low-budget film and multimillion-dollar blockbusters. A simple story line, based on the battle between good and evil, is mandatory. Action films sell well if presented with a different twist (familiar situations presented in different and new ways). At times when the market is flooded with action films, you'll have a tough go unless you feature a name star.

Action-Adventure usually sells well but demands exotic, or at least highly interesting, locations (e.g., the Indiana Jones trilogy).

Art Film is the most difficult genre to get financed and distributed. Such a film is hard to market. There are, however, some small distributors who, in moving a few prints from theater to theater, do an excellent job. Do not expect to make any money on your art film, yet as you exhibit it at various film festivals (not markets) and—it is hoped—garner some awards, you gain exposure for yourself and your work of cinematic art (e.g., *La Strada, Lili, Marty*).

Comedy, if the script offers hilarious situations and twists, is always a seller. Usually it does better domestically than overseas (e.g., *Some Like It Hot*).

Romantic Comedy, if featuring two well-known stars, is another marketable vehicle. Without name stars, romantic comedy is more difficult to sell (e.g., *The Graduate, Desk Set, The Quiet Man, High Society,* all the Spencer Tracy–Katharine Hepburn films).

Docudrama features a story based upon a nonfictional frightening, unusual, or controversial event. Theatrically and in home video this genre has proven to be less successful, but is always needed for cable and network TV (e.g., *All the President's Men, Paths of Glory, The Right Stuff*).

Mystery. The traditional mystery has by now been firmly entrenched in TV programming, and is therefore less prevalent on the big screen (e.g.,*The Third Man, Dr. Crippen on Board, Murder on the Orient Express*).

Horror is an old standby that never fails to attract viewers. Blockbusters of course depend on extraordinary—and expensive—special effects. But even a low-budget film will find buyers if based on an interesting premise (e.g., *The Creature from the Black Lagoon, Frankenstein).*

Psychological Thriller. The psychological thriller has replaced the traditional murder mystery on the big screen. If your psychological thriller has believable characters and an extraordinary hook, then go for it (e.g., *Fatal Attraction*).

4. *Title.* It is a must to carry the high concept over to a film's title; a film's title presents the audience with the hook about its content.

As you think about the best title for your movie, ask yourself:

What does the title mean and/or what message does the title communicate?

What emotion does the title evoke?

The working titles of many of my films were changed by the distributor for catchier ones. Here are a few examples:

Revenge	to	*Lady Streetfighter*
Chill Factor	to	*Frozen Scream*
Bikers	to	*Hellriders*
The Idol	to	*Jungle Trap*

Granted, all the above titles were chosen for low-budget films, but the principle applies to multimillion-dollar productions as well.

5. *Visual Interpretation of Ideas.* Beware of any ideas that depend upon the verbal expression of goals and/or emotions primarily. Always keep in mind that film is a visual medium that fosters visual expression. (Most stage plays that were adapted to the screen turned out to be photographed renderings of the play, and therefore failed to grab the movie audience's empathy.) This does not imply, however, that a film depends upon the director's expertise in creating unique camera setups and moves. Fact is, many a film failed to

grip the audience's response (and therefore failed at the box office) because its cinematography did draw too much attention from the movie's pictorial aspects, instead of focusing on the director's responsibility *to tell a gripping story.*

6. *Twists in Concepts and Ideas.* Let's face it, writers of novels and screenplays have only a limited number of basic plots at their disposal. Even magazine stories and news reports seem to repeat the same incidents over and over again. Then why do we read books, go to the movies, and watch TV? We do, because the old and familiar has been changed in such a way as to make it new and exciting.

Take another look at the previously discussed fairy tales and you will discover that a host of movies has developed from their basic—and very simple—concepts. Here are but a few examples, randomly selected:

Jack and the Beanstalk
A young boy outsmarts a powerful giant.

Burning Bed
A woman escapes from her abusive husband.

Cinderella
Prince Charming saves Cinderella from her mean stepmother and ugly stepsisters.

Pretty Woman
A girl who makes her living as a prostitute meets the man who "saves" her.

Hansel and Gretel
The witch lures children into her gingerbread house.

Silence of the Lambs
A psychopath imprisons young girls and kills them.

Snow White
The queen tries to kill her rival—the beautiful Snow White.

Dressed to Kill
A cross-dresser stalks attractive women.

Therefore, if you find a story or idea that seems suitable, if a little trite, try to turn it upside down, adjust it, change it, create new characters, and you'll be surprised about the unique concept you'll come up with.

Advertising

As the producer, you will eventually have to pay for the release prints (about $1,500 for each 35mm print). Contrary to common belief, the distributor *does* *not* pay for the prints. The distribution company only *advances* the required sum, and—never forget this—is first in line for recoupment. Moreover, most distributors attempt to put some of the advertising expenses upon the producer's shoulders.*

The following are the traditional advertising tools employed:

Trailers for theatrical promotion (teasers)
Trailers for TV promotion (spots)
Radio blurbs
One-sheets (posters)
Mats for newspaper advertising
Sell sheets
Box cover for home video release
Screening in foreign film markets

If you, the producer, are able to pay at least partially for the prints at the movie's release, you'll have a strong negotiation point as far as advertising is concerned.

Trailers. Here we are speaking about two kinds of trailers: the "teasers" customarily shown in theaters and the spots shown on TV. While the cost of a teaser is negligible, since it involves only some expenses for editing and printing, TV spots—especially if shown in prime time and in major cities—may run into millions. (Needless to say, a low-budget film does not require any TV spots.) TV spots are also important for a film's home video sales; wholesalers tend to hinge the size of their order upon the scope of the motion picture distributor's TV advertising.

Radio blurbs. Radio blurbs are an excellent and not exorbitantly costly advertising tool, if your film has either a strong musical score or catchy, unusual auditory moments.

One-sheets (posters). The advertising tool demanding close attention is the one-sheet (poster), not as much for its value as a lobby display as for the fact that all graphic advertising (sell sheets, newspaper mats, and home video box covers) is based upon the eye-catching and emotional-reponse-demanding one-sheet. My advice is that you begin working on the concept of your one-sheet as early as your film's preproduction time. Many producers even have

---

*The producer's participation in advertising expenses will be discussed in the chapter on distribution.

their one-sheet's concept ready for their offering and/or prospectus. Some producers, getting ready to offer their films at the film markets, even create one-sheets for films that neither are in preproduction nor have acquired funding.

Here are some pointers about your one-sheet key art:

- Keep the concept strong but simple.
- Do not include too many details. Keep in mind that your key art has to work in reduced formats. Even a very small newspaper ad has to convey the film's hook.
- Remember that your full-color one-sheet will be printed in black-and-white for newspaper advertising.

Title treatment is equally important, and as with your graphic art it must reduce well. The one-sheet shows two title elements: the copy line and the tag line. The copy line is placed *above* the film's title. It sets up what the film is all about. It has to grab the viewer's attention and emotional response immediately. For this very reason the copy line is imperative for the low-budget film. Here are a few examples:

COPY LINE: They came out of the grave . . .
TITLE: *Scalps*
COPY LINE: Beware rapists, killers, and muggers . . .
TITLE: *The Executioner*
COPY LINE: The dream you cannot escape . . .
TITLE: *Nightmare*

If these copy lines seem a bit too colorful—read "cheap"— don't worry, major studios use similar scintillating "orations" to sell their product. (Your art film, of course, demands a more subdued way of advertising.)

The tag line appears *after* the title and acknowledgments:

TITLE: *Scalps*
TAG LINE: . . . to get revenge.
TITLE: *The Executioner*
TAG LINE: . . . is back to get you.
COPY LINE: *Nightmare*
TAG LINE: . . . you haven't got a chance.

Once your film ad receives favorable reviews, add those blurbs to your tag line.

Shop around for your artwork. It is not unusual to spend several hundred thousand dollars (or more), but there is no doubt that you can obtain highly satisfactory artwork for about $5,000. All you have to do is shop around.

Here are a few suggestions:

Contact local art schools or the fine arts department of a university or college. You may put an inquiry on their bulletin board or enlist the assistance of one of the instructors.

A small ad in the "wanted" column of local newspapers should get you in contact with free-lance artists.

If you have some contact with one of the big studios, you may be able to find out whether someone on their staff might be willing to moonlight for you.

All students, and some free-lance artists, will gladly accept a lower fee in exchange for printed samples for his or her portfolio.

Presently distribution companies prefer illustrations for their key art. These illustrations are derived from either sketches or photos.

Once the artwork has been completed to your and the distributor's satisfaction, an offset printer will do the color separations, add the copy, and do the actual printing.

Sell sheets. Sell sheets are used as "throwaways" at film markets and are given to home video retailers. They advertise either a specific film or a number of films. Sell sheets will be printed both in color and in black-and-white.

Mats. This term derives from the old "hot type" era, and refers to your film's ads for newspapers and sell sheets. You need mats in several sizes to fit various printing requirements and ad spaces.

Home video box cover. Your home video distributors either supply the wholesaler with sleeves to be inserted into the plastic envelope covering the box or have cardboard boxes printed.

Except for blockbuster movies, it is packaging that makes a modestly viable theatrical film into a hot one for home video. The cover is the key element of the home video release. With your home video sale in mind, and knowing that your one-sheets will adorn the home video box, you should choose a strong color scheme. Don't ever try to save money by deciding upon a black-and-white box cover; no one will look at your film, much less rent or buy it. A *three-color* job is a must for your one-sheets. Still, you can save a bundle of money and give your one-sheets the desired three-color effect by choosing colored stock on which you print *two-color* key art. For my film *Night of Terror* we used black stock and had the artwork printed in red and silver.

Publicity

Publicity, if thoughtfully orchestrated and combined with effective advertising (P&A), can be immensely helpful. Needless to say, the publicity campaign *should not* be employed in lieu of advertising.

Publicity consists of your film's free exposure via magazine and newspaper articles, TV talk shows, and news shows. You'll need a press kit and electronic press kit and, most important, a public relations (PR) firm to handle your publicity. Granted, a PR firm, if well connected and established, is expensive. True, there are many PR firms around, but only one with clout will do you and your film any good. Don't be taken in by sweet words and flashy pamphlets. Before you hire a PR firm, interview several firms, *ask for client lists* (including telephone numbers), and call these clients. In addition, take a look at magazines and newspapers featuring articles or pictures about the firm's clients. Make certain the firm's sample press releases are recent. Question every PR firm long and hard. Find out whether the firm is familiar with PR techniques pertaining to motion pictures, and if it has excellent media connections.

The effective PR firm *must* have nationwide contacts. After all, you want to read about your movie in national magazines, and you want to see your stars on network or syndicated TV.

Obviously, all publicity concentrates on your stars and—if well known—your director. Don't expect, however, that you, the producer, will be part of the "hype." Accept the fact that you, the person who has nurtured the project through all the travails of rewrite, financing, casting, and so on, are not appropriate fodder for the media.

Don't hesitate to negotiate the PR firm's fee. All PR firms demand retainer fees. You'll have to apply a (hefty) monthly fee regardless of whether any promotion results from the firm's effort. And this is the catch: You'll pay for their efforts and not the results.

It is obvious that, for a small art film seeing territorial distribution only (we will discuss distribution patterns later on) and being exhibited in a few selected theaters, an expensive nationwide PR campaign is a waste of time and money. For your art film you'll do best to hire territorial PR firms and have your film given some exposure in national magazines catering to the audience interested in art films only.

It is a must to get in touch with PR firms as soon as possible, and it is a good idea to have at least *some* publicity material ready before you contact any of them. A long "lead-in" period is mandatory. Magazines have to be approached about three months (if not longer) prior to the publicity target date. Therefore, if your film has been scheduled for a summer release, your PR firm *must* contact magazines no later than March.

Should a magazine insist upon screening your movie, make arrangements to do so about five to six months before your movie's release date. But here's a word of warning: Do not get suckered into showing a rough cut of your as yet uncompleted film.* Since magazine editors are not accomplished filmmakers, your film, at best, won't be reviewed; at worst it might be set up for poisonous barbs.

Once you have decided on a PR firm, provide them with all the photos, dates, and written material they require. They will need these materials to put together a press kit and an electronic press kit.

Press kit. Think about publicity while your film is in production. You will need a still photographer to shoot "stills" throughout the production. (You'll need plenty of stills anyway for your foreign market, where lobby displays of stills are very much in vogue.)

Electronic press kit. An electronic press kit may be as short as five to seven minutes, or it may stretch into a full thirty-minute documentary. Domestically only short versions of a press kit are asked for, while a number of overseas TV stations (Germany, Italy, France, Spain) gratefully accept (free of charge) your documentary. The electronic press kit is a combination of "behind-the-scenes shots" of the filming of your movie, some actual film clips, and interviews with the stars. The behind-the-scenes segments are easy to do. Here are a few suggestions:

* Actors: Actors in makeup session
           Actors and crew at lunch
           Actors rehearsing

*A "rough cut" refers to a film that is incomplete as far as final editing, music, and sound effects are concerned.

* Director: Conferring with script supervisor
Setting up a shot
* Stunts: Preparation for a stunt
Rigging of stunt vehicles

And don't forget the "in-depth interview" with your stars. By the way, have you ever wondered why a world-renowned movie star granted your local station's anchorperson an interview? Well, here is the answer: While shooting your movie, you'll tape your star's answers to questions that appear character generated (printed) on a tape between the answers. Your local station edits their anchorperson in, and presto you'll have a "personalized" interview.

It's as easy as that, and it looks great.

My advice is that you have about a thousand electronic press kits ready at your PR firm. Editing and duplicating a press kit on tape is inexpensive.

Screenings. All major studios and a great number of independent distributors test the market via prerelease screenings.

Testing the market consists of specific tests in three or four different TV spots and in a number of newspaper ads featuring different artwork, titles, copy lines, and tag lines. The film is previewed in a variety of areas on the East and West coasts, in the Midwest, and in the South, as well as in various theaters located in different socioeconomic areas. According to the audience's response, the film will be targeted (advertised) to a certain socioeconomic group and therefore will be more heavily promoted and exhibited in certain areas, while not shown in others.

Audiences respond to the film via questionnaires. The following questions are those most likely to be asked. Respondents rate their answers on a scale of 1 (highest) to 4 (lowest).

Your favorite scenes
    action scenes _____
    love scenes _____
    scenes between Lydia and James _____
    others _____
Your least-liked scenes
    boxing scenes _____
    love scenes _____
    family reunion scenes _____
    others _____

Your favorite character
    Lydia _____
    James _____
    Bill _____
    Rita _____
What did you like best in the movie? _____
What did you like least in the movie? _____
Would you recommend the movie to your friends? _____
Total overall rating:
    Excellent _____
    Very good _____
    Good _____
    Poor _____

Considering the questionnaire's results the distributor may increase or decrease the film's advertising budget and change the ad campaign. For instance, if the film had been targeted as an action film but the questionnaire revealed the love scenes as audience favorites, the film's one-sheet (artwork and copy) will be changed accordingly.

If the film tested poorly with affluent audiences, it will be targeted (posters, TV spots, radio blurbs) to a more middle-class audience. If the film tested poorly in rural areas but did fairly well in urban areas, the distribution pattern will follow course.

Prerelease screenings, a.k.a. sneak previews, are expensive, at times helpful, but most often confusing. The result of a sneak preview may compel the producer to change the film via reediting or (worse) reshooting. As a result, there is always the chance that such a "reworked" film may lose the story's basic direction and possibly the film's theme as well.

Granted, market research serves its purpose, but I'm afraid it is a far less powerful device than most distribution executives claim. Who knows whether the questionnaires have been filled in thoughtfully and specifically? Many people don't care. Some put marks wherever their pencil happens to land. Some resent having to fill in these "darned" cards; they come to the movies to be entertained, not to be part of a survey. Others enjoy the opportunity to "cut those Hollywood characters down to size." Comparatively few viewers take the time to answer thoughtfully.

And there are producers who participate in the not-uncommon practice of bringing suitcases full of filled-in cards to their screenings, all—naturally—waxing enthusiastic about the movie.

In my opinion it is a toss-up whether a considerable amount of money (and time) ought to be spent on sneaks. While changing promotional and distribution patterns has some validity, I doubt the merit of any last-minute reediting or reshooting. If you have targeted your film wisely from its conception on and are working with a distributor experienced in your film's genre, you may as well forgo market research.

Promotion for the Special Elements of Movies Made for Home Video

Admittedly, the extensive promotional pattern discussed in this section does not apply for the low-budget film that has been produced for the home video market, one that sees a token domestic theatrical release only.

Let's not kid ourselves. A made-for-home-video movie can in no way compete with any major film that, because of its theatrical exposure, has enjoyed extensive promotion. This in no way indicates that the made-for-home-video film is in any way inferior to its major-studio counterpart. The fact remains, however, that it did not enjoy the latter's promotional advantage, and therefore, at least in the retailer's mind, is second-rate.

You, the producer, have to supply the distribution company with almost life-size standup "cutouts" of your star (or the movie's main promotable element), participate in advertising your film in the appropriate home video magazines, and last but not least, supply the key art and copy for an eye-catching box cover.

In short, you'll have to spend your advertising dollars wisely.

2.

The package:

how to put together

your offering/prospectus

Your chances of attracting a studio deal, independent distributor, and investors hinge on a complete and effective presentation of your *offering/prospectus*—in short, the package. (You will approach investors with an offering, and studios with a prospectus.) You have to convince investors, studio and distribution executives alike, that you, the producer, are able to helm the project. If you are a novice, you of course have to work harder than your more experienced counterparts. Your offering/prospectus must look and sound professional, that is to say, impressive but not flashy. You achieve this by creating a complete and convincing combination of artistic and promotable elements that provide a picture of the film's favorable economic prospects.

You should also at this point (if you are not pursuing a studio deal) obtain competent legal advice. Financing a movie (or any other venture) is fraught with problems, and I cannot emphasize strongly enough the importance of having an expert entertainment attorney on your team. All materials of your offering and all documents you may attach should be approved by your attorney.

The four key elements of your package are

1. The film's creative elements (artistic merit):
   Screenplay
   Stars

Director
Locations
2. The film's promotable elements:
Star
Genre
Hook
3. The film's positive financial elements:
The producer's expertise (track record, showing that producer has brought in previous films on time and on budget)
The film's viable financial structure (budget)
4. The film's sales potential (a letter of intent from a reliable distribution company) if you are trying to interest investors

After reading the above list, you'll realize that you have to give your prospective investors not only a strong economic incentive but also the confidence that the project is viable, that is to say that others, all experts in their fields, are interested in participating. You'll have an excellent chance of getting your project off the ground if you have letters of intent from a reliable distribution company, known directors, and a recognizable star.

In regard to the above elements, you are facing a Catch-22 dilemma. Many stars, directors, and distributors refuse to commit themselves unless the project has been financed. On the other hand, investors are reluctant to "sign on the dotted line" unless the above elements are attached to the project. The only way to overcome this seemingly insurmountable hurdle is to ask your prospective investors for a letter of interest. Such a letter does not represent a commitment on anyone's part, but does confirm an enthusiasm for the project.

In case you have entrusted an agent with the task of interesting a director and stars in your project and this agent works for an agency known to package* films, you may face the danger that the packaging agency contacts *your* investors, firms the deal, and leaves you out in the cold. You should protect yourself against such practice by having your attorney draw up agreements, binding your prospective investors to deal only with you and your attorney on "said" project (your film).

On the other hand, if you do not look for financing, but are pursuing a

---

*"Packagers" are agencies providing a project with the necessary elements: stars, writer, director, who are under contract with the agency. The agency submits the project to major studios.

studio deal,* it is best not to contact any stars or a director, but to wait for the studio's suggestions.

And now, let's discuss your package in detail.

How your offering/prospectus (package) should look.

Your offering/prospectus must have a professional appearance:

- Have a competent typist type your presentation.
- Choose a plastic spiral-bound folder.
- Use heavy paper stock for your cover.
- *Do not* stamp the front cover with a "confidential" stamp (there is nothing confidential about your project); such labels smack of amateurism.
- *Do not* include photographs of stars or locations (again, this gives your presentation an amateurish look).
- *Do not* clutter your presentation with graphic designs (these make your presentation difficult to peruse).

Now that your package looks professional, let's discuss what should be included in it. The following is a list of the main elements:

Cover Page
The Offering
Legal Entities
Story Synopsis
Script and Story Outline
Stars and Director (Letters of Interest)
Producer
Key Personnel
Distribution Agreement (Letter of Interest)
Project Status
Financing
   Budget
   Risk-Return
   Fiscal Control
   Investor's Protection
   Overall
   Share of Profits

*A major studio finances and distributes your film.

Marketing
  Promotable Elements
  Advertising and Publicity
  Viability
  Suggested Distribution Plan

Cover page:
  Title of your film
  Project description: A motion picture project
  Brochure description: A financing outline
  Name of production company and logo
  Name of producer
  Date

The offering. This is a statement of what you are offering prospective investors: "Offering [amount of monies to be raised] in limited partnership, corporation, or joint venture interests in [name of production company] to finance the motion picture [title of your movie]."

It is very important that (after discussing the matter with your attorney) you add the following qualifying clause: "These securities [partnerships] are offered pursuant to an exemption from registration with the United States Securities and Exchange Commission. The Commission does not pass upon the merits of any securities [partnership shares], nor does it pass upon the accuracy or completeness of any offering or other selling literature."

Legal entities. This segment shows the legal form of your venture. Again, in establishing the decided upon legal entity, your attorney's advice is urgently needed. The basic options are as follows:

• *Limited partnership.* The investors become Limited Partners, whereas the producer remains the General Partner. The Limited Partners are protected from any liability in excess of their investment. The General Partner does not enjoy this protection.

• *Corporation.* The investors acquire *nontransferable* shares of stock in the production company.

• *Investment contract.* The producer and/or the production company contracts with the investors re interest rate (not profits) to be received from the invested monies.

• *Joint venture/general partnership.* A few partners share risk and profit with the producer.

The merits and pitfalls of each venture will be discussed in detail later. Since financing is such a wide and, let's admit, complicated field, an entire chapter will be devoted to it. (See chapter 8.)

Story synopsis. Make certain that the synopsis contains all marketable/promotional aspects of the prospective film. For this purpose I like to submit a teaser and the story outline. The teaser, very much like the one used on a home-video box cover, highlights the film's promotional aspects. The following teaser was used in the offering for my horror film *Frozen Scream.*

> Two misdirected scientists think they have discovered a technique for achieving immortality: lowering body temperatures to slow down the aging process. But this technique has one fatal flaw—a mind- and soul-altering effect that turns the patients into frozen zombies.
>
> When Ann discovers her husband's poisoned body, she goes into shock and is hospitalized. The doctors try to convince her that Tom, her husband, died of a heart attack, but her nightmarish visions lead her to believe otherwise. Her curiosity takes her to the doctors' secret laboratory where she discovers a freezer full of frozen zombies—including Tom.
>
> Ann escapes the zombies' violent attack, but others are not as fortunate. Soon the zombies are everywhere, attacking and "recruiting" new victims for the mad doctors' experiments.

Keep the story's details for the story outline. And be aware that unless you are offering an art film, or asking for a grant, you should not go into your film's theme, that is to say, your concerns about esoteric issues that are important to you. Remember, the partners you are soliciting will join you in your venture for one reason only: They want to make some profit. Films that deal with issues don't have "legs" (don't sell well).

Script and story outline. Include the completed script as well as a detailed story outline in your package.

Stars and director. We already discussed the dilemma faced in trying to obtain the precious letters of intent. But in lieu of those you should at least try to obtain letters of interest. Although these letters aren't a commitment to anything, they look good in your offering.

Unfortunately, for the beginning producer it is not easy to get the cooperation of recognizable actors and actresses. This difficulty is compounded by the fact that the first-time producer most likely has no development funds earmarked to pay options to a prospective star.

Over and over I've heard stories about scripts delivered to stars and agents that were never read; about telephone calls that were never returned. Let's assume these eager-beaver producers went about their business the wrong way. They sent their scripts to actors who, commanding "honoraria" of four to five million dollars, were far beyond the producer's status in this industry. Or they sent their scripts to one of the big agencies, such as William Morris, CAA, ICM. Now don't get me wrong, if you submit a terrific script to be packaged by the respective agency, as a first-time producer you have at least a fighting chance to be invited for an initial interview. (It goes without saying that your script *must* have been written by a recognizable writer and *must* qualify for the standard budget of between ten and twenty million dollars.) But no major agency will consider any low-budget not-yet-funded script if asked to interest one of their stars in the project.

So what is the first-time producer going to do? After all, a recognizable star is the key element in any offering. There are a few simple steps that should result in recognizable names providing letters of interest. First discuss your project with some medium-sized distributors. If you do not find willing ears, contact a reliable "distributor for hire."* Show your script and show your budget. (In case you do not live close to a metropolis, consult the respective film market issues of *Variety* and *Hollywood Reporter* for names and addresses. You can gauge a distributor's importance by the size of their ads.) Try to get the distributor's letter of interest. Even if you should fail to do so, ask the distributor to suggest a few names, people he/she thinks are right for your project, that is to say, are recognizable. This in turn means these names may not be recognizable by the public at large, but are known to the industry domestically and overseas. But be well aware that the *recognizability* of any name hinges upon the size of your budget. For a budget ranging in the vicinity of one and a half million, you will attract a "better" name (not necessarily a better actor) than for a budget of $750,000. After you have collected a few names, call your local SAG office and ask for the actor's agent's name and address. Don't send your script out cold. Call the agent first, tell him/her that you have a terrific script with an excellent part for his or her client, and that the distribution company has not only shown interest in your script, but also

*More about the "distributor for hire" in chapter 5.

has suggested the agent's client for the lead. Then submit your script and your budget, and watch the ball roll.

Producer. Do have an experienced producer on board as one of the key elements of your package? He or she has to have a track record—has to be known to bring in a film on budget and on time.

My advice is that for your first project you hire a skilled producer, and content yourself (if you are instrumental in obtaining financing) with the title of executive producer.

And now, please hold your horses and don't throw this book aside. The following advice comes straight from my heart: If you, the producer, also are the screenwriter with as yet no directing notches on your belt (regardless of whether you attended directing courses), please do not insist that you and only you can direct the film. Many otherwise promising projects have run aground on the treacherous rocks of a writer-producer-director's contention "Only I will provide the film with the artistic and creative elements it deserves. Only I ought to direct the film." True, you probably know your script and your movie's theme better than any other person in this world, but remember, investors invest in a movie for one purpose only, to make money. You, the novice director-producer, by polishing your brainchild's minute details, may be tempted to go over time and budget. The experienced director, on the other hand, though as excited about the project as you are, views a film objectively, maintaining necessary emotional distance.

And even the experienced director needs an equally experienced producer, one who adheres to these principles:

- Choose a well-constructed script, featuring a clear plot line that is based on honest human emotions.
- See to it that the film is competently acted, directed, and photographed.
- Always be aware of the film's promotional hook.
- And last but not least, remember Billy Wilder's famous advice: "Thou shall not bore."

Key personnel. It is absolutely essential that your offering/prospectus name certain key people as part of your team. These include a production manager, a production accountant, an art director, and a cinematographer.

If the project at hand is your first attempt at producing, you ought to contact a *production manager* (PM) who has a mile-long credit list. Quite naturally, the financing sources assume that in case you encounter difficulties, the PM will jump into the breach. The PM is the liaison between the producer and the "shoot." He or she hires crew and equipment, searches in concert with the director and art director for locations, and is responsible for the sufficient delivery of raw stock for each day's shooting. One of the PM's most difficult tasks is to keep the production running, that is to say, to make certain that each scheduled setup has been shot and that the production does not run into "golden time." If you remember that crew and cast will not only receive overtime pay but also "meal penalties" (for meals not provided for overtime work), you will agree that staying on time is mandatory. Also, if for any reason any scheduled setups have to be carried over to the next day, the following problems may arise: The shooting schedule may have to be revised; the location needed may not be available for another day; or one of the actors may be unavailable.

You will agree, the PM's job is not an easy one. Frictions occur between the director and PM, as the director insists on "one more take" (which stretches into five takes), the cinematographer opts for a more elaborate light plot, and the star demands more close-ups.

Since it is *your* job to keep the show running smoothly—that is to say, to keep each situation from exploding—the PM will ask you to make the final decisions. It is exactly for this reason that you must have either solid producing experience or have hired a well-qualified PM.

Traditionally the PM writes the budget and breaks down the script into a realistic shooting schedule. I advise strongly that the producer does this job first, then with the PM finalizes the budget, and, adding the input of the PM, director, and cinematographer, goes over the breakdown again. It is during the preproduction period that disagreements can be settled most easily, and areas where frictions may arise can be anticipated and may be dealt with.

Many investors insist that they hire the *production accountant.* He or she is the production's watchdog, who turns in daily and weekly production accounts. Insist that the production accountant is present on the set, takes care of the miscellaneous items to be paid out of petty cash, and pays the bills for rentals, crew salaries, permits, and minor daily locations. The weekly accountings will include payments for cast, locations, lab fees, and raw stock, and later on sound lab and editing expenses. The production accountant is a blessing in disguise, as he or she keeps the PM from dealing with minor monetary matters. The daily expense account keeps the producer abreast of expenditures (seemingly minor ones may turn into an avalanche), while the weekly reports do point out any area where the production is in danger of going overboard. It is important that copies of both daily and weekly reports be sent to each investor.

Technically neither the *cinematographer* nor the *art director* is a key person on a project, yet it is wise to list their expertise in the offering/prospectus. Both have to be experts in their respective fields. It is the art director who gives a film its look and atmosphere. Take a good look at the art director's portfolio:

- Do sets/locations express the film's mood?
- Do sets/locations fit the film's theme?
- Are sets/locations unique or run-of-the-mill?

Discuss your budget requirements with the art director and see whether he or she can meet your time and budget demands. And always remember, it is the art director who, with the director and cinematographer, brings the script's idea and theme to life.

It is the cinematographer who has not only to bring in a visually acceptable film but also who, in many instances—because of slow setups and overly complicated light plots—may contribute to a film's going overtime and consequently going over budget. Before looking at any cinematographer's demo reel,* get names and addresses, as well as telephone numbers, of his or her previous employers. Contact these producers, and ask about the cinematographer's

- Work habits
- Attitude
- How he/she got along with others—the crew, director, and producer
- Setup times (fast or slow)
- Light plots (effective or ineffective). Additional requirements that are costly, such as scaffold lighting or excessive use of tracks for camera movements

As you look at the cinematographer's "demo reel" do not be taken in by the beautiful vision you see on the screen. Ask your director to check out:

---

*A demo reel is a tape that shows excerpts of the cinematographer's previous work.

- How is a scene lit? Does lighting help to set the mood and atmosphere of the scene?
- Are actors lit attractively?
- Transitions. As the film moves from scene to scene, is the lighting appropriate? Is there a smooth change in color values?
- Framing of shots. Will they adapt to later TV conversion?
- Are camera moves executed professionally?

Get together with the director and cinematographer, discuss your film, find out whether they see the film in the same way you do. Probe whether the cinematographer will go along with your ideas and will support these with creative suggestions of his/her own.

Distribution agreement. To negotiate a binding distribution agreement is unusual, unless you are a successful producer known to produce films that "have legs" (sell well). And don't forget, a distribution agreement is only worth the paper it is written on, even if the distribution company (regardless of size) is known as a reliable one. A distribution agreement issued by a fly-by-night company will do your project more harm than good. As previously mentioned, most distributing companies are more than reluctant to furnish you with a letter of intent unless you have your financing in place, and the best you can expect is the letter of interest. But don't let this deter you. Simply point out the unshakable truth—that a more favorable distribution agreement can be obtained once the film has been completed and a release print can be shown.

Project Status (Time line)

Twelve weeks—preproduction (before shooting commences)
    Polishing the script in concert with the director
    Location scouting
    Studio rental
    Conferences with key personnel (art director, cinematographer, stunt coordinator, special effects lab and person)
    Crew assembly
    Interviews with editor, production manager, musical director
    Discussion with agents regarding stars
    Final preparation of budget

Location breakdown and final shooting script
Hiring of key personnel
Callbacks of secondary actors
Conferences with postproduction facilities (lab, sound lab, editing)
Four weeks (before shooting commences)
Final casting of actors
Rehearsal of actors
Contracts with editor, labs, editing facilities, musical director
Contracts with production and postproduction facilities
Wardrobe designs and fittings
Contract locations and/or studio
Commence building sets (if applicable)
Set insurance, completion bond (if necessary), obtain city and/or county permits
Six weeks
Principal photography
Begin preediting dailies
Eight weeks (postproduction editing phase)
Edit film
Edit sound (dialog and sound effects)
Edit music
Six weeks (postproduction—final phase)
Mix and foley
SD/FX
Negative cutting
Opticals
Optical soundtrack
Titles
Timing of answer print
Answer print

Financing. It is important that you submit as detailed a budget as possible. The following is the budget for the motion picture project *High Treason** (International Film Partnerships) for a motion picture budget for $2.5 million. This budget serves as an example only—every film has to be budgeted differently.

*By permission of International Film Partnerships, Michael R. Gardina, general partner.

Maybe you'll have to spend more on locations, the star, special effects, or stunts—it all depends on your film.

The term "above-line cost" refers to the money paid for story and rights, producer's unit, direction, cast, agent's fee, and above-the-line fringe benefits, while "below the line" refers to the cost of actually shooting the film, including such diverse items as lab cost, locations, crew salaries, equipment rental, cost for editing, and music. These items include a 10 percent contingency fee, covering legal expenses, finder's fee, and so on.

The total sum of these below-the-line expenditures are called the *bottom line.*

The sum total of above- and below-the-line costs (including the completely finished and acceptable release print and at least some advertising material such as trailers, radio blurbs, and newspaper mats, and one sheets) is called the *negative cost* of a film.

Traditionally, the above-line cost of a film should be one-third the below-the-line cost, two-thirds of the negative cost. That is to say, if a film has been budgeted for $2,500,000, then the above-line cost should not be more than $833,000. In today's market, however, where even minor stars (deserving or not) demand fees of $1,000,000, and where well-known names, especially for home video and foreign sales, are mandatory, the picture has changed. Still, do not let the production values of your film suffer; it is not the dollar amount that shows on the screen, but the producer's and everyone's expertise.

Here are some suggestions:

- Consolidate locations. If you have scheduled the Smiths' living room at location A, and the Millers' living room at location B, consolidate by shooting both at location A. A clever art director can give a room many different looks.
- Consolidate light plots. Discuss all light plots at length with your cinematographer. Work out a general light plot that covers an entire area, and change lights as required to shoot specific areas.
- Change night shots to "day-for-night" shots. Night shots are expensive to set up and to light. By attaching specific filters to a camera's lens, one can change daylight to night. It helps, of course, if one is blessed with bright sunlight. The sunshine translates to eerie "moonshine."
- Move quickly from one set to the next by having your art director's

crew "dress" (set up props, furniture, draperies, and so on); have the light crew light set #2, while you shoot on set #1.

- If you have many exterior locations scheduled, always—being observant of poor weather conditions—schedule interior shots as a stopgap measure.
- Make sure your actors are well rehearsed.
- Hire only actors who have on-camera experience.
- Watch out for temperamental actors. Find out whether or not an actor/actress follows the director's suggestions willingly and easily. Replace an ego-centered actor with another, better-adjusted, one.
- Investigate whether expensive special effects can be made more palatable price-wise, by building miniatures. This advice holds especially true if you work with explosions or burning buildings.
- If you have only on-set rehearsals, have your director rehearse actors while lights are being changed. (Light changes take long; he/she will have plenty of rehearsal time.)
- Avoid time-consuming shots, of planes landing, busy city streets, shorelines, gambling places, nightclubs, party scenes, church interiors and exteriors. Buy "stock shots" instead. These are unused outtakes other production companies have sold to labs. You'll find addresses of these firms either in a production Blue Book (any bookstore specializing in theatrical and film books carries it) or by inquiring with a lab.
- And most important: Do not cut your preproduction time short. Preproduction is the key to a film's being brought in on time and within budget.

BUDGET

1100	Story and Rights	
	01. Screenplay	$25,000
	02. Idea for screenplay	5,000
	03. Printing	500
	Subtotal:	$30,500
1200	Producer's Unit	
	01. Executive producer	$ 75,000
	02. Producer	75,000

	03. Associate producer		7,000
	08. Legal and auditing		25,000
		Subtotal:	$182,000
1300	Direction		
	01. Director		$50,000
	02. Assistant director		8,000
		Subtotal:	$58,000
1400	Cast		
	01. STAR: (either alternate I or alternate II)		
	Alternate I:		
	Star A		$1,000,000
	Alternate II:		
	Star A		500,000
	Star B		500,000
	02. Supporting		
	Costar		50,000
	2 or 3 supporting stars		20,400
	3-day players		3,600
	15, 1-day players		6,300
		Subtotal:	$1,080,300
1500	Agent's Fees		
	01. 10% Star's Salary		$100,000
	02. 10% Actor's agents		8,030
		Subtotal:	$108,030
1900	Above-the-line Fringe Benefits		
	01. Writer's WGA pension, H&W (12.5%)		$ 3,125
	02. Producer's units		-0-
	03. Director (non-DGA)		-0-
	04. Cast SAG pension, H&W (12.5%)		10,037
	Star SAG pension, H&W (12%)		125,000
		Subtotal:	$138,162
2000	Production Staff		
	01. Manager		$10,000
	02. Script supervisor		6,000
	08. Production accountant		3,000
		Subtotal:	$19,000

2200	Set Design		
	01. Art director		$ 9,000
	02. Assistant Art Director		3,200
	03. Purchasers		5,000
	04. Rentals		3,000
	05. Damages		1,000
		Subtotal:	$21,200

2300	Set Construction		
	01. Construction		$ 2,000
		Subtotal:	$ 2,000

2500	Set Operation		
	01. Key grip		$ 3,600
	02. Second grip		3,000
	03. Slate		3,000
	04. 3 Grip assistants		5,400
	05. 2 Production assistants		1,200
	06. Equipment rental		4,200
	07. Damages and losses		1,000
	08. Purchases		500
		Subtotal:	$21,900

2600	Special Effects		
	Generator rental		300
	Oil and gas		50
	Fogger		300
	Liquid fog		100
	Gun rental		200
		Subtotal:	$950

2700	Set Dressing		
	14. Purchases		500
	15. Rentals		500
	16. Damages		200
		Subtotal:	$1,200

2800	Petty Cash		
	16. Petty cash		$1,200
		Subtotal:	$1,200

2900	Wardrobe		
	Purchases		$5,000
	Cleaning		300
	Wardrobe girl		1,800
		Subtotal:	$7,100

3100	Makeup and Hair Dressing		
	01. Key makeup person		$3,000
	02. 2 Assistants		3,600
	03. Purchases		1,000
	04. Special effects makeup		200
		Subtotal:	$7,800

3200	Lighting		
	01. Gaffer		$ 6,000
	02. Best boy		3,000
	03. Assistant		2,400
	11. Burnouts, carbons, gels		2,000
	12. Purchases		1,500
	17. Rental		12,800
	18. Repairs		500
		Subtotal:	$28,200

3300	Production Sound		
	01. Mixer		$ 6,000
	02. Boom man		3,000
	03. Tape		300
	06. Equipment rental		8,000
		Subtotal:	$17,300

3400	Camera		
	01. Director of photography		$12,000
	02. Camera operator		6,000
	03. Focus assistant		4,800
	04. Loader		3,000
	05. Still man		2,400
	16. Purchases		2,700
	17. Camera maintenance		300
	19. Loss and damages		1,000
	20. Camera package rental		26,000
		Subtotal:	$58,200

3500	Transportation		
	11. Grip truck rental		$2,400
	20. Limousine (star)		2,400
	21. Rental trailer		3,000
	23. Expenses preproduction		2,000
		Subtotal:	$9,800

3600	Location Expenses		
	30. Preproduction		$ 2,000
	32. Catered meals		10,000
	33. Miscellaneous		2,500
	40. Location rentals		18,000
	41. Fire safety officer		900
		Subtotal:	$33,400

4400	Optical		
	11. Optical		$5,000
		Subtotal:	$5,000

4500	Editing		
	01. Supervising editor		$29,000
	02. Assistant editor		11,000
	03. Sound editor		8,000
	04. Music editor		2,400
	11. Coding		2,000
	14. Projection (dailies)		3,800
	16. Purchasing		2,000
	17. Equipment rental		12,000
		Subtotal:	$70,200

4600	Music		
	01. Composer, conductor, musicians, recording		$50,000
		Subtotal:	$50,000

4700	Postproduction		
	11. Sound transfer		$12,000
	12. Magnetic film		18,800
	13. Foley		5,100
	15. Sound FX		2,400
	20. Music recording		5,000

	21. Dolby stereo mixing		34,000
	25. Dialog recording		4,488
		Subtotal:	$81,788
4800	Film and Laboratory		
	08. 35mm raw stock		$17,600
	09. Developing		11,000
	10. Printing		14,000
	11. Negative cutting		6,200
	12. Sound negative dolby		4,140
	14. Answer prints		8,520
	15. Release prints		8,520
	85. Coding		2,000
	89. Tax		6,039
		Subtotal:	$78,019
6500	Publicity		
	01. Unit publicist		$10,000
		Subtotal:	$10,000
6700	Insurance		
	01. Cast, crew ($5 million)		
	02. Negative film, errors, and omissions; faulty stock, camera, and equipment; third-party property damage, workers' comprehensive and umbrella liability		
		Subtotal:	$54,000
6800	General Expenses		
	11. Telephone		$3,000
	12. Xerox		500
	13. Location accountant		5,000
	14. Office supplies		500
	15. Office costs		500
		Subtotal:	$9,500
7800	Indirect Cost		
	A. Cost overrun acct.		68,375
	B. Commission (10%)		250,000
		Subtotal:	318,375
		Total:	$2,500,124

Risk-Return. It is imperative that you are absolutely frank with your prospective investors. Naturally, you are eager for them to invest in your project, and you are almost certain that your film, special as it is, will not only return their investment but will also earn them a handsome profit.

Don't promise any castles in Spain. Your film has to go through many stages; it has to clear a number of hurdles to reach its break-even point. Make your investors aware that investing in a movie is a high-risk proposition and that they could suffer the total loss of their investment. Granted, legally you are not required to add a risk clause to your offering, but morally you are.

In discussing any potential returns, you must make it clear to your investors that you are not guaranteeing any returns. No one can predict a film's profit or loss. The success or failure of any film depends largely on the audience's reaction and the existing worldwide political and economic situation at the time of the movie's release. It is, therefore, an unrealistic practice—regardless how often employed—to compare one's project with similar films that are presently, or have been recently, on the market. One has to take into consideration that audiences' reactions are unpredictable, and that the rule of thumb—comedies and escapist entertainment sell well in troubled times, while dramatic films do better in emotionally calmer periods—does not necessarily hold true. Nevertheless, do acquaint your prospective investors with the following lucrative sources of income (both domestically and foreign):

Theatrical release (domestic)
TV network sale (domestic)
Cable sale (domestic)
Home video sale (domestic)

Theatrical release (worldwide)
TV, cable, home video sales (worldwide)*

Book about film (if applicable)

Merchandising—toys, games, outfits (if applicable)

Next you may present your investors with a hypothetical cost-income scenario based upon your film's budget. The following scenario is based on

---

*The difference between domestic and worldwide sales will be discussed in the chapter on distribution.

an overall cost of $2,500,000. This budget in today's market denotes a low-budget project that has been produced primarily for home video and all areas of foreign distribution.

Impress upon your investors the fact that the given scenario is a hypothetical one, and should not be employed as a basis for any risk-return assessment.

Production Cost. $1,725,000 above- and below-the-line cost.
400,000 production company's participation in
P&A (prints and advertising)

Possibly your investors have not funded your project directly, but have supplied you with letters of credit (LC), which guarantee that investors will pay back the bank loan in case of the producer's default. In short, an LC gives you the opportunity to borrow money from a bank (more about LCs in chapter 8). Borrowing money from a bank will add about a 15 percent interest rate to your film's cost. And remember, you'll have to pay until the loan interest has been paid off, which, if the film has no legs, may take several years. Furthermore, depending on the economic situation at the time of the loan approval, your interest rate may be higher or lower than the hypothetical 15 percent. The sum of $375,000 interest reflects interest payment for one year. You will, without any doubt, save money if you withdraw money only as needed.

Income. $100,000—domestic theatrical release.

The scenario assumes that the production company hires a distributor to distribute the picture *domestically.* (As we'll find out later on, in the chapter on distribution, such a limited domestic theatrical release is of utmost importance for the film's cable, home video, and foreign [all areas] release.) The shockingly small amount of $100,000 refers to the production company's take after the exhibitor's* *share* and distributor's *fees* have been deducted.

$1,500,000—domestic cable, negative pick-up
500,000—domestic home video, negative pick-up

A negative pick-up means that the cable and/or home video distribution company pays one-quarter of the agreed-upon amount upon delivery of the

*Exhibitors will be discussed in the chapter on distribution.

picture, and the rest in quarterly installments. Domestic cable will insist upon a *window,* a time period in which the film cannot be marketed in home video retail stores.

$400,000—TV rights
 250,000—TV syndication rights

Payments of TV and TV syndication rights dribble in within about five years, as your film will be sold for areas as a "package" with other films.

$1,000,000—foreign rights worldwide

The above foreign incomes have been calculated after distribution fees and related expenses have been deducted.

Our hypothetical scenario gives us the following income picture.

Cost $2,500,000
Income   3,100,000

This is the income to be earned during the picture's first year. The second year will see some insignificant worldwide income, whereas the film will bring about $650,000 during the following five-year period.

After the initial investment has been paid back the investor will share the first year's profit of $600,000—and the following profit of $650,000—with you.

As far as the scenario is concerned, be advised of the following:

- The scenario reflects that the producer hires a distributor (we will discuss the pros and cons of such practice in the chapter on distribution).
- That the investors provided the producer with LC only (if they choose direct investment, they save a bundle on interest rates).
- The given scenario reflects cost and income at the time of writing (these amounts, all based on supply and demand, change from year to year).
- Do not get tied down in guaranteeing profits.

Fiscal control. Specify that all funds obtained from investors will be held in escrow until the needed sum has been raised. If the producer should fail to raise the required sum within a given period, monies collected will be returned without interest. Once the production is under way, a production accountant of the investor's choice will handle the daily expenditures and will supply the investor with weekly financial reports.

Investor's protection. Since a number of independently produced films are not completed, some investors insist upon a *completion bond.* A completion bond is expensive, and many low-budget films do not qualify to apply for one. (The firm issuing the bond guarantees the completion of the film, in case the production goes over budget.) In any event, with or without a completion bond, you should point to your team's (producer, production manager, director) track record, to satisfy any investor that the production will be completed.

Overcall. No *overcall* (monies needed should the film go over budget) will be collected from investors. The general partners may advance or borrow funds to be repaid prior to the returns due to the limited partnership. The respective percentage interest of each partner will NOT be affected.

Share of profits. It is mandatory that you inform your prospective investors that profits are not to be shared until after the costs of the film have been paid back to the investors. The traditional profit participation is 50/50, that is to say, 50 percent of the profits go to the investors and 50 percent of the profits go to the producer. Investors share their profits based on the percentage level of investment. Profits will be shared on net profits only. (Later, we will discuss the delicate balance between net profit and gross profit, since accounting concepts do vary from distributor to distributor and studio to studio.)

The traditional view that a picture has to bring in three to four times its cost before a new profit will be achieved, refers to *studio*-financed and -distributed films. The average low-budget film, employing a distributor for hire and contracting with a representative for worldwide distribution, enjoys net profits much sooner.

Marketing. Your marketing information has to support the financing program you have outlined. It contains:

1. Your film's promotable elements
2. Advertising and publicity
3. Concept viability
4. Suggested distribution plan

1. *Promotable elements.* A list of all of your film's promotable elements (stars, director, story).

2. *Advertising and publicity.* Explain the advertising and publicity tools you plan to employ. Having already contracted a well-known PR firm helps. Concentrate, as discussed in chapter 1, on advertising and promotional tools appropriate to your film's genre. It's an excellent strategy to attach samples of one-sheets and sales flyers (to be distributed at the international film markets) and, if you primarily go after the home video audience, cassette box covers, as well. Remember the old proverb "A picture is worth a thousand words," and give your potential investors a visual idea of the planned movie.

3. *Concept viability.* Much has been written and even more has been said during the past years about a film's viability. Much money has been spent on researching the "moviegoing market" based on family income, sex, and regional aspects. The research suggests that a larger number of mature people are available for theater attendance, but that mature *young people* constitute the important swing that can make a movie a hit.

Very well, that's this year's conclusion, but will it hold true for next year and the years to come? Who knows? When we consider the fact that it takes at least one year from the commencement of the screenplay to the release date of a film, we know that the applied research is yesterday's news and might not necessarily be applicable to your project.

It is far better to acquaint your investor with the film's intended target audience:

Art theater sophisticated audience
General release
Cable release
Home video release
Worldwide (all areas release)

Most likely your film has been targeted for a combination of release areas.

4. *Suggested distribution plan.* Ideally you'll have a distribution plan for your picture. But since no distribution company, even if it signed a letter of intent, will commit more fully to your project by establishing a distribution plan, you'll have to steer clear of specifics and remain on general terms. The following distribution plan is based upon our previous scenario of a film budget for $2,500,000:

- The film will be ready for release early fall.

- The film will be distributed on a limited domestic theatrical run; 50 prints during the months of September, October, November (these months are generally favorable for this type of film, as they do not interfere with the major summer and Christmas releases).
- The film will be shown on cable.
- The film will be exhibited at the major film markets (MIFED, Milan, Italy, October; Los Angeles Film Festival, Los Angeles, California, February; Cannes Film Festival, Cannes, France, April for all foreign rights sales).
- The film will be shown on TV, and syndicated TV.

Prospectus

While you need an offering to attract investors, you will submit a prospectus if you are interested in a studio deal.

Cover page
Highlights
Story synopsis
Story outline
Script
Promotional hook
Shortened version of budget
Producer's résumé

While it is mandatory that you present the studio with a final script and budget (once a studio accepts your project, both script and budget will undergo numerous changes), it is wise not to submit letters of intent from either stars or director. You may, however, suggest some names. Always keep in mind that studio executives have their own ideas about stars and directors who are "simply perfect" for this film.

The following is an example of a typical prospectus. The prospectus of my low-budget horror film *Frozen Scream* has been attached.

Sample: Cover Page

Ciara Productions, Inc.

A California Corporation*
Chill Factor
A Motion Picture Project

Renée Harmon, president
Address
Telephone Number

*You do not have to be incorporated to submit a project to a studio.

Highlights

THE PROGRAM

Ciara Productions, Inc. intends to produce a film with the current working title *Chill Factor* (the motion picture).

The original screenplay has been written by Renée Harmon. The film will be produced by Renée Harmon (the producer). Producer has a history of bringing her films in on schedule and within budget. Each of the producer's films has returned a profit. Producer is experienced and has demonstrated her ability to provide or obtain essential supporting cast and crew suitable to needs of this production. Producer's track record shows ability to deliver film on schedule and within budget. The producer has committed to bring the film in on time and within the budget.

The Motion Picture

The motion picture, a full-length feature film, is to be produced from the original screenplay by the working title *Chill Factor*. It is to be filmed in 35mm.

Project Status

SCRIPT: The script has been written. Script may be revised or polished in preproduction.

LEGAL STATUS: The production and creative team, including but not limited to, producer, director, writer, editor, etc. are to be considered independent contractors.

Sample: Story Synopsis

This story deals with the occult concept of age-old entities prolonging their lives indefinitely by taking over, and inhabiting, human bodies.

At the small Southern California college of South Coast University two scientists, Sven Jonson and Lil Stanhope, are convinced that by keeping a person's body temperature close to the freezing point, human life can be extended to near immortality.

Their assistant Tom Gerard dies of a heart attack. His wife, Ann, suspects he was murdered. No one believes her except Detective McGuire, who, nonplussed by the previous disappearance of two of Sven's students, eagerly helps her to find the murderer. He is sure that Sven Jonson is the culprit; he is also sure that some gruesome experiments took place.

Matters become more complicated. Not only do McGuire and Ann fall in love but also Ann encounters Tom—or someone like Tom—alive. She is determined to find out about Tom's death or disappearance.

Sample: Story Outline

Tom Gerard is chairman of the psychology department of South Coast University, a small private college. He is young and ambitious, and he has found the perfect partners for the breakthrough in longevity (leading to immortality) he is hoping for. His partners are Sven Jonson and Lil Stanhope, psychiatrists with strong interests in biochemical research.

His wife, Ann, a brittle young woman, is troubled by the secrecy of her husband's work, although she understands it involves altering animal metabolism as a technique for retarding aging.

Upon returning home from a Midsummer Eve party, Ann finds her husband dead. She is told that Tom had a heart attack, but she believes Tom has been murdered. She suspects Sven to be the killer. Ann has a breakdown. After several weeks in the hospital she returns home. Upon Lil's—her best friend—urging, she hires Tom's former assistant, the beautiful young Cathrine, as her nurse.

There is another mystery. Early in the summer two of Tom's students, Kirk and Bob, vanish. Detective Kevin McGuire of the San Luis police is under pressure to locate them. He suspects that drugs as well as criminal experiments on humans are involved in the case. He attempts to learn more from Ann about the nature of her husband's experiments. The two agree to collaborate. Soon they are following several promising leads. There are indications that the beautiful, young Cathrine is really an eighty-year-old woman, artificially kept young. Bob's landlady, Mrs. Gregory, reports of having seen Bob alive, if greatly changed in appearance. Ann is certain there is a secret lab where dark experiments take place. Yet every lead ends up on a dead-end street. There are logical explanations for everything, until Sven Jonson is found murdered. Now, in rapid succession, strange things begin to happen that make Ann suspect a dark force at work.

Through all of it, Lil stands by Ann in true friendship, and Ann's relationship with Kevin deepens. She knows she has fallen in love with him.

Ann has to live through a number of frightening experiences. On one occasion, she encounters Bob's apparition; twice she sees Tom's ghost. Shortly thereafter she recognizes a very-much-alive Bob in a supermarket and follows him to an abandoned cottage that—much to her surprise—is located in a straight line from Sven's mansion. Shortly after she has to flee her home, as it becomes invaded by unexplainable forces. She moves in with Mrs. Gregory. Visiting an antique market, she sees a man who she knows is Tom. That same evening Tom calls, asking her to meet with him. He promises to explain what is happening. Ann drives to Tom's apartment, which turns out to be a half-demolished tenement in Los Angeles. Ann follows Tom's voice from floor to floor, and she ends up in a dark room. Tom's voice turns out to be a tape-recorded message, and to her horror Ann discovers that had she taken another step she would have fallen to her death; she stands in front of a gaping hole in the wall.

Ann decides against telling Kevin about her experience. Things have changed. She does not trust him anymore. Neither does she trust her friend Lil any longer. Lil has drawn the man Ann loves into the circle of her unexplainable power. And, in a mysterious way Ann feels her own strength and will weaken. She knows she will be Lil's next victim, and she also knows the day of her death will be Lil's Summer's End party.

Lil tells her, gleefully, that she is a witch. It was she who has murdered Tom as well as Sven, as both men came too close to the true secret of her power: immortality. Lil's explanation pulls Ann out of her almost catatonic state. An inner force commands her to expose Lil. The only chance to do so, she knows, is to find the secret lab. She remembers the ruins of the old house that is located above Sven's mansion. She assumes that a tunnel connects the ruin, Sven's mansion, and the abandoned cottage. Somewhere in between, she suspects, must be the lab. She finds the entrance to the tunnel and fights her way through it but finds no secret lab. Yet in the root cellar of the cottage she discovers a huge freezer. Here she finds the frozen bodies of Lil's victims, now mindless and soul-less robots. Tom and Cathrine are among the robots. Ann takes photos and is about to leave when one of the corpses, Bob, becomes animated. Ann escapes. Bob chases her. Ann finds refuge in an old factory building. She calls the police and hides. A man enters the building. It is Bob.

Bob is ready to kill Ann by injection when Lil arrives and intervenes. She begs Ann to join forces with her and help with the project of immortality. Yes, she admits, the masses of people will be robots without emotions and wills of their own. Only a few intellects will receive the gift of true immortality, and those will rule the world. Ann refuses Lil's offer. Lil is ready to kill her, when Kevin and a few FBI men arrive on the scene. Ann by now is convinced that Kevin is part of the deadly game Lil had been playing all along. But her fears prove to be false. Kevin arrests Lil for murder. The moment the handcuffs touch her wrists Lil begins to age—her hair turns white, her features sag, she becomes an old, old woman. Next her flesh falls off her bones, until her skull is revealed, and then suddenly she shoots up in flames.

Kevin explains to Ann that he is an important FBI official. He had been informed about criminal experiments at South Coast, and had sent two of his most experienced agents, Bob and Kirk, to investigate. They were undercover pretending to be students. When both agents vanished, he decided to investigate the case himself. Ann was one of his prime suspects. True, he met her to find out about the experiments, but soon he fell in love with her. His proposal was not part of the game; he loves her and wants to marry her.

Ann listens to Kevin, but his words do not touch her heart. She walks out of the room. Kevin goes after her, but in the hallway he runs past her. Ann knows she is invisible. She is not surprised about it. She walks all night long. And as she walks Lil's secret reveals itself to her. Lil was not a witch, she was a human body housing an age-old entity, and this entity has inhabited human bodies from time immemorial. She has flashes of memories that are not her own, but the ones of the immortal entity that has taken over her body.

Sample: Promotional Hook

When Ann discovers her husband Tom murdered, she goes into shock. Everyone tries to convince her that Tom died of a heart attack, but her nightmarish visions lead her to believe otherwise. Her curiosity brings her to a secret laboratory where she finds him, a frozen zombie.

Many films promise terror, but this is truly frightening.

CHILL FACTOR (WORKING TITLE)

Exterior Country Road. Night.
A lonely country road pelted by sheets of rain. The camera takes in the dim outline of a small building sheltered by trees. A red neon sign flashing through the darkness designates the building as the Dew Drop Inn.

The headlights of a car cut through the rain. A car approaches and stops in front of the inn. PULL IN as Ann, a young woman, gets out of her car. PAN with her, as she walks to a public phone situated at the side of the building.

PULL IN to MEDIUM, as Ann fishes in her purse for a coin. The heavy rain makes her task difficult. She shivers in her lightweight cotton dress, pushes her wet mane of red hair out of her face, finally finds the coin, deposits it, and dials.

> ANN
> Tom, I'm sorry . . . but I'm a little late. . . .

Exterior Tom Gerard's House. Night.
A small, Victorian house, its outline—the veranda and the turret—are barely visible in the rain.

> VO ANN
> . . . you know how Sven is . . .

DIFFERENT ANGLE. A shadowy figure slips around the corner of the house, hesitates for a moment, then looks up.

> VO ANN
> . . . once he starts talking, he finds no end. But
> after all, he is your boss . . .

The shadowy figure's POV, a lighted window.

> VO ANN
> . . . and since you did not want to attend his
> Midsummer Night's party . . .

Interior Tom Gerard's House. Study.
A book-lined study. The corners of the room are steeped in shadows, only a lamp on Tom's desk spills a pool of light on his face. He is in his middle thirties, kind of ascetic looking.

> TOM
> Honey, you didn't have to trek out in this
> weather. You ought to have stayed at Lil's. . . .

Dimly the sound of humming voices comes up. Tom looks over his shoulder.

> TOM
> You shouldn't have left because of me.

Exterior Inn. Telephone. Night.
MEDIUM on Ann

> ANN
> You sounded so strange this afternoon, just before
> I left.

Interior Tom Gerard's House. Study. Night.

> TOM
> I was just a little upset. I'm all right now . . . really
> I am.

The sound of the humming voices increases.

> VO ANN (filtering through)
> If you really want to know, I was feeling a little
> homesick for you. . . .

Exterior Inn. Telephone. Night.

> ANN
>
> I love you so, Tom. . . .
> I'll love you forever . . .

Interior Tom Gerard's House. Study. Night.
Tom sits very still, as if frozen.

> VO ANN
> . . . and ever . . . see you soon.

> TOM (with difficulty)
> Yes, hon, real soon.

Exterior Inn. Telephone. Night.

> ANN
>
> I love you.

She hangs up, turns, and walks toward her car.

CU SHOCK ZOOM the car lights. Sound of humming voices, suddenly interspersed with the sound of a clock ticking.

Interior Tom Gerard's House. Night.
CU on clock ticking, louder and louder; the dial shows about two minutes to midnight.

Finally Tom puts the receiver back into its cradle. He looks at the telephone. After a while he picks up Ann's picture.

CU on Ann's picture.

CU on Tom, as he reacts to his wife's picture.

Exterior Tom's House. Night.
PAN with the shadowy figure walking to the door.

MEDIUM on figure, its face hidden by a black hood; a hand reaches out. CU on hand turning the doorknob.

Interior Tom Gerard's House. Study. Night.
CU on hand dialing a telephone number.

PULL BACK to TIGHT MEDIUM on Tom:

> TOM
>
> Hello? This is Dr. Gerard again. Is Father O'Brian back from the church yet? Any minute? Yes, well please have him call me as soon as he arrives. Tell him it's urgent . . . life or death.

Tom hangs up, hesitates, then opens a desk drawer.

CU on Tom's hand reaching for a gun.

Back on TOM. He checks to see whether the gun is loaded, and it is. He puts the gun in front of him. The SOUND OF HUMMING VOICES has decreased somewhat, but all of a sudden the sound of a CLOCK TICKING cuts through the HUMMING VOICES, louder and louder.

(The rhythm becomes faster; cross cutting adds to the increasing speed of the scene.)

Suddenly the phone rings. Tom, relief on his face, answers.

> TOM
>
> Father O'Brian, thank God, I can't hold off any longer, it's happening tonight . . . and . . . he'll . . . Who is this?

There is a long pause. Then a husky voice answers.

> VO VOICE
>
> The angels will be there in a few moments. Be ready for them.

The phone clicks off. Sound of hollow dial tone.

Exterior Inn. Night.
Ann approaches her car, gets in, slams door shut.

Interior Tom Gerard's House. Hallway. Night.
TIGHT MEDIUM on black-clad arm, hand closes the front door ever so carefully. PULL BACK to reveal a black-clad, hooded figure.

Interior Tom Gerard's House. Study. Night.
Tom grabs his gun.

Interior Tom Gerard's House. Staircase. Night.
CU on feet walking upstairs (flashcut).

CU of hand on banister (flashcut).

Interior Tom Gerard's House. Study. Night.
Tom is on the phone, his voice thick with fear.

> TOM
> Beach Station? Give me Sgt. McGuire right
> away. . . . Yes . . . please . . . Tom Gerard . . .

Exterior Road. Night.
On Ann's car, speeding; her headlights cut ribbons of light through the rain.

Interior Tom Gerard's House. Upper Hallway. Night.
CU on feet walking.

Interior Tom Gerard's House. Study. Night.

> TOM
> . . . it's an emergency . . . tell him . . .

Tom is interrupted by the sound of heavy footsteps. He drops the receiver, hurries to the door.

He throws the door to the hallway open.

Interior Tom Gerard's House. Upper Hallway. Night.
Tom's POV. The empty hallway.

INSERT the phone receiver dangling.

> VO MCGUIRE
> Hello, Tom . . . Tom . . . answer me. . . .

CLOSE ANGLE on Tom standing motionless at the top of the stairs. Sweat builds on his temples, as he listens for a sound . . . any sound. Yet the night remains deadly quiet.

Tom descends the stairway cautiously.

ANGLE on Tom's gun pointed straight ahead.

ANGLE on Tom stopping at the bottom of the stairs. He breathes heavily as he checks around for danger. LOW LIGHTING of heavy shadows, the possibility of lurking danger, ready to strike.

Suddenly there is a whisper.

> VO VOICE
> Time to pay your debts to science, Tom Gerard.

Tom whirls around.

His POV. At the head of the stairs, bathed in blinding white light, stands the hooded figure.

Titles begin to roll

Sample: Budget

At the inital stage of contracting a studio, a shortened version of your budget will suffice. Needless to say, the sample budget given is too small to interest any major studio in the proposed film. Since, however, our film *Frozen Scream* (working title *Chill Factor*) obviously was a low-budget film (the film was distributed by the independent company 21st Century Distribution), I feel that a comparative budget ought to be given as a sample. The following is the shortened version of the budget listed in the offering.*

BUDGET

1100	Story and Rights	$ 30,500
1200	Producer's Unit	182,000
1300	Direction	58,000
1400	Star	1,000,000
	Supporting Cast	80,300
1500	Agent's Fees	108,030
1900	Above-Line Fringe Benefits	138,162
2000	Production Staff	19,000
2200	Set Design	21,200
2300	Set Construction	2,000
2500	Set Operation	21,900
2600	Special Effects	950
2700	Set Dressing	1,200
2800	Petty Cash	1,200
2900	Wardrobe	7,100
3100	Makeup and Hair Dressing	7,800
3200	Lighting	28,200
3300	Production Sound	17,300
3400	Camera	58,200
3500	Transportation	9,800
3600	Location Expenses	33,400
4400	Opticals	5,000
4500	Editing	70,200
4600	Music	50,000

*The given budget does not reflect the actual budget of our film *Frozen Scream*.

4700	Postproduction—Sound	81,788
4800	Laboratory (developing and printing)	75,019
6500	Publicity	10,000
6700	Insurance	54,000
6800	General Expenses	9,500
7800	Indirect Cost	318,375
		Total: $2,500,124

Sample: Producer's Résumé

Renée Harmon

Renée Harmon produced and wrote the screenplays for the following motion pictures:

Jungle Trap	World Inter Media Distribution, Palace International, Korea Raidon Home Video, USA, 1991
Revenge	World Inter Media Distribution, Palace International, Korea Raidon Home Video, USA, 1991
Red Satchel	Schau Mal Home Video, Germany, 1990
Escape from the Insane Asylum	Cinevest Entertainment Group, USA and Overseas, 1989
Run Coyote Run	World Inter Media Group, USA and Overseas, 1988
Night of Terror	Video Pictures Distribution, Mid American Home Video, USA, 1987
Executioner II	21st Century Distribution, Worldwide, Continental Home Video, USA, 1986
Hellriders	21st Century Distribution, Worldwide, Transworld Home Video
Frozen Scream	21st Century Distribution, 1985
Lady Streetfighter	Scope II Distribution, USA, 1982

3.

From literary property to screenplay: what you need to know to acquire and create a promotable concept

No movie can be offered and subsequently produced without its basic requirement: the *property*. The property can be a stage play, novel, short story, nonfiction essay, newspaper, or magazine article. Regardless of the source of your property you, the producer, have to make certain that you hold the right to the property.

You must *option* the literary property. The option agreement states the option fee and the purchase price, as well as the time period during which the producer has the exclusive right to the property. To option a property you'll have to pay between 5 and 10 percent of its purchase price. Each additional option fee should be based upon the original one. Whether these option payments may be deducted from the eventual purchase price is open to negotiation.

Remember one important fact: The producer must option the property, and money—even if it is only one dollar—*has* to be exchanged. A handshake won't do. A little-known actuality is the convention that "who owns the property owns the project." Consequently, even though the author will not interfere with your developing the property, he or she is at liberty to interfere with your choice of star, director, location, and so on.

Therefore, prior to optioning any property you should understand exactly what the "producer's rights" are.

1. First, make certain that the author owns the property. Who has retained the copyright? The author or the publishing company? Who has retained the motion picture rights? If in doubt, search the Copyright Office in Washington, D.C. The motion picture rights to the property must be acquired from the party holding these rights.

2. The producer has the right to develop the property, that is to say, he/she will have the screenplay written, work on the budget, contact directors and stars, negotiate with distribution companies, and obtain publicity for the project.

3. The producer has the right to change elements (plot, characters, locations) of the literary property. (Sadly, this is the point of most contention—and often litigation—between author and producer. It is also the reason that at times a movie based upon a well-loved book disappoints us once we see it on the screen.) Incidentally, the right to change the plot and characterization does not apply to a stage play. A stage play must be presented word for word as written. And this, again, is the reason that a filmed play remains a play in every respect and often lacks the reality we associate with a film.

The Literary Purchase Agreement

I cannot stress enough that no producer, regardless how experienced, should either write or accept a literary purchase agreement unless he or she has consulted a well-versed entertainment attorney. There are several ways to find the entertainment attorney who's right for you (don't forget, attorneys' fees do vary widely):

Ask your attorney for a referral.

Call your local Bar Association.

Contact: Volunteer Lawyers for the Arts
 1560 Broadway, Suite 711
 New York, NY 10036

An entertainment attorney should check the literary purchase agreement, or even better, *write* it; after all, contracts and agreements are the entertainment attorney's field of expertise.

This brings me to "boilerplate"—those contract forms one buys in any stationery store specializing in motion picture and publishing forms. Boilerplate or model contracts—since they open the door to all kinds of legal loopholes—simply won't do.

The purchase agreement becomes effective as soon as the option is exercised. There is no set rule about the amount to be paid for the property. (This does not apply to the purchase agreement for a screenplay written by a member of the Writers Guild of America. We will discuss the WGA rules and regulations later on, as we deal with the screenplay per se.) For a literary property (book, article, short story, newspaper, or magazine account), the purchase price may be as small as a few hundred dollars, or it may skyrocket into millions.

The following are the most salient points any literary purchase agreement must contain:

1. Title of literary property.
2. Author's name, address, and social security number; WGA membership number if applicable.
3. Publisher of book, short story, or magazine/newspaper article.
4. Copyright information.
5. Purchase price.
6. The right to exhibit a film based upon said property in theaters.
7. The right to exhibit a film based upon said property nontheatrically, such as:
   Home video
   Cable
   TV
   Institutions, ships, airplanes, oil rigs, university, and school campuses.
8. The right to:
   Publish the screenplay issuing from said property in book form.
   Novelize (unless based upon novel) the motion picture based upon said property.
   Publish stills of the film based upon said property in book form.
9. The right to broadcast excerpts of the film based upon said property via radio (this right authorizes the producer to advertise the film via radio).
10. The right to publish the films, based upon said property, songs, and score.

11. The right to merchandise items (toys, T-shirts, posters) bearing the likeness of characters appearing in the film based upon said property.
12. The right to produce the film based upon said property for TV or cable in lieu of the planned theatrical production.
13. The right to publish synopsis of story content of film based upon said property for promotional purposes in newspapers and magazines.
14. The right to option any sequels of said literary property.
15. The right to withhold a part of the author's payment until after the film's release, since it is impossible to detect whether any literary property contains infringing material.
16. The right to assign rights in the literary property to third parties. Any bank or investment group financing your picture will *insist* that the literary property be assigned to them. (Remember: The one who owns the literary property, owns the project.)

A Look at Author's Rights

So far we have viewed the purchase of literary property from the producer's point of view. Yet I feel it is only fair to concern ourselves with the author's rights as well; after all, you, the producer, want a fair deal for all. Besides, this segment will help readers who are authors *and* producers.

The author may be asked to sign a *grant of rights* in lieu of the more traditional option. The grant specifies:

Payment for the initial grant.
Purchase price for the literary property. Reversion of the property to the author in case the producer fails to pay the payment for the initial grant.

Payment of purchase price for the literary property.

Reversion of property to author (or holder of copyright) in case the producer fails to pay the agreed-upon purchase price.

It is the last clause that makes the grant of rights agreement tricky. If the production company, after having paid part of the purchase price, goes into bankruptcy, then the literary property becomes *part of the production firm's assets.*

Since the author has to wait in line with all the other creditors, his/her property may be tied up for years.

It is for this reason that I advise the author to choose the traditional option.

In addition the author should retain the rights to any sequels of his/her property, as well as the rights to use the original property's characters, names, and location for sequels, and any literary property not connected to the property optioned.

The author should request that the following clauses be included in the literary purchase agreement:

1. A definite purchase price.

2. A definite payment schedule:

   Partial payment to begin at the commencement of preproduction.
   Partial payment at commencement of principal photography.
   Partial payment at delivery of answer print.
   Final payment after commencement of domestic release.

3. An *outright date,* a time that payment is due, even though the film has not commenced shooting. (Be aware that a film's date of principal photography might be delayed indefinitely.)

4. Your credits should read:

From the _____ by _____. They have to appear on the front titles on the same title card with the screenplay writer's name.

In case your contract stipulates that you, the author, will receive net profits, make certain that these net profits are in concert with the net profits earned by producer, director, and stars. An author's net profits should *never* be deducted from the producer's net profits.

How to Find a Terrific Screenwriter

You have optioned a screenplay and wish to have a screenplay written, or you may be in the market for an original screenplay—in short, you need a screenwriter. Unless you like being bombarded with, and finally suffocated by, an avalanche of poorly written screenplays do not advertise for one in any of the trade papers, or even worse, your local newspaper. You may, however, decide upon one of the following:

1. If you have optioned a literary property that is destined to become a major studio deal (and if you have the funds to pay a hefty advance), your best bet is to contact one of the Big Four: William Morris, CAA, ICM, and Triad.

The William Morris Agency
151 El Camino Drive
Beverly Hills, CA 90028

CAA
1888 Century Park East, #1400
Los Angeles, CA 90067

ICM
(International Creative Management)
8899 Beverly Boulevard
Los Angeles, CA 90048

Triad Artists
10100 Santa Monica Boulevard, 16th Floor
Los Angeles, CA 90067

Since Hollywood still seems to be the hub of the motion picture industry you may want to contact a number of smaller but highly respected and well-established agencies, such as:

Robinson-Weintraub-Gross & Assoc.
8428 Melrose #C
Los Angeles, CA 90069

Paul Kohner Inc.
9169 Sunset Boulevard
Los Angeles, CA 90060

The Lantz Office
9255 Sunset Boulevard #505
Los Angeles, CA 90069

Mitchell J. Hamilburg
292 S. La Cienega Boulevard, #212
Beverly Hills, CA 90211

The Gage Group
9229 Sunset Boulevard, #306
Los Angeles, CA 90069

Or you may contact the Writers Guild of America West for a list of agencies:

Writers Guild of America West
8955 Beverly Boulevard
West Hollywood, CA 90048

Needless to say, if you plan to employ a WGA writer, your company has to be signatory with WGA. That is to say, your company agrees to abide by WGA rules and pay scales. Even if you have not yet formed your company, you'll still have to sign a WGA agreement. This contract must be signed up front,

The screenwriter has to be paid for his/her services. No writer may write on spec [speculation]—the promise of future payments. The payment schedules vary and are subject to negotiation. Usually the writer receives a specified amount at the commencement of his/her work, additional payments for each rewrite, and the final payment either upon delivery of the final script and/or at the time of the movie's release.

The producer must pay basic scale. This scale varies, and the producer should get in contact with the local chapter of WGA to determine current rates. At the time of this writing the following royalty scale was in effect:

$25,000—basic minimum scale for a full-length feature film script.

$25,000—basic scale for a full-length feature film script for cable.

For the theatrical film the WGA writer receives residuals for TV network and TV syndicated exhibition, as well as cable sales. For home video sales the WGA writer receives royalties. These royalties are to be negotiated, and are based upon the number of cassettes *purchased,* while residuals depend on the number of times the film is *being shown on the small screen.*

For TV the following minimum pay scale applies at the time of this writing:

$21,359 for each one-hour segment of a miniseries and/or movie of the week.

$14,560 for each half-hour series episode (prime-time); $7,529 (syndicated).

A royalty of 20 percent of the initial fee paid for up to five reruns. No royalties are due after the fifth rerun. For syndication, a royalty of 10 percent applies.

In addition to the fee paid to the screenwriter, the producer has to pay WGA specified amounts for health and retirement plans.

If the writer wrote the original screenplay (one that is not based on a literary property), he/she will retain the screenplay's publication rights, called "separation rights." These rights, however, cannot be exercised until six months after the picture's release. The producer, however, retains the rights to publicize promotional synopses.

A producer signatory to WGA is free to hire a screenwriter who is not signatory to WGA, but a WGA signatory writer cannot work for a nonsignatory producer.

You should also take into consideration that pay scale and additional requirements and fringe benefits change whenever WGA negotiates a new contract.

2. As you can tell, contracting a top screenwriter is expensive. Still, the producer of limited means need not despair.

He or she can obtain an excellent screenplay for an honorarium below WGA basic scale by contacting:

DG
The Dramatists Guild
234 W. 44th Street
New York, NY 10036

3. There is no reason to believe that a nonunion writer's skills are inferior to a union counterpart's. Many talented and highly professional writers all across the country are nonunion for the simple fact that they have not as yet been hired by a WGA signatory production company. All these writers know their craft, are familiar with screenplay construction, and—happily and eagerly—will do a great job. You'll find such writers by contacting your local university's or college's cinema department. Ask for the instructor who teaches screenplay writing and enlist his or her help in finding a graduating student well versed in screenplay structure, and who possibly might have written a viable screenplay. Do not get pawned off to the English department.

True, English majors may have learned to write stage plays, but they are as yet unfamiliar with a screenplay's stringent demands.

Possibly you may contact a local institution that teaches screenplay writing. But watch out: Some of the courses offered are excellent, while others are too short to be of any value to the students. These "screenplay writing made easy" sessions simply teach some basic facts about a complicated matter.

If you hire a nonunion writer, you may be able to defer his or her salary to commencement of the film, completion of the film, or the film's net profit.

Since a beginning producer's first venture most likely won't bring in any net profits, I think it is more honest to sign the writer on as partner in a joint venture partnership, rather than grant the writer net profit participation.

The Screenplay

This segment pertains to an original screenplay (a screenplay that is *not* based upon a literary property) as well as a screenplay derived from literary property.

After the literary property has been purchased, the producer assigns a screenwriter to write the screenplay. Sometimes the author will want to write the screenplay. (This request will be granted only if the author is a best-selling writer who has clout.)

One has to remember that screenplay writing is a craft all by itself; its techniques differ greatly from the writing skills necessary to write a novel or an article. Unfortunately, only a few authors (fiction and nonfiction) take the time and effort needed to learn the mechanics of screenplay writing. Therefore, it stands to reason that even though a famous author wrote the first draft based on a literary property, sooner or later a professional screenwriter will be assigned to the project.

A screenplay moves through the following stages:

TREATMENT

A synopsis of the plot; a short description of main characters and locations. The synopsis is about ten to fifteen pages in length.

FIRST-DRAFT SCREENPLAY

The scenes are fully written, and some dialog has been added. This is the time when director, star, and the distributor—if you have signed with one—will put in their "two cents' worth" of advice. This is the most harassing time for both the screenwriter and the producer. The distributor—understandably—is concerned about the promotable aspects of the project. The star worries about the effectiveness (read: size) of his or her part. The director has artistic considerations and the producer deals with budgetary fears.

It is now that a film based on an excellent literary property (or on an original screenplay) may lose its center core by splintering into various directions.

You are faced with the difficult and often thankless task of listening to all demands, of considering their merits, of sorting the chaff from the wheat, of discarding what obscures the screenplay, but most of all of keeping the script on a straight path, so as not to obliterate the literary (or original screenplay's) core.

A discussion about the importance of keeping the literary property's basic ideas intact may seem out of place in a book dealing with financing a movie, but financing your movie begins with the film's conception. If the basic idea of a film, because of additions and/or deletions, becomes obscure, you'll open the door to reshooting and reediting—both time- and money-consuming processes.

It is easy to lose a handle on your film's concept as you fight your way through the jungle of rewrites and refinements. Many of the suggested changes may be excellent. However, many terrific but isolated moments do not necessarily add up to an effective cinematic matrix. Remember to keep these few simple facts in mind when you are dealing with an avalanche of suggested changes:

1. *Basic Idea.* Has the property's basic idea been preserved?
2. *Intent.* What does the screenplay intend to show to the audience?
3. *Emotion.* What feelings should the screenplay evoke in the audience?
4. *Theme.* The theme keeps the movie's core together by clearly expressing three main ideas:
   This movie is about _____
   This movie establishes a strong belief in _____
   This movie intends to prove _____

5. *Goal.* The theme leads to an understanding of why the protagonist (hero) pursues his or her goal.

Has the main question, "Will _____ achieve _____" been clearly established and satisfactorily answered?

WHAT YOU NEED TO KNOW ABOUT STRUCTURE

The screenplay's structure keeps your audience's interest in the movie alive.

1. Have the *who* and *where* been established clearly? Some scripts make the mistake of revealing the *what* (what is going to happen) and *why* (the motive for the main character's actions) just a little too early. Yes, the audience must know about the *what* and *why*, but first it has to meet the main characters *(who)* before it will care about what is happening to them.

The relationship between the main characters *(who)* and their environment *(where)* should be made known as early as possible. It is their relationship that explains the *why*.

2. Does the script contain any *twists,* and are they placed correctly? *Twist at the end of Act I:* An event occurs that sets up the main plot *(what)* and the main character's motives subplot *(why).* These motives lead to the protagonist's (hero's) goal and the antagonist's (villain's) countergoal. This twist asks the main question: "Will _____ achieve _____?"

Twist I in the middle of Act II: Keeps the story going, possibly turns it in a different direction and repeats the main question. *Twist II at the end of Act II:* Pulls the story toward Act III and to the plot's climax and denouement.

3. Does the *what* and *why* grow out of the relationship between the main characters, or has it been imposed upon them for the purpose of creating an exciting plot? The *what* and *why* sets the story in motion:

What the story is about determines the main plot and the film's line of action. *Why* determines the main characters' motives, leading to goal and countergoal. *Why* establishes the film's subplot, which examines the film's theme.

4. Is the subplot strong enough? The subplot reveals the "human element" of your story. It gives your story depth, keeps your characters from becoming "cardboard figures," and demands the audience's empathy. Here are some guidelines:

- The subplot must be part of the story, not a story by itself. While the main plot tells the story, the subplot focuses on the relationship between people. Often, the subplot is the stronger and more interesting one, but it is the plot that causes the actions the characters take, and as such holds the film together (in *Kramer vs. Kramer* the subplot deals with the couple's relationship to each other; the plot deals with the custody case).

- Once you have clarified your plot-subplot structure you will have to check the structure of the subplot: The subplot has the identical structure as the main plot; it has a beginning, a middle, and an end. It has twists of its own.

- The subplot twists should be placed as closely as possible to their respective main plot twists. If you are struggling with a script, most likely you are facing faulty main plot–subplot integrations.

The Middle (Act II). Act II is where your screenplay should develop into an increasingly gripping matrix. At times, unfortunately, Act II may drag after an interesting beginning (Act I). Besides main plot and subplot twists and the integration of both, you need the following to keep Act II alive:

Momentum
Graduation
Suspense
Foreshadowing
Dark moment
Highlight scenes
Obstacles and conflicts

Momentum. Momentum simply means that a story gains in strength. This is achieved by the application of graduation and suspense.

Graduation. Check your story. Are all events on the same high- or low-interest level, or do they vary in strength? Interest level must move up even though you should give your audience plateaus when "nothing much happens." Does the final (and highest) graduation lead into the dark moment and from there into the twist that propels the story into Act III?

Suspense. While graduation keeps the audience's interest alive, it is overlapping suspense that holds Act II together. Act II consists of a series of overlapping suspense sequences, each headed by a goal that has to be either frustrated or satisfied. The point is that a new overlapping suspense sequence begins before the denouement of the previous one.

Make certain that the suspense sequence B has been set before the denouement of suspense sequence A has been delivered.

The denouement of the various suspense sequences must be delivered at the end of Act II; then only the main question needs to be answered.

Never fail to make your character's expectations of the outcome clear to your audience. Remember, your audience expects some outcome. It is fun (and makes for an exciting film) to manipulate this expectation.

1. The denouement does not happen as anticipated—surprise.
2. The audience at this point does not expect a denouement—shock. (This technique was used to great effect in the original *Halloween*.)
3. The denouement happens as expected—satisfaction.

It is obvious that an always satisfied anticipation becomes as boring as a continually frustrated expectation becomes annoying.

Foreshadowing. Foreshadowing is another integral part of momentum. Any event needs to be foreshadowed twice. Audiences should not become aware of foreshadowing; they should remember, however, that the foreshadowed event has taken place.

Dark moment. The twist at the end of Act II features the dark moment, when everything seems lost. It is imperative that at this point the main plot and subplot twists are closely integrated, and that the main plot twist moves the story in a different direction. (The dark moment occurs in *Jungle Trap* when everyone but Chris and Leila has been killed.)

Highlight scenes. A highlight scene resembles a plot within a plot. The highlight scene is an excellent device that keeps the middle of a motion picture from dragging. It is most effective if it occurs immediately after the first twist.

1. The highlight scene ought to be an integral part of your film; it should not take off on a tangent of its own.

2. The highlight scene should not last more than five to seven minutes.

3. A highlight scene, starting from a point of departure, features a beginning (Act I), a middle (Act II), and an end (Act III). A twist occurs at the end of Act II.

Obstacles and conflicts. Obstacles are barriers that keep a character from reaching a goal. Obstacles are important because they give you, the beginning producer-director, the chance to "prove character in action," that is to say, characters have to react to obstacles in keeping with their established personality: A braggart will not react humbly; a sensible person will not turn reckless, unless the secondary trait of recklessness has been established (foreshadowed) prior to the event.

Obstacles are closely connected to *conflict.* All conflicts need to be established clearly; at times they need to be foreshadowed. Never expect your audience to guess who is in conflict with whom or what, *but spell it out.* Only three conflict patterns are possible: Man against man/woman; man against nature; and man against himself.

If your script lacks suspense, I recommend that you investigate the obstacle/conflict area. Ask yourself:

1. Has an obstacle or a conflict been established early enough to cause audience anticipation?

2. Do the opposing forces have an *equal chance* to reach their goal? If not, the script will lack *suspense.* If John and Jerry court Miss Beautiful, but all advantages are on John's side, no suspense is evoked. But if the chance of success is equally distributed between the two, then we, the audience, are interested in the outcome of the competition.

3. Are goal and countergoal clearly stated, and are both focused upon the same area? Mary and Beth are both up for the starring role in an Off-Broadway play. The girls are equally compelled to win the role, but they have never met, and they do not know of each other's existence—same goal, but no conflict, and therefore no suspense. But if Mary and Beth are friends and devious Beth does everything in her power to discredit sweet Mary, then we have a countergoal, conflict, and suspense.

The End (Act III). Do NOT: introduce any new characters or any new events.

End your subplot before the climax begins. The climax focuses on the *main plot only.*

But DO: let the climax build up swiftly, tie up all loose ends, and answer the main question.

DELIVERY OF THE FINAL SCRIPT

A word of warning: Even after a script has been polished (has had a final going-over), it should never be termed a "final script," as lines and scenes may be changed during shooting.

The considerate producer will give the screenwriter between three and six months from commencement of writing to delivery.

4.

*D*istribution:

a primer for professionals

The distribution game is complicated. It is a contract-driven game, where each aspect of a contract must hinge upon the next. No producer should venture into this game without having an experienced attorney and a knowledgeable accountant on his or her side. Distribution is a game that requires a team approach.

This chapter, and I cannot emphasize this enough, tries to give you some very basic knowledge about the ways distribution works, the pitfalls one might encounter, and the maze of various distribution practices. *In no way* does this chapter stand in lieu of any legal advice given by an attorney, or financial advice given by an accountant. This chapter shows the facts; it is up to your attorney and accountant to interpret them.

There are various ways to distribute a film. It is the distributor's responsibility to find the best one for your picture:

Distribution by saturation
Platform release
Limited engagement
Market-by-market saturation
Four-walling

DISTRIBUTION BY SATURATION

Only major studios can afford saturation, since as a blockbuster opens simultaneously in several thousands of theaters nationwide, it must be supported by enormous—and very expensive—national and local advertising.

The rationale is that the blockbuster must earn the greatest dollar amount in the shortest time period.

PLATFORM RELEASE

The same as its counterpart, the motion picture release by saturation, the film given a platform release opens *simultaneously* nationwide. But it opens in fewer theaters and usually in major cities only. From there the film moves into secondary markets, smaller towns, and smaller theaters. Advertising thrusts toward local newspaper, radio, and TV ads. The platform-released picture relies heavily upon the previously discussed press kit. Most major studios release their "run of the mill" film, as well as all films that have been picked up by a major studio-distributor on a platform-release basis.

LIMITED ENGAGEMENT

Such a film opens in just a few select theaters in Los Angeles, New York, and Chicago, and from there—if the audience response warrants it—makes its way into the other major markets.

Advertising for a limited-engagement film has to be geared to an identifiably sophisticated audience. Some major studios prefer to release films of artistic merit but limited audience appeal in this manner.

MARKET-BY-MARKET SATURATION

A film of special appeal to certain geographic areas and/or socioeconomic groups does best if distributed market-by-market. A rather small number of prints, rarely more than about two hundred, supported by adequate but not expensive local advertising, moves from territory to territory. Most independent distribution companies employ market-by-market distribution, by "farming" a picture out to territorial subdistributors. Both distributor and subdistributor (called "territorials") share the advertising cost. Of course, ultimately you, the producer, will pay for these. A film distributed market-by-market does not utilize any national advertising.

If a small number of prints have to be circulated, the producer might elect to bypass a distributor altogether by contracting subdistributors operating in various territories. These territorials do not necessarily distribute state by state. A California-based territorial, for instance, may service part of California, plus Arizona and Nevada. Most likely the territorial subdistributor requires that you advance most of the advertising cost.

FOUR-WALLING

In case a producer has been unable to interest neither independent distributor nor territorial subdistributor, the producer might consider four-walling by contacting theater owners directly. Areas can be worked one at a time with just a few prints. You'll have to supply all advertising, such as one-sheets, newspaper, mats, and—if warranted—radio blurbs. In a way, you *rent* the theaters by paying the exhibitor either via a specified rental amount or a certain percentage of the box office intake. Needless to say, such a practice does not work with any national theater chain such as Mann's or Loew's, or any of the privately owned multiplex theaters. Four-walling is a viable way of getting your picture into distribution, if you are dealing with one of the quickly disappearing mom-and-pop theaters. After deducting your advertising costs, I doubt whether you may break even by four-walling your movie. But, if you need a domestic release in order to gain a more lucrative home video contract, four-walling might be the way to go.

Now that we've discussed how to distribute your film, let's talk about where to distribute it.

Majors*

Before the Paramount consent decree, studios controlled distribution by owning theaters outright. Since then the major studios' influence on distribution has been somewhat diminished; still, they are "the big fish in the pond."

*Disney, Universal, Warner Bros., Paramount, Sony (Columbia), 20th Century Fox

After all, majors maintain nationwide and worldwide distribution networks, and they do run the distribution game. Certainly, every major studio finances and produces a number of films but picks up the majority of its releases from well-established production companies.

Since $20 million is the *average* budget for a film produced by a major studio, it is understandable that generally only well-known and well-connected producers who can show a track record of successful films will be given the opportunity to ally themselves with a major studio.

Yet, one never knows what will happen: A beginning producer who owns a terrific project might be able to interest a studio. Consequently, it is necessary to take a long and hard look at the "studio deal."

At this point you'll have to distinguish between the studio deal (a major studio finances and distributes a picture) and the "pick-up deal" (a major distributor agrees to distribute a film that had been financed by an outside source). In the first instance you, the producer, exchange most if not all artistic control for a lucrative salary; in the latter, you retain artistic control but have to take the chance that your investors might see no profit, and stand in danger of recovering possibly only a fraction of their investments.

Frankly, both the studio deal and "studio pick-up"—unless you have secured the now all but extinct "negative pick-up"*—are not quite as sweet as they seem. Still, the fact remains that seeing your film released by a major studio gives you and your picture the kind of prestige that will make it easier for you to negotiate a favorable distribution contract with one of the mini-majors, as you develop your second film.

The Formal PD Agreement (Production-Distribution Agreement)

A major studio requires that the producer enter into a production-distribution agreement, called the PD agreement.

The studio, fully aware of the fact that the financial opportunity is vested in distribution, will spend millions on your film to make millions more.

---

*Upon delivery of the film, the distributor pays and agrees upon the amount, usually some percentage above the film's production cost. Payments will be made in four quarterly installments.

First, a word of advice regarding the studio deal. If you have visions of sending your script directly to a major studio, forget it. Studios do not accept scripts from unknown producers or writers. There are only three ways to approach a studio:

1. Submit your script (not your offering) through a well-established agency.
2. Submit your offering (not your prospectus) to one of the big agencies (such as William Morris, CAA, ICM) that package projects.
3. Submit your *prospectus* (as discussed in chapter 2) directly to the major studio.

1. *Have your script (not your offering) submitted to a studio by a well-established agency.* Make certain that the agent under consideration not only has contacts in the motion picture industry, and will target your script only to these major studios and mini-majors, for which your script's genre is just right, but also target it to an executive with enough clout to start the process. Let me warn you, if your agent does not have strong connections, your script will end up in a studio's story department for evaluation. There an assigned reader synopsizes the submission and recommends the project for further consideration or rejection. Unfortunately, the majority of these readers are people on the first rung of their career ladder, who have not as yet developed the talent necessary to "sense" a viable project among the many less desirable or frankly amateurish ones they have to evaluate. Also, it is understandable that these readers hesitate to put their limited expertise on the line by recommending a project.

The scripts that have passed through the readers' "sieves" are submitted to the story department, where the story editor has a chance to either reject a script or move it on to the vice president in charge of production for further evaluation.

2. *Submit your offering (not your prospectus) to one of the big agencies (such as William Morris, ICM, or CAA) that package projects.*

Your project will have a fair chance of success if one of the big agencies handles the package, as the agent in charge (bypassing the story editor) gets in contact with the vice president of production. Furthermore, the big agencies know about the kind of projects currently demanded by majors and mini-majors.

And now a word about the package. First, submit your offering but not your prospectus. Agreed, the offering, having been tailored to attract investors, is not the document that the packager submits to the studios, but it gives an overview of your project, its costs, and possible commercial viability. At this point it is better not to have solicited any letters of interest from either director and/or stars (and positively no such letter from any distribution company; after all, the majors and mini-majors are not as much interested in producing your film as in distributing it). As far as actors and director are concerned, letters of interest present a severe hindrance. It is in the packager's interest to supply talent from his or her own pool of clients.

In turn, the packager writes a proposal, including those segments of your offering deemed important.

And in both cases, regardless of whether you work with an agent or a packager, you must sign a release before your script will be submitted.

3. *Submit your prospectus directly to the major studio and/or mini-major.* If you are in the very fortunate position of having the opportunity to submit your prospectus (not your offering) to a studio or mini-major, be advised *not* to suggest names of stars and directors. One studio's beloved star might be another one's deplorable monster. Patiently wait for the studio's casting suggestions.

And now, after this necessary detour, we'll go back to the major studio's production-distribution (PD) agreement.

Before entering into a PD agreement you must negotiate your position in the deal:

1. The producer (you) forms a corporation. It is the corporation, not the producer, who enters into the PD agreement with the studio.
2. The producer enters into the PD agreement with the studio.

(Please do not confuse the PD agreement with a distribution agreement; in the first the studio finances and distributes the picture; in the latter the studio only distributes the picture.)

And now let's illuminate the pros and cons of both situations:

The corporation enters into the PD agreement with the studio. Most likely, a producer entering a PD agreement with a major studio, being a well-known producer, already heads his or her own corporation. It is, however, at times far better to form a corporation for each individual of your studio-financed project. True, corporation status may limit tax advantages, but the benefits the producer gains from his or her corporation's status far outweigh the tax disadvantages. The corporation, and this is the salient point, applies corporate assets to the motion picture in production under the auspices of the PD agreement. That is to say, the film listed in the PD agreement is the corporation's one and only asset. In case of breach of contract, the corporation (not the producer) will be held liable only for the amount of money the motion picture in production represents. The producer's other film and personal assets are protected.

The advantages and disadvantages of this type of agreement are listed below and should be considered.

Advantages	Disadvantages
The producer retains day-to-day control over the project.	In case of disagreements between producer and talent, labs, production entities, and so on, the studio—since its rights are derivative—may be of little help to the producer.
The producer retains the right to contact talent and key personnel.	
The producer has somewhat more input as far as creative control is concerned.	
	Unless the studio has guaranteed the contract signed by the producer, the producer has sole responsibility.
It is not easy for the studio to move away from a project protected by the no-asset corporation.	

The producer enters into a PD agreement with the studio. If the producer is not protected by a no-asset corporation, he or she will be responsible personally for all damages that may arise during the production or in the event of breach of contract.

Advantages	Disadvantages
The studio is responsible for all contracts signed.	In case of takeover, it is easier for the studio to remove all personnel (including the producer) from the project. A takeover, of course, can take place under the no-asset PD agreement, as well, but then the procedure is difficult and time-consuming.
It is the studio's responsibility to intermediate if disagreements arise between producer, labs, talent, and so on.	

Advantages	*Disadvantages*
	The studio has the right to assign a studio representative to the project.
	The producer loses the day-to-day control over the film.
	The producer may lose creative control over the film.

And now I'd like to draw your attention to the fact that the discussed points are supposed to give information only. The scope of this book does not permit a discussion of legal details. And it is impossible to determine whether a producer/PD agreement or corporation/PD agreement is the most beneficial; it differs from film to film. Therefore, it is imperative that you discuss the pros and cons of each with your attorney, as well as have the PD agreement itself scrutinized closely.

Regardless of which type of setup seems best for your project, always be aware of the fact that you, one way or the other, are in the studio's employment. Therefore, make certain that you are a well-paid employee. Rather than accepting a sizable net profit participation, have your attorney negotiate a higher salary and a lower net profit participation.

Why? Aren't your pictures going to make millions?

Sure, your picture will make millions of dollars, but how much of the fortune will trickle down to you is rather dubious. So, take a deep breath before reading the next few pages, in which I'll try to shed some light on the most common studio accounting practices.

The following is a *hypothetical* cost and profit scenario for the average $20 million studio-financed distributed motion picture.

Actual production cost	$20,000,000
15% studio overhead	3,000,000
10% interest on both production cost and overhead.	2,300,000

These interest rates will run (hopefully) for about two years, if we assume one year's duration for preproduction, production, and postproduction, and another year for distribution. Make certain that interest is charged *only* from the commencement of each period, and as funds are released to you.

Print and advertising expenses to open the film amounting roughly to about half of the production cost	10,000,000
10% interest rate on costs for prints and advertising	1,000,000
So far the film has accrued a negative cost of	36,300,000
For argument's sake, let's assume the film in domestic theatrical release played in (earned).	$40,000,000

This amount does not reflect the box office receipt but the amount due to the distributor. From this amount the distributor will deduct:

40% cost for additional prints and additional advertising.	16,000,000
30% distribution fee	12,000,000

Next the film goes into overseas distribution for all areas (theatrical, TV, cable, home video)

Assuming the film plays in another	$40,000,000
35% (sometimes 40%) distribution fee	14,000,000
If a subdistributor has been employed his or her fee has to be deducted	4,000,000
10% for additional advertising overseas	4,000
10% interest rate on additional advertising	400
For auxiliary rights, such as home video, cable, network, and syndicated TV, receipts for 20 percent distribution fee	$15,000,000 3,000,000

And finally (yes, there is no end to it) the studio takes on a 5% gross participation fee on *all* receipts. These receipts amount to the receipts received, and do not deduct expenses.

5% gross participation fee on all receipts	4,775,000
Receipts domestically	$95,000,000
Expenses:	
Prints	
Advertising	
Overhead charges	
Distribution fee	
Interest	$90,079,400

As you can tell, the profit margin is slim. If you wonder why a studio remains in business, and even prospers, remember that studios are in the distribution business. They make their living even though a film may barely break even, or might be considered a flop. For this purpose we will compare *actual* expenses with fees and interest rates.

Expenses	
Production expenses	$20,000,000
Studio overhead	3,000,000
Print and advertising expenses (to open the film)	10,000,000
Additional prints and advertising	16,000,000
Subdistributor fees overseas	4,000,000
Total expenses	$53,000,000

You see, the fairly modest budget of $20,000,000 has almost tripled by the time all expenses have been added. Now take a look at the amount of fees and interest rates the studio charges. (As far as interest rates are concerned, we must remember that the studio must pay interest, too.)

Fees and Interest Rates	
10% interest on both production cost and overhead	$ 2,300,000
10% interest rate on prints and advertising needed to open film	1,000,000
30% distribution fee domestically	12,000,000
35% distribution fee overseas	14,000,000
10% interest rate for additional overseas distribution fees	400,000
20% distribution fee for auxiliary markets	3,000,000
Total amount of fees and interest rates	$32,700,000
Plus 5% gross participation fees (based upon the entire amount of gross receipts.)	1,600,350

The Formal PD Agreement

The studio and the corporation and/or producer enter into a formal PD agreement. Most likely a studio will submit to you a lengthy (between twenty and fifty pages) standard contract, called a "boilerplate." Changes, omissions, and revisions are always negotiable. Before entering into any agreement, discuss the changes. Find out which clauses are readily changed and which ones are likely to be sticky issues. The following gives you a picture of the most important clauses of the PD agreement:

1. Contracting Control
2. Artistic Control
3. Financial Control
4. Breach of Contract
5. Takeover
6. Termination of Project
7. Over-Budget Penalty
8. Interest Charges
9. Overhead Charges
10. Insurance (liability, negative insurance, cast insurance)
11. Union Contracts
12. Producer's Warranties
13. Producer's Billing
14. Delivery of Motion Picture
15. Accounting Rights
16. Assignment of Rights
17. Producer's Payment
18. Producer's Profit Participation

Only the most basic points of each clause will be discussed. Everything mentioned has been written to give you facts, but, as mentioned before, it is your attorney's responsibility to interpret these facts and to negotiate the most favorable terms for you.

1. *Contracting Control.* Under the producer PD agreement the studio contracts creative talent and key personnel, while under the corporation PD agreement, the control remains with the producer. The studio, of course, will take an assignment of each contract, or will receive a power of attorney from the producer.

2. *Artistic Control.* Artistic control rests (depending on the contract) with either the studio or the producer. To avoid disagreement, the PD agreement should identify these controls. The fairest way to handle artistic control is to have the producer propose names but give the studio the final decision. In

practice, the convention of proposal selection applies to stars, director, art director, composer, and director of cinematography. All other assignments are usually left to the producer's discretion.

3. *Financial Control.* Since financial control is one of the most important (and most controversial) clauses of any PD agreement, the following need to be identified in unmistakable terms:

Studio commits to finance the total cost of picture, such as production costs, prints, and advertising.

The producer is not responsible for any production and/or distribution costs. The producer will not be liable for any over-budget costs arising from:

Acts of God
Defaults by third parties (actors, labs, etc.)
Changes requested by the studio

Since you can expect arguments about this particular addition, you may sweeten the pot by providing a *completion bond*. A completion bond is a type of special insurance that guarantees additional funds in case the picture should go over budget. Since the cost of such a bond is rather high, it behooves the producer to have this amount tacked on to the production cost of the film.

The studio usually takes copyright ownership (that is to say, the studio owns the literary property, and whoever owns the literary property owns the project). In some cases (under a corporation PD agreement, for example), the studio takes a security interest in the copyright of the literary property plus the preprint material. The monies needed to produce the film are considered loans, and the studio, understandably, receives interest on them.

- The studio will require having a production account opened in a bank of its choice.
- The studio will require having a production accountant of its choice assigned to the project.
- The studio will assign one of its production executives to the picture.
- The studio reserves the right to take over the production in case of default, breach of contract, and/or over budget.

Since the studio may keep the terminology of those clauses rather loose, it is your attorney's responsibility to clarify each.

4. *Breach of Contract.* Clarify *all* conditions that may be construed as breach of contract. Most likely these will be:

- Picture went considerably over budget.
- Picture was not delivered on time.
- Picture's concept was changed *without* studio's approval.

Do *not* accept as breach of contract any damages resulting from defaults by third parties (actors, labs, locations).

5. *Takeover.* In case a studio takes over a picture, the studio has the right to remove and replace all personnel (including the producer) connected to the project. It is important to have the following provision spelled out in the PD agreement: A person can only be removed from the project if he or she has acted in an irresponsible or egregious manner (believe me, that is hard to prove).

6. *Termination of Project.* Generally a project will be terminated as a measure of last resort, and only if a production threatens to go out of control completely. Since closing a production and opening it again is costly, a studio takes this measure seriously.

7. *Over-Budget Penalty.* A picture is considered over budget if the monies spent on production exceed the approved budget. It is customary, and no studio will object, if the producer adds a 10 percent contingency for unforeseen expenditures. The following should not fall within the area of over budget:

- Unforeseen raises in guild salaries
- Additions and changes requested by the studio
- Acts of God

The producer should foresee any difficulties arising, and have the attorney ask for:

- Exclusions
- Definition of over budget and over-budget add-back penalties

Most likely the over-budget cost will be subject to interest rates:

Production	$20,000,000
Over budget	5,000,000
10% add-back penalty	500,000
10% interest	275,000

Needless to say, the studio will charge the customary interest rate of 10 percent on over-budget and add-back penalty, in which case the producer is liable to pay interest on the additional $5,500,000.

8. *Interest Charges.* A studio's interest rate exceeds the customary prime rate of 2 percent. It is important to clarify the commencement of interest payments. A studio may hold the position that interest commences as soon as the production loan has been approved, while producers contend that interest ought to be charged in concert with monies received for the production.

9. *Overhead Charges.* As discussed in our scenario, a studio charges 15 percent overhead on production expenses. You, the producer, are entitled to charge overhead (during preproduction, production, and postproduction) on the following items:

Office rental
Secretary salaries
Office supplies
Telephone
Attorney's fees

10. *Insurance.* It goes without saying that the PD agreement demands that the producer arrange for proper insurance:

1. Production liability insurance
2. Errors and omissions insurance. At times the studio will provide this type of insurance protecting the studio as well as the picture from claims such as:
   Invasion of privacy
   Libel
   Slander
   Copyright infringement

Most likely the above claims arise from material contained in the literary property. It is for this reason that if the producer deals with a controversial script and/or idea, "errors and omissions" insurance should be obtained prior to contacting a studio.

If you are shooting a scene including "civilians" (onlookers who have not been hired as extras), have every one of them sign a release form.

The errors and omissions insurance should be obtained to cover not less than $10,000,000 with a deductible of $100,000.

Raw Stock Insurance. Since suppliers of raw stock limit their liability to replacement of faulty raw stock only, raw stock insurance covers the cost of having to reshoot scenes.

Negative Insurance. This insurance protects the negative of your film against damage incurred when stored in the lab, or during transportation from studio and/or location to lab, and from the lab to editing facilities.

Miscellaneous Insurance:

Workers' Compensation
Fire, theft, property insurance
Third-party liability insurance

Cast Insurance. Most likely the studio carries an umbrella cast insurance. Again, some producers prefer to be covered by an insurance policy of their own. The cost of cast insurance depends usually on the proposed film's negative cost. The basic premium covers six people: the director and five actors. All persons covered have to submit to medical examinations by a physician appointed by the insurance company. If a person does not meet the requirements, this person may be excluded from the policy, or (more likely) a higher premium will be collected. Cast insurance comes into effect if an actor or director is injured or dies. For this reason the production company *must* sign an affidavit stating that none of the insured personnel will engage in any hazardous activities, and that for such activities stunt personnel are to be employed.

In case of an actor's death, the options are whether to replace the actor and reshoot segments of the film, or to terminate the project. Even though a producer and studio favor reshooting, the insurance company usually opts for termination of the film.

11. *Union Contracts.* The producer is responsible to enter into agreements with unions. It is interesting to note that there are no reciprocity agreements between the unions. A producer may choose to become signatory with one

but not with any other union. This does not hold true if you are producing a movie for a major studio; in this case you'll have to sign with all unions. (Yet, even if you are producing a low-budget film and have SAG actors on your casting list, you *must* sign with SAG [Screen Actors Guild]. SAG will agree to reduce scale for its members if you are producing a film budgeted under $1 million. You must, however, observe SAG regulations pertaining to overtime and meal penalties, and are to pay certain amounts to the SAG pension fund.) Also, be advised that you cannot employ SAG and nonunion actors on the same shoot. If one actor on your shoot is a member of SAG, *all* actors must be SAG members. But don't worry; if during your casting sessions you discover a terrific actor who happens to be nonunion, all it takes is a letter from you to SAG requesting to have this actor admitted to the union. Furthermore, to assure that actors will be paid the producer must deposit a bond securing actors' salaries. This bond must be deposited with SAG.

The following is a list of unions you will, or may have to, deal with:

- Screen Actors Guild (SAG)—actors
- Writers Guild of America (WGA)—writers
- Directors Guild of America (DGA)—directors, assistant directors, production managers
- Screen Extras Guild (SEG)—extras
- American Federation of Musicians (AFM)—musicians, composers, arrangers
- Theatrical Stage Employees Union (LATSE)—grips, gaffers, transportation workers
- Cinematographers Union—cinematographers, camera operators, loaders

12. *Producer's Warranties.* The studio will require the producer to submit what is called a "chain of documents" regarding the literary property. This chain refers to the documents the producer has previously obtained from the copyright holder of the literary property. In addition, the following documents have to be submitted:

- An errors and omissions insurance policy (in case the studio does not carry one).
- Agreement that the producer will refrain from placing a lien on the project.

- The producer indemnification against any claim arising from breach of contract by third parties.
- Agreement by the producer not to obtain a loan based upon expected net profits.
- Agreement by the producer not to assign any sum due him or her to any third party.

It is obvious that the producer has no remedies against the studio. In case of alleged breach of contract, the producer can sue for monetary damage only, and cannot keep the studio from distributing and/or merchandising the picture.

13. *Producer's Billing.* The typical standard or boilerplate contract contains several clauses regarding the producer's billing.

The producer's screen credits have to be positioned on a single title card, and must roll before the director's credit on front titles.

The producer's credit has to appear in proper size on one-sheets, and *all* newspaper advertising.

The producer has the right to supply the studio with billing requirements.

Laboratory Pledge-holder Agreement. The studio customarily will use in-house lab and editing facilities, or will assign a lab of its choice to the production. In the event the producer has been permitted to employ a lab of his or her choice, the studio retains the legal title to the motion picture via a "laboratory pledge-holder agreement," guaranteeing that only the studio will have access to the negative.

14. *Delivery of Motion Picture.* The studio reserves the right to the final cut of the picture. The items to be delivered are discussed in detail in the Distribution Agreement on pages 90–91.

15. *Accounting Rights.* Most PD agreements provide for quarterly accountings during the film's first two-year run. After this time period the producer receives semiannual and finally annual accountings.

16. *Assignment of Rights.* In the event the producer elects to dispose his or her net profits, the producer agrees to offer these to the studio first.

17. *Producer's Payment.* Once a studio has accepted a project for development, the studio will have to pay the producer a nominal fee (about $25,000) plus compensation of all expenses incurred in the project so far. If the project goes into "turnabout," that is to say, if the studio has lost interest in the project, the producer is entitled to a small compensation, usually not exceeding $30,000.

Once the studio has approved your production, you should negotiate for a set payment schedule:

10% of the producer's compensation in biweekly installments during the preproduction period

50% of compensation in weekly installments during the production period

10% of compensation at delivery of picture

or:

1/3 of compensation at the commencement of preproduction

1/3 of compensation at commencement of production

1/3 of compensation upon delivery of picture

18. *Producer's Profit Participation.* At times, the producer's profit participation gives rise to heated negotiations. (We will discuss gross and net profit in detail a little later.) Suffice it to say that if you have any doubts about the studio's accounting, you have the right to audit the studio's books. Such an audit is expensive, and the results are doubtful. In any event, you have the right to audit receipts and expenses applying to *your film only*. For this reason the following information, pertinent to your audit, is difficult if not impossible to obtain:

Was the film used to cross-collaborate a less successful picture? There is always the possibility that the loss on one film has been offset with the gross profits of another film as far as distribution expenses and advertising are concerned.

Yet you should have no difficulty obtaining the following information:

1. Has my film been given sufficient play dates?
2. Was enough money spent on prints and advertising?

The "Pick-Up" Deal: The Producer's Distribution Agreement with a Studio

The distribution agreement comes into play when the studio agrees to distribute a picture that has either already been financed, or has been completed, especially for foreign distribution.

The financial scenario, except for the amount spent to produce a film, is the same as for the studio-produced-and-distributed motion picture.

The distribution contract, however, differs greatly. Again, as in the PD agreement, do not tackle the distribution agreement by yourself, but enlist the help of an attorney and an accountant. Even though most distribution agreements are standard boilerplate, they contain many clauses requiring negotiation and/or clarification. The following is an example of a distribution agreement:

1. Date
2. Picture
3. Elements: Producer
   Director
   Screenplay written by
   Screenplay based upon the following literary property
   Stars
   Running time
   Production year and rating
4. Budget
5. Production company (called grantor)
6. Distribution company (called grantee)
7. Delivery date
8. Distribution period (usually perpetuity)
9. Territories: listing territories (usually universe)
10. Rights granted:
    Producer grants the distribution company all rights to the picture, including the copyright.
    Distributor has the right to distribute the picture (listing medias).
    Distributor has the right to music publishing and merchandising.
    Distributor has the right to all underlying rights in and to the picture.
    (Note: Make certain that *all* rights are spelled out.)

11. Gross Receipts:

Determines the accounting of gross receipts. (Note: Gross receipts ought to include *all* monies received and/or credited from all media.)

12. Net Receipts:

Determines the amount to be paid to the production company.

Determines the way distribution fees and distribution expenses are to be deducted from the gross receipts.

Determines that all third-party profit participation has to be deducted from the producer's profits.

Determines the producer's participation in net profits.

13. Accounting:

Determines the producer's right to audit books.

Determines the distributor's accounting period, usually quarterly and delivered sixty to ninety days after the reporting period. (Note: Try to negotiate for a sixty-day period.)

14. Advance and/or Minimum Guarantee:

Determines whether or not the distributor will give an advance or minimum guarantee. (Most likely a distribution will grant neither to the first-time producer.)

15. Distribution Expenses:

Determines the distribution expenses.

16. Distribution fees:

Determines the percentage the distributor collects from the gross receipts; usually between 30 and 40%:

- Domestic theatrical
- Cable
- Network television
- Syndicated television
- Theatrical, television, home video—overseas

Determines the percentage of the royalties the distributor receives from domestic home video sales.

Determines the agent's fee (if an agent was involved in any of the above transactions. The agent's fee should not be higher than 10%).

17. Delivery of specific items:

Film:

Original negative

Optical soundtrack negative
Three-track magnetic master of the soundtrack
Answer print
Color-corrected interpositive
Titles
Titleless background
Separate soundtracks: dialog track
sound-effects track
music track
M&E track
Outtakes and trims
Television cover shots
Video:
Digital video master: one in NTS format
one in PAL format*
Digital television master: one in NTS format
one in PAL format
Digital trailers: one in NTS format
one in PAL format
Trailer:
Picture negative
Optical soundtrack negative
Magnetic soundtrack negative
Answer print
Textless background
Soundtrack
18. Publicity: Producer grants distributor the right to promote and advertise the picture.
The producer has to submit the following materials:
Stills and negatives: black-and-white and color.
Color slides
Electronic press kit
19. Aspect ratio: Standard theatrical 1:85 to 1
20. Rating: Distributor has the right to submit picture to the MPAA for rating. Rating fee has to be paid by producer.
21. Artwork: Distributor is responsible for the creation of artwork.

*Overseas studios demand PAL formats.

22. Editing: Distributor reserves the right to reedit the picture.
23. Dailies: Distributor reserves the right to view dailies.
24. Warranties: Producer warrants to keep distributor free of all liens and claims.
    Producer warrants that there are no claims, legal actions, or suits against the picture or the company.
    Producer warrants that all third-party participations have been disclosed.
    Producer warrants that he or she has the right to enter into said agreement.
25. Security interest: Distributor will be granted security interest in the picture. (Note: This clause should be omitted unless distributor has given an advance or participates in financing the picture.)
26. Termination
27. Indemnities:
    Producer shall hold distributor and its subsidiaries, distributors, officers, and representatives harmless from all obligations arising from claims, damages, etc.
    Distributor grants identical warranties to producer.
28. Residuals: Producer shall be liable to pay residuals.
29. Act of God (Force Majeure):
    Distributor has the right to discontinue marketing picture in case of acts of God.
30. Documents: Producer has to deliver the following documents to distributor:
    Laboratory access letter
    Sound laboratory access letter
    Original screenplay
    Script supervisor's notes
    Dialog spotting list
    Synopsis of screenplay
    Music cue sheets
    Credit list, and screen credit obligation list
    Talent agreements
31. Legal documents: Producer has to deliver the following documents to distributor:
    • Copyright certificates (U.S. copyright registration certificates issued by the Library of Congress)

- Copyright report
- Notarized assignment of rights
- Music licenses

32. Errors and Omissions Insurance: Producer shall furnish distributor with a copy of errors and omissions insurance.
33. Conditions Precedent: This clause lists conditions, if not met, rendering the contract null and void. (Note: Have your attorney negotiate each and every clause listed.)
34. Governing Law: This clause deals with arbitration and/or legal actions in case of disagreements.
35. Signatures: The standard distribution agreement has many points in common with the PD agreement. Do not sign on the dotted line until your attorney and accountant have scrutinized the document carefully.

    The average distribution agreement runs between twenty-five and thirty-five pages. A volume of fifty pages is not unheard of. Each and every clause warrants your attention and has to be dealt with thoroughly.

    Have your attorney negotiate terms that are either vague or seemingly unfavorable for you. Discuss financing clauses and distributor's demands with your accountant.

    And always remember, distributors do not grant you a favor by taking on your film. They need films to stay in business.

Mini-Majors

Mini-majors are powerful companies that operate very much like the major studios. They finance and distribute pictures of high artistic quality and strong audience appeal, and at times pick up a film here and there. In order to gain access to the more lucrative domestic and foreign markets, they distribute their products through the major studios.

Unfortunately, mini-majors do not weather economic changes as well as the majors do, and a company that did fantastically initially might be out of business after a few years. How come? Well, in today's world, major studios are but divisions of huge corporations. Losses sustained by the film division of a conglomerate are easily, and at times gladly, absorbed by the parent corporation.

Mini-majors do not enjoy the financial umbrella of their major studio counterparts. A number of unsuccessful films can wipe out a company.

The advice given about PD agreements and distribution agreements in the section on major studios applies to the mini-majors as well.

5.

Other distributors,
other deals

And now let's take a look at the independent distributor. The success of your film depends on its successful distribution. The right independent distributor can make a small film "take off," while another, seemingly equally well qualified independent keeps your film toddling along on the road to oblivion. Therefore, take time before you approach any distributor. Find out about the distributor as much as you possibly can. While it is difficult to ascertain an independent distributor's financial strength, you'll find out easily enough:

Does the distributor handle your film's genre?

Does the distributor handle films that are budget-wise similar to your film?

What is the distributor's main area of concentration?
Domestic distribution
Foreign distribution
Home video
Cable

Once you have decided upon an independent, you'll have to think about the correct approach. Admittedly, you are in a better and far stronger position if you approach an independent after your film has been completed. (Yet, as things stand at the time of writing of this book you do need a distributor's letter of intent, or at least a letter of interest, to obtain financing.) On the other hand, if you approach the distributor after your picture has been completed, you are missing out on highly important and helpful input. The distributor knows what sells, and usually will be able to sense what might be selling a year from now, when your picture is completed. For this reason the distributor's input, as far as story line, stars, and director are concerned, can be invaluable.

But you also have to be very careful not to sacrifice your prospective film's theme and visualized mood. Always be wary that the distributor might try to fit your prospective movie within the framework of all the films he or she distributes generally.

Probably the most unsatisfactory approach is to film a demo tape for prospective distributors. I am amazed how many beginning producers still believe in this method, and how much time and, even more important, money they waste by pursuing this ill-fated approach.

Remember, a demo tape *never* shows what the finished film will be like. No distributor can decide upon acceptance or rejection of your film on a five- or ten-minute demo reel.

And this brings us to the sad truth that producers often tend to view distributors—whether major studio, mini-major, or independent—as money-grabbing machines. True, it seems unreasonable for distributors to charge interest rates, take their fees off the top of box office or foreign receipts, and disregard the producer's responsibility of paying back bank loans and bank interest charges and/or partner investments. But remember the enormous overhead majors have to absorb by maintaining costly studios and an extensive national and international distribution network. Independents, on the other hand, while not faced with these expenses, do advance—as do the majors and mini-majors—extensive sums for prints and advertising as well as to foreign sales agents. (We will discuss domestic and foreign distribution next.)

So why not forget about the distributor as the ogre, and instead look at the distributor as the producer's partner. Don't ever forget, the distributor needs you, the producer, to supply the product, and you need the distributor to get the film to the people; it is as simple as that. Granted, the distributor has not chosen this line of work for purely altruistic reasons; the distributor is in it to make money and so are you: Don't ever lose sight of that.

Consequently, don't approach any distributor with naive trust or antagonistic wariness, but from the very beginning of your negotiations look upon him or her as your partner. This approach, however, should not keep you from being concerned about your own interest, that is to say, evaluate each and every clause in your distribution contract carefully, and have your attorney and accountant negotiate unsatisfactory points, as well as clarify the opaque ones. It is true, such negotiations might lead to heated arguments, but it is far better to straighten things out in the beginning of a relationship (the producer-distributor relationship is a close one) than to stew, pout, argue, and possibly litigate later on. It is equally true that bringing forth your demands might cause the distributor to lose interest in your project. And this is just as well, because this particular distributor would have been wrong for you anyway.

As you and your attorney look at your prospective distributor's distribution contract, keep in mind that this contract—the same as the major studio's PD agreement—is heavily loaded in favor of the distributor. Still, after you have made your demands known, there is no reason why distributor and producer should not work together amiably. (By the way, the independent distributor's contract is almost identical to the one favored by the majors and mini-majors we discussed in the last chapter.) Make certain that the contract contains the following provisions:

- The amount spent on P&A *must* be specified (never forget that you the producer have to pay for these expenses later on).
- Have recoupment and gross profit defined in clear terms.
- Clarify whether any interest rates will be charged on the P&A expenses (most likely interest will be charged).
- Clarify whether or not exhibitors will participate in advertising expenses. Find out about the percentage rate of participation.
- Set a ceiling for both prints and advertising expenses.
- Determine which amount is considered the base for the distributor's 30% distribution fee:
  - Box office receipts
  - The distributor's share of box office receipts

A few years ago independents paid a sizable advance to the producer, and even gave negative pick-up deals. Those times have passed, and I doubt whether they will ever return. Independent distributors now refrain from even giving a minimum guarantee.

It is no secret that independent distributors face certain difficulties in obtaining theaters *and* collecting money from the exhibitors, both resulting in reduced box office receipts. Independents distribute relatively few pictures a year and have less leverage with exhibitors; they therefore see their films booked into less desirable theaters, theaters that show rather small box office receipts. Still, distributing your film through an experienced independent gives your product an excellent chance for not only recouping the investor's money but making a small profit as well.

After this lengthy but necessary introduction, let's take a careful look at the independent's areas of distribution: domestic distribution and foreign distribution.

Domestic Distribution. Domestic distribution refers to domestic playdates within the United States and Canada. While the major studios operate their own domestic and foreign distribution facilities and are dealing with major theater chains only, the independent has to rely upon domestic territorial subdistributors. Territorial subdistributors, also called territorials, may represent one territory, or they may work in several areas. A California-based territorial may supply exhibitors in California, Arizona, and Nevada.

Usually distributor and subdistributor share advertising expenses (they do not share cost of prints). This cost sharing is called "cooperative advertising." The exhibitor usually takes 20 percent "off the floor," that is to say, 20 percent off the box office receipts. The remainder will be shared according to the exhibitor's share of advertising payments; for example, exhibitor/distributor participation may be 20/80, 30/70, 40/60* or—the most common —50/50.

At this time it might be a good idea to dispel some of the box office myths. Agreed, we read about box office receipts ranging in the tens of millions. A $50-, $75-, or even $90-million domestic box office is not unheard of. But remember: Only majors take in such fantastic amounts of money; these box office receipts apply to blockbuster Christmas and summer releases; and, most important, the studios receive only about half of the box office intake.

To get an accurate picture of an independent's "strength," you must ask these questions:

- Will my film be distributed in the off-seasons (April–June, August–November)? Your film has a much better chance to succeed if exhibited in the off-seasons.

---

*40% to the exhibitor, 60% to the distributor.

- What specific areas will be targeted for distribution of my film? If your film is an action and/or horror film you are far better off if it is exhibited in areas not favored with major studios' second-string films.
- How many prints will be cut? It is more advantageous to the producer if a smaller number of prints (about 200 to 500) make the rounds.
- What is the extent of advertising? (Look at the media list. Ask for tear sheets of ads.)
- Will I receive copies of the distribution schedule and box office receipts?
- Will the distributor handle the auxiliary markets of home video, cable, network, and syndicated television?

The following is a hypothetical scenario illuminating the domestic release picture, including the auxiliary market:

Production cost of film	$ 2,500,000

(We assume that the film was financed by partnership investment, and therefore no interest rates are to be considered.)

Distribution expenses	
500 prints at $1,500	$ 750,000
10% interest rate	75,000
Advertising expenses	1,000,000
if shared 50/50, with territorial advertising cost charged to producer	500,000
10% on advertising cost	50,000
Total distribution costs:	$ 2,375,000
Box office receipts	$10,000,000

Fees to be deducted from box office receipts
20% off the floor to exhibitor $ 2,000,000
Participation in box office receipts
50/50 share of remaining box office receipts. After the
exhibitor's off-the-floor fee has been deducted the
distributor will take in $4,000,000.

Amounts to be deducted from gross box office receipts of	$ 4,000,000
Cost for prints	750,000
Interest rate	75,000
Advertising expenses (distributor's share)	500,000
10% interest rate	50,000
30% distribution cost on distributor's take of $4,000,000	$ 1,200,000
Total amount to be paid by producer	$ 2,500,000
Income from auxiliary markets	
Cable sales	$ 2,000,000
Home video sales	1,540,000
Network and syndicated sales	500,000
Total amount of auxiliary sales	4,000,000
If your distributor handles these sales a fee of 20% will be deducted	808,000
Amount due to producer	$ 3,232,000

The above scenario assumes that the exhibitors do pay the amounts due to the distributor, and that both exhibitors and distributor pay promptly.

And now a few words about auxiliary sales:

Since home video (theatrical and instructional) has become such a vital part of today's distribution picture, an entire chapter has been devoted to it. (Presently, we will examine cable and TV sales.) First, a producer does not necessarily need a distributor to arrange auxiliary sales. A savvy producer can easily manage these sales. Nevertheless, if your film is on the upper scale— say, between $2,500,000 and $5,000,000—it is probably more advantageous to have your distributor handle the auxiliary sales. In fact, most medium-sized independents insist upon handling auxiliary rights.

About auxiliary rights the producer has to know that:

- There is a window (a certain, negotiated time period) between your film's theatrical exhibit and its cable exposure.
- Most likely cable will either give the producer an advance, or buy (negative pick-up) the film outright.
- Advances and negative payments are usually stretched out over one year. You'll receive your payment in four equal installments.
- A $5,000,000 film may bring in about $2,500,000 to $4,000,000.

- There is another window of about six months to one year between cable and home video exhibit of your film.
- The advance for a film depends on how successful a film has been theatrically. And this is the reason, as mentioned previously, that a domestic theatrical release is imperative for any producer. Most likely your advance for a $5,000,000 film will run between $750,000 and $1,000,000.
- You may expect about 200,000 tapes to hit the video stores. If the tape sells for $30 wholesale, you may expect the following scenario:

Wholesale price of one unit (tape)*	$30
60% discount (combined discount for wholesaler and retailer) per unit =	$18
25% to manufacturer (if tape is not being made by major studio) Percentage to be deducted from wholesale price of $30	$ 7.50
From the adjusted gross profit per unit of $4.50, the distributor deducts 20%.	$ 0.90
This brings the producer's net profit to	$ 3.60

Considering that 200,000 tapes have been distributed to retailers, you may expect a windfall of about $720,000.

A net profit of $720,000 is nothing to be brushed off if, and that is the point, *if* all your tapes sell. All manufacturers permit retailers to rerun tapes, and most likely between 30 and 50 percent of the tapes will be returned, to be sold for a discount later on.

After a certain time period (window), network TV, and later on syndication, will show your film. Usually some income trickles in for about five years.

Since your film is in a package with a great number of other films, it is difficult to ascertain the amount of money the producer will actually receive. Also, remember that the *producer*, not the exhibitor, is responsible for the

---

*The following scenario pertains to theatrical videos only, and does not apply to instructional tapes.

residuals because of actors appearing in the films. But take heart; you, the producer, do not have to employ a full-time bookkeeper; SAG keeps track of residual payments due their members.

Foreign Distribution. Some independents distribute domestically as well as overseas. Most of them work together with agents specializing in overseas sales. (If, however, you have a distribution agreement with a mini-major, don't fail to have your attorney add the following clause to the distribution contract: "The United Kingdom, Australia, France, Germany, Italy, Spain and Japan *will not* be licensed on an outright sales basis." The other territories, of course, will be sold on an outright basis, that is, for a fixed sum.

The independent distributor who handles foreign sales does not have the sales access the majors and mini-majors enjoy, and does not deal with the buyers purchasing films for important territories. As the independent deals with a number of small territories only, it is far better to accept a fixed sum that includes theatrical as well as home-video and possibly cable and TV.

Your film will be sold at all film markets. These, I can assure you, are not the glamorous affairs as pictured in glitzy novels and entertaining films and TV shows. These so-called festivals are hard-nosed sales conventions. Here is how they operate: Several hotels are taken over by the sellers. Majors and mini-majors occupy entire floors (they are the ones who throw elaborate parties); the run-of-the-mill seller rents a room in one of the big hotels. This room plays host to a number of TV sets, one next to the other, all showing the distributor's films over and over. Buyers walk from room to room, take a short look at the displayed wares, take the sell sheets the distributor hands out, and if interested return to watch one of the tapes.

But let's go back to the film markets. First of all, do not confuse them with the many, many film festivals that are held all over the United States and Europe. Film festivals are concerned with a film's artistic merit; film markets are concerned with a film's monetary prospects. While some films made their way from festivals to the film markets, most fail to do so. These are the film markets where your film, you hope, will be shown and sold:

Cannes Film Festival   Cannes, France—April
This festival has been geared primarily to the requirements of majors and mini-majors. Cannes may show some profitable sales for the medium-sized independent, but this market is a waste of time and money for the small-time distributor.

MIFED   Milan, Italy—October
This is the most lucrative market for the distributor of low-budget films.

Los Angeles Film Market   Los Angeles, California—February
Somewhat in between Cannes and Milan, as far as importance is concerned. The Los Angeles Film Market attracts new majors as well as the small distributors and buyers.

Foreign sales are complicated at best, and no producer should even think about selling films at one of the film markets without help. Each territory (country) has different import and tax regulations that must be met. The smaller independent distributor works with a number of sales agents, all well versed about the regulations, taxes, and customs of their respective territories. Film markets are expensive. The independent distributors charge:

40% distribution fee
10% foreign agent's fee or 20% subdistribution fee

Expenses include advertising and film market overhead (such as distribution booth rental, hotel, flight, meals, and entertainment). You see, expenses encompass a wide area, and it is for this reason that the producer ought to set a ceiling on distribution expenses.

At times, an independent distributor prefers to work with a foreign subdistributor instead of an agent. If your film is technically and artistically well done, you have a good chance that the subdistributor will pay an advance against the independent distributor's expected gross receipts. The subdistributor keeps all gross receipts until the advance and the 20 percent distribution fee have been recouped.

The money the distributor receives is called an "overage." From this amount the independent distributor draws between 30 and 35 percent distribution fee. If the distributor works with an agent instead of a subdistributor, the distribution fee ranges between 35 and 40 percent.

Unfortunately, monies earned through foreign sales are not as readily available as you might wish. Here's the typical chain of events:

1. The foreign buyer sends a letter of credit (LC) to the foreign distributor, who in turn submits the LC to your U.S. distributor.

2. Sometimes the LC has a due time of several months (and you hope that the LC won't be canceled).
3. Not until the LC comes due, and has been cashed, are you expected to submit the following items to the foreign buyer:
   Negative copy of the film
   Optical soundtrack
   Dialog track
   Sound effects track
   Music track (if requested, and paid for by foreign buyer, the producer has to submit a foreign dialog track)
   Titles
   Textless background (for titles)
   M-E track (magnetic soundtrack)
   Cover shots for television
   Digital video master
   Digital TV master
   Trailer
   Black-and-white stills
   Color slides
   Advertising material (artwork for one-sheets and mats)
   Script (English version)
   Production book (copy of script supervisor's notes)
   Cover shots (some foreign countries rightfully are opposed to violence, and more palatable scenes have to be submitted. It is a good idea to include these cover shots in your production schedule)

As you can tell, the materials to be submitted are plentiful and costly. And, yes, it is the producer's responsibility to pay for them.

This is a foreign sales scenario:

Income from 10 territories	$10,000,000
Expenses	
20% distribution fee for foreign distributor	$ 2,000,000
35% for independent distributor	3,500,000
Distribution expenses	500,000
Materials submitted to foreign buyers (If possible, the producer should pay for the material expenses,	50,000

because if the distributor advances the needed amounts, the producer will have to pay a 10% interest rate. If you have an acceptable credit rating, labs manufacturing these materials will defer.)

Total expenses $ 6,050,000

Total due producer $ 3,950,000

Again, a word of warning: while your first year of foreign sales is the strongest and most lucrative, do not expect to sell all territories. Looking at the scenarios, both domestic and foreign, you'll notice the producer's net profit—after production costs have been recouped—amounts to about $800,000. If shared 50/50 with the investors, the producer takes home $400,000. The investor's percentage return amounts to less than 10 percent.

And now another important point. All scenarios given in this chapter are purely hypothetical. One can estimate the cost of a film, but no one can ever predict domestic box office receipts and foreign sales. The given amounts are examples and should not be used to predict a film's box office draw. Your movie might take in more money, or it might be a loss. No one knows.

Distributor for Hire

Let's assume you have produced a small, low-budget film, and your production costs were not above $500,000. The film, shot on 35mm, is of good technical quality, and you even have a secondary but acceptable star on your cast list. Needless to say, you won't ever think of approaching a major or mini-major with your project; even a run-of-the-mill independent distributor will decline to distribute your film.

Granted, compared with the previously discussed budgets, a budget of $500,000 seems to be a meager one. Yet the innovative producer (who most likely is also the screenwriter and possibly director) will be able to pull it off if he or she is a professional who knows the craft of filmmaking.

To produce a salable film on a tiny budget, be fully aware of the following:

Your film won't be accepted by an independent distributor.
Your film won't find an extensive domestic distribution.
Your film's primary profit areas are:

Domestic (U.S., Canada): home video
Foreign: all areas

Your film, even though it has been shot for home video, needs domestic distribution. The problem is that no independent distributor will handle it. What you need is the "distributor for hire." A number of highly skilled and very reputable companies specialize in your kind of film. Aware of the fact that your film's domestic distribution is a lost cause financially, they charge about $100,000 for their services. In addition, you have to supply them with:

25 release prints
One-sheets
Newspaper advertising mats

To be sure, you'll have to pay for prints and advertising materials. Conservatively speaking, you'll have to add $150,000 to $200,000 to your production budget for advertising purposes.

Give your distributor about six months to "bicycle" your film around the country. Don't dream to see your film exhibited in major cities or main multiplexes. Your film in "multiples of three or four" finds its niche in obscure areas in small, privately owned theaters. The distributor for hire pays a nominal amount to the exhibitor. In addition, the exhibitor retains all box office receipts. You don't see a penny of the box office receipts, but your film proves its all-important domestic release.

In some instances the distributor for hire four-walls your picture. This practice usually applies to theaters that show higher box office intakes than the tiny mom-and-pop theaters.

If you, the producer, have but a few prints (three to five) at your disposal and if your budget in all honesty cannot carry the services of a distributor for hire, you should try to do some four-walling yourself.

Granted, four-walling involves legwork and your film won't have the exposure of a film handled by the distributor for hire, but you'll save money.

Foreign Distribution. Let me advise you not to attend any foreign markets. First of all, booth rental is exorbitantly expensive, even if you were to partner with a number of small-time producers. And without a booth, there are no sales possibilities. You do far better by entrusting your film to one of the many experienced but small foreign distributors. You'll find their names and addresses in the film market issues of *Variety* and *Hollywood Reporter*. (The film market issues are published about fourteen days prior to each respective market.) Approach a small foreign distributor who handles but a handful of films. Don't expect to sell your film to any lucrative foreign territories. Your markets are the small territories in Southeast Asia, South and Central America, and Africa, plus a few European territories. You'll have to supply your distributor with:

One-sheets
Sell sheets (flyers to be handed out)

As with his or her bigger counterpart, your foreign distributor will charge distribution expenses (make certain to set a ceiling) and a distribution fee that ranges between 35 and 40 percent. The rights to your film will be sold primarily for theatrical and home video release, even though your contract reads "all areas." It is because of the foreign theatrical market that you *must* (forget what some people say) shoot your film on 35mm. A film shot on 16mm simply won't do.

Don't be disappointed if your film sells to but a few territories its first year out. Your small, low-budget film, after all, has a foreign sales life of about three years. Payments come slowly, but regularly.

Home Video. Just because your film is on the bottom rung of the distribution ladder, don't hesitate to approach the big home video distributors first, then make your way down to the medium-sized ones. Have confidence in your film, and don't hesitate to ask for an advance. The usual advance is between $300,000 and $400,000 (yes, in this area your film compares favorably with its higher-budgeted counterpart). If your film should turn out to have legs, and sells units exceeding the recouped advance, you are entitled to a 20 percent royalty of the tape's wholesale price.

If the distribution company does not pay an advance, you are entitled to a 25 percent royalty off the wholesale price of each unit sold. Agreed, you will never really know how many units have been sold, but you have to rely upon your distributor's honesty and desire to distribute your future films.

You do not require either an agent or a distributor to contact prospective home video distributors, but you yourself should approach each firm's director of acquisition.

Again, you'll find the names of home video distributors in the film market issues of *Variety*, 1400 N. Cahuenga Boulevard, Los Angeles, CA 90028, and *Hollywood Reporter*, 6715 Sunset Boulevard, Hollywood, CA 90028.

And now a word about home video distributors. Except for the home video departments of the major studios, the home video field is a highly fluctuating one. A distribution company may open today only to be gone tomorrow. Find out about the company you intend to do business with. Grit your teeth, pay an entertainment attorney, and find out:

How long has the distributor been in business?
Is the distributor known to be reliable?
Does the distributor advertise his products sufficiently?
Is the distributor known to pay promptly?

Cable and TV. Your chances of getting your film into cable distribution are small. In comparison, you have a good chance to have your film picked up for a *syndicated* TV package. But the revenue is small and trickles in over about five years. And even the small, low-budget producer has to pay residuals to the actors.

This is the expense/income scenario for a small, low-budget film:

Expenses	Production expenses	$600,000
	Prints and advertising	50,000
	Distributor for hire	100,000
Income	Advance home video (since you arranged the sale yourself, no distributor's percentage is due)	300,000
	Syndicated TV sale	100,000
	20% agent's fee	20,000
	Foreign sales (10 sales @ $100,000)	1,000,000
	40% Foreign distributor fee*	400,000
	Distribution expenses	50,000
	Materials submitted at $5,000 per film	50,000

*The higher percentage on the distributor's fee reflects the fact that usually no agents are involved in the sales.

Total Expenses	Production expenses	600,000
	Prints and advertising	50,000
	Distributor for hire	100,000
	Agent's fee, syndicated TV sales 20%	20,000
	Foreign sales distributor's fee 40%	400,000
	Distribution expenses	50,000
	Materials submitted	50,000
Total Incomes	Home video advance	300,000
	Syndicated TV sales	100,000
	Foreign sales	1,000,000
	Total income	$1,400,000
	Total expenses	$1,270,000
	Profit	$ 130,000

As you can tell, in terms of income your small, low-budget film compares nicely with its high-budget counterpart. But, and this is a point I wish to stress, an income scenario comparable to the one given occurs *only if your film is of excellent technical and artistic quality.* Your film must *look* like it cost about $2 million. Home video is a highly competitive business. No distributor wastes time on a mediocre film. Here are a few pointers:

Interesting, *professionally* written script
Promotional hook
Recognizable star
Professional screen actors (stage actors won't do)
Experienced key personnel
Good-quality services (labs, etc.)

Experience counts if one produces a small, low-budget film.

6.

All about profits,

gross and net

n any business, except the motion picture industry, *gross profit* (receipt) refers to income received, but *no* deduction taken; *net profit* refers to income received *after* expenses have been deducted; and *break even* has been achieved when income *equals* expenses.

Unfortunately for films, such simple equations do not hold true. The interpretation of gross, net, and break even changes from distributor to distributor, and at times it even changes from movie to movie. Since these terms are endowed with such dangerous elasticity, it behooves the producer to have them not only defined but also to have the definition spelled out in the PD agreement and/or distribution contract.

Since so much confusion arises because of the terms, and so much disagreement is inherent in them, let's take a close look at:

Gross profit (receipt)
Break even
Net profit

Gross Profit

The following is a breakdown of domestic gross profit participation.

Box office receipt deductions:

Exhibitor's "floor," the exhibitor's expenses for rent, upkeep, overhead, and salaries.

Exhibitor's advertising expenses

The remaining gross profit will be shared by distributor and exhibitor depending on the percentage of the exhibitor's promotional participation. The usual split is 50/50.

From the remaining gross profit the *distributor* deducts distribution expenses:

Distributor's advertising expenses (eventually the producer reimburses the distributor):
Taxes

Prints (another expense the producer has to carry eventually)

Overhead

Shipping charges*

The savvy producer ought to be well aware of the following distribution practice: Since the distributor receives distribution fees from the gross, the distributor gains income by keeping the gross as high as possible by postponing payment of distribution expenses as long as possible.

That practice obviously yields a higher income for the distributor, and to avoid this pitfall your attorney should add a clause stating that for the purpose of calculating participation, gross receipts received should be changed to "adjusted gross receipts," a sum that is considerably smaller, since distribution expenses have been deducted. In this scenario, the producer shares in adjusted gross once the film reaches the break-even point. If the

---

*For foreign distribution these costs will be added: collection conversion, transfer, licenses, export fees.

distributor—and watch out for this loophole—incurs additional distribution expenses, the distributor will recoup these costs before the producer can claim profit participation. Therefore, the producer must have his or her attorney add a clause to the contract, setting a ceiling on distribution expenses, that is to say:

> Distribution expenses have to be kept within a certain negotiated amount.

> The distributor needs the producer's *written* approval if distribution expenses are to be increased.

The producer who has to deal with third-party participation—the investors who'll recoup their investment plus percentage or profit participation; the writer, actor, director whose contracts stipulated points—faces deductions of his or her own.

From gross profits received from all sources (domestic and foreign, all area distribution) the *producer* will further deduct:

Taxes
Deferments
Interest rates (if bank loans were used)
Bank payments
Distribution expenses
Distribution fees

Break Even

Break even is the point when expenses equal income. Clearly, then, if expenses and income can be balanced no gross profit has been reached. Some distributors keep this balance by favoring a "rolling break even," which means they add new distribution expenses whenever a break even threatens. Therefore, to safeguard against such practice, the producer ought to insist that the two clauses discussed in the previous segment (distribution ceiling and producer's approval if expenses have to be increased) are contractually defined and added.

Another device that keeps a film from reaching a break even is called "cross-collateralization." The distributor offsets the income of a number of films with their respective expenses. For instance: If film I produced by producer A earns a gross receipt of $1,000, and film II produced by producer B loses $1,000, film B's loss is deducted from film A's gross receipt; in other words, both films are "cross-collateralized."

Such collateralization, no doubt, is unfair to the producer. On the other hand, if the distributor collateralizes the profits your film achieved in one area—cable, for instance—with the losses suffered in another area such as domestic distribution, collateralization is most acceptable.

So, whenever the question of cross-collateralization comes up, have your attorney make certain (and state it in the contract) that your film cannot be collateralized with any of the distributor's other films.

Net Profits. There is no standard net deal. Remember this before you, your attorney, and your accountant head for the distributor's office. And also remember that most distributors will try to convince you to settle for a 100 percent* net deal. This particular deal permits the distributor to recoup all expenses and to collect all fees before the producer sees any money. This, in my opinion, is an unfair situation. Let's not forget that the producer has the responsibility to recoup the investors' investments, and—it's hoped—pay them a little profit, while struggling to pay off a high-interest bank loan. While it is true that the fair "first-dollar gross"† deal is all but extinct, you should never agree to the 100 percent net deal. Instead you may consider (and fight hard and long for) one of the following net profit participation arrangements:

1. The distributor takes all expenses off the top and splits the remainder 50/50 with the producer. The distributor's split is considered part of the distribution fee.

Advantages	*Disadvantages*
A fair deal if you know the distributor is a reliable one, and have worked with him or her previously.	Risky if the distributor is an unknown entity, as the danger of a rolling break even lurks.

*Yes, the producer receives 100 percent of the net, but *after* the distributor has recouped distribution expenses and the distribution fee.
†The producer receives 30 percent of the distributor's gross until a negotiable point of expenditures has been reached.

2. If the producer participates in advertising expenses (but not expenses for the prints), the distributor/producer split should be 40/60. The distributor recoups expenses for prints. The distributor's split is considered part of the distribution fee.

Advantages	Disadvantages
10% higher profit participation.	For a mere 10% higher profit participation, the producer is stuck with part of the advertising cost.

3. If the producer participates in prints and advertising expenses, the distributor/producer split is 30/70. Distributor split is considered part of the distribution fee.

Advantages	Disadvantages
The producer has control over all expenses. Fraudulent distribution practices are unlikely.	Depending on your movie's scope, the monetary outlay may be excessive.

And last but not least, a few words of warning:

- Do not agree to anything and do not sign anything without your attorney's and/or accountant's advice.
- Demand straightforward answers to your questions.
- Insist that all clauses pertaining to gross and net are spelled out, and are clear and short.
- Have all distribution expenses listed in detail.

7.

Contracts:

five important contracts

every producer must

negotiate carefully

No book on the business of making a movie is complete without some advice about contracts. There are a host of contracts to be considered. Some contracts, being mostly standard boilerplate (crew, key personnel, day player), have little if any impact on a film's final budgetary success. Other contracts have to be negotiated carefully, as not to put the picture over budget and/or cause friction between producer and artist. Clearly, then, we'll have to take a close look at these five contracts:

1. Director's contract
2. Actor's contract
3. Star's contract
4. Cinematographer's contract
5. Music/Composer's contract

Director's Contract

SALARY

If you are a director who is a member of DGA (Directors Guild of America) you'll have to abide by this union's *current** rules and regulations regarding salary requirements, fringe benefits, pension, and welfare payments.

1. The DGA requires that the director be compensated for a minimum number of weeks for preproduction, principal photography, and postproduction. (The number of *minimum weeks* is based upon the film's budget.)
2. If the director works for DGA minimum salary, the DGA demands that such salary as well as a minimum number of weeks be guaranteed.
3. If the picture is delayed for a period of not more than six weeks, no additional fee is due; if the film should be canceled, the director's entire salary must be paid.
4. The following payment schedule applies:
   - 20% of salary in equal weekly installments during preproduction.
   - 60% of salary in weekly installments during principal photography.
   - 10% of salary at the time of delivery of director's cut.
   - 10% of salary upon delivery of the release print.†
5. During the course of preproduction, principal photography, and postproduction, the director is prohibited from working for a third party.
6. The producer has to deposit a specified amount for pension and welfare into a DGA account.

Fringe Benefits. The director's contract covers the following fringe benefits:

- First-class transportation if shooting on location.
- First-class hotel accommodations.

---

*Regulations change whenever the union negotiates new contract requirements.
†Release print refers to the prints exhibited in theaters.

- Office and secretary during preproduction, principal photography, and postproduction.
- A car and driver during the above-listed periods.
- A trailer during principal photography.
- Additional payments (TDY)* for time spent on location.

Billing.

1. The director's name must appear on the film's front title, immediately after the producer's credit.
2. The director's name must appear on a single title card.
3. The director's name must appear on *all* one-sheets and newspaper advertisements.

Creative Control. Once you have contracted a director, you, the producer who has nurtured the film from its conception, will have to step back and watch another person bring your project to its fruition. And that, believe you me, is not easy to do.

During preproduction the director—in concert with the producer and writer—decides upon the final script, star, cast, and other issues of vital importance. These are areas that may lead to friction and disagreements. Therefore, it is almost imperative that the director's contract decide *who* has creative control—the producer or the director. Traditionally the producer exercises supervision (notice the fine line between the terms "creative control" and "supervision") over the director, but a well-known director yields, nevertheless, a great deal of artistic control.

Once a film "goes on the floor" (commences principal photography) it is the director who runs the show; you the producer have to step aside.

A director who shows little or no budgetary sensibility might insist upon an expensive—usually unnecessary—location, or be determined to include setups that add little to the film's effectiveness. If you are burdened with an overly "creative" (read: opinionated) director, pray that you have a good production manager on your side who keeps you abreast of any incidents that threaten to push your film over budget.

Director's Cut. The director has the right to supervise the editing of the film during its first cut, called the "director's cut." At times the director has

*TDY refers to payments actors receive on location for such things as travel, meals, hotel, etc.

the contractual right to two cuts. The director's cut must be completed within a certain stipulated time limit (usually three months), and once the director's cut has been delivered the director's artistic control has ended. The producer and eventually the distributor have the right to reedit the picture.

Actor's Contract

Should you plan to produce a low-budget film (below half a million dollars), and if you have decided against casting a "star" (after all, it is almost impossible to interest a "name" to work for a fee small enough to fit your budget), then you'll do well to cast nonunion actors.

It is a fallacy that SAG (Screen Actors Guild) actors are more talented or skilled than their nonunion counterparts. Many SAG actors who have little or no acting experience or training joined the union via a commercial shot by a SAG signatory company.* Let me explain: In order to be accepted by SAG as a member, an actor has to work one day on a commercial shot by a SAG signatory production firm, or three days on a SAG signatory TV show or film.

If you have cast a "star"—that is, a recognizable name—your production company *must* become signatory to SAG, which means you are permitted to cast SAG members only. You are prohibited from employing union and nonunion actors on the same shoot. Yet, if you have decided to add a nonunion actor to your cast, a letter to SAG stating your request to have the actor granted membership will take care of the membership rules.

Once your company is SAG signatory, you'll have to adhere to these regulations:

1. A SAG actor cannot work below minimum scale on a day-to-day or week-to-week basis. In addition, the producer has to pay set amounts for pension and welfare, as well as a 10 percent agent's fee on top of the actor's salary (if the contract has been negotiated by the actor's agent).

2. The SAG actor is permitted to work only a specified number of hours daily. If the actor works over the allowed time, overtime has to be paid.

---

*The SAG signatory company adheres to all SAG rules and regulations.

Furthermore, the actor must be provided with meals, customarily breakfast and lunch. Child actors work fewer hours. In addition, a teacher and social worker must be present on the set and/or location whenever child actors are employed.

3. If an actor has been cast for the entire duration of principal photography, and if the production does not commence on time, then a "free period" sets in, which means the actor has to render his or her time without pay. The same holds true for reshooting of scenes and looping (rerecording of dialog).

Additionally, the actor has to render his or her services free for publicity purposes, wardrobe fittings, makeup tests, and rehearsals to principal photography.

4. As far as auditions are concerned, SAG demands the following:

- The actor must be given the opportunity to pick up his or her "sides" (pages of script) at the production office three days prior to auditioning.
- Auditions are not to be paid. The same holds true for callbacks. Two callbacks are free, the third one must be paid for.

5. Actor's compensation is to be paid weekly.

6. All actors' names not appearing on the front titles must appear on the "crawl."*

Star's Contract

While actors' contracts are pretty much standard, it is your star's contract that needs your attorney's attention.

Stars, like directors, demand, and get, the usual fringe benefits:

- First-class travel if shooting on location.
- First-class hotel accommodations.

---

*"Crawl" refers to the end titles of a film.

- Additional daily payments (TDY) if shooting on location.
- A car and driver during rehearsals and principal photography.
- A trailer on the set.

As far as responsibilities are concerned, the star must give his or her time "free" for rehearsals prior to principal photography, for wardrobe fittings, makeup tests, and publicity shots. And again, even the star cannot demand any payment for loopings and reshooting of scenes. Yet, if a film goes into overtime, the star has more clout. Stars usually demand a "stop date," after which they will no longer be available. Given the fluctuating ways of film production, most producers resist the imposition of a stop date.

If a star has some measure of clout, his or her agent works diligently to establish the star's power over producer and director by demanding amendments such as:

1. The star has script and cast approval. (The wise producer tries hard to have this clause changed to give the star the right to "consultation" rather then "approval.")

2. The star's role cannot be diminished. Since this clause demands that *all* of the star's scenes in the script will be shown in the release print,* it might be a good idea to humor your star in case the film offers strong and competitive roles for other, less well-known, actors.

On the other hand, the producer should safeguard his or her rights:

1. All rights to the results of the actor's service (the film) belong solely to the producer. That is to say, the producer has the right to use the footage in which said actor appears in *any* future motion picture (sequel or otherwise).

2. In case the producer should decide to cast another actor in the role said actor had been cast for, the producer retains the right to do so—"pay or play"—as long as the producer pays the replaced actor the agreed-upon compensation. The same applies if a producer decides to use only parts of an actor's performance. It is easy to understand why actors resent the pay-or-play clause and why agents work hard to have it omitted in their star clients' contracts.

*Prints shown in theaters.

3. The producer retains the right to use a double for any dangerous and/or stunt scenes the actor is involved in.

4. If the star (or any actor, for that matter) should breach the agreement, the producer has the right to suspend the actor.

5. The producer reserves the right to obtain injunctive relief against the actor.

Even though "breach of contract" seems obvious on the surface (the star does not show up for work), it is difficult to prove and therefore promises to become a tricky legal matter, since breach of contract can only be established if shooting had to be suspended solely on the grounds of the actor's absence and that due to the actor's action the production company suffered a "severe loss." Take my word for it, unless you enjoy sticking your hand into a legal hornet's nest, try to solve any breach-of-contract situation amicably by shooting around the star.

- Find an alternate scene and/or location that does not require your star's presence.
- "Double" your stars by using your star's "stand-in."* Of course, you can show the stand-in's back only, or show a frontal from a safe distance. If you use "over the shoulder" shots you'll have to dub in your star's dialogue later.
- Negotiate, negotiate, negotiate with your reluctant star.

Billing. Without any doubt your star's name should appear prominently on a separate title card on the front titles. If you have cast a well-known star, and two other recognizable names of less stature, your "star" will supersede the two other names. If, however, you have cast three actors of equal name value, you may have to do a tricky balancing act.

The crucial question of any artwork (one-sheets, mats) is "above title" billing. You may face difficulties if an equally well-known name directs your film.

I suggest that you solve this problem by showing *both names* above the film's title. For example:

---

*A person looking very much like the star, and identically dressed like the star, who stands in for lighting and rehearsal purposes.

A William Directwell Film
starring
Anita Gorgeous
in
"The Guppie Attacks New York"
with
James Strongarm and Rob Muscleman

Another sensitive issue is size, type style, and color of the star's name in artwork, where type and size of letters have to be identical to the film's title. No doubt, any secondary lead will negotiate to have his or her name preceded by the word "and" on film titles and artwork:

and
Alice Sweet as Goldilocks

If you have cast a number of equally important actors (called an "all-star cast"), the "most-favored nation" clause comes into effect. This clause specifies that in case one star receives more favorable terms than the other stars, these will receive the latter star's terms as well. But make certain that the "most-favored nation" clause does not extend to billing.

Cinematographer's Contract

The cinematographer's contract mirrors the director's contract.

Music Contracts

After your film's principal photography has been completed and as you go into editing, the question of music comes up. You have three choices:

1. An original score will be composed.
2. A synchronization license has to be obtained for music that has already been recorded.

3. You'll use "canned music," music that has been recorded, and for which a synchronization license already has been obtained.

Original Score. The composer works out the film's main musical theme, music to underscore the mood of a place, situation, or character's emotion, and music needed for scene transitional purposes.

The composer is responsible for arranging and orchestrating the score, to conduct the score or electronically synthesize it. In this respect the composer—according to AFM (American Federation of Musicians)—becomes the production company's employee.

The production company is responsible for (and has to pay for) musicians, rehearsal and recording facilities, and any incidentals such as meals, pensions, and welfare.

The company owns the score and the copyright to it. If, however, the production company operates a music publishing department, such as Warner Bros. does, the composer in addition to his/her salary receives a royalty as any published composer would.

Usually the composer and the publisher divide royalties from record and sheet music publishing sales as regulated by ASCAP (American Society of Composers, Authors and Publishers). In this respect the composer should make certain that his or her contract includes a clause stating that the music publisher (not the motion picture company) takes full responsibility for payment of the composer's share of royalties.

The royalty is based on the *wholesale* price of records, tapes, discs, and sheet music.

Contractually the composer's name must appear on your film's front titles, before the producer's credit.

You see, composed music can become a major item in your budget. In some instances, it might be a better choice to use canned music, or—if you have at least somewhat of a budget—to invest in a package deal. You have two choices:

- Hire the composer on a *package basis.* You pay a flat fee, and the composer is obligated to compose, orchestrate, and record the score.
- For a *flat fee* the composer composes the music and synthesizes it. This method, next to canned music, is the most economical way to solve your music problem.

Prerecorded Music. If you are shooting a period film that requires music popular in, say, the thirties or forties you'll have to look for prerecorded music. Prepare yourself to face some hassle and—assuredly—an extraordinarily high music budget.

First determine whether the music you have your heart set on is still in copyright.* If so, you'll have to obtain a synchronization license.

Contact the U.S. Copyright Office in Washington, D.C. (Copyright Office, Library of Congress, Washington, DC 20559) to inquire about the music's original publisher. Should the music still be protected by copyright, the producer has to negotiate a synchronization license with the music publisher. (Only the publisher can grant synchronization rights; neither ASCAP nor the U.S. Copyright Office, as some people assume, is authorized to do so.)

As you apply for a synchronization license, please remember that the license applies to the music's *theatrical* (on-screen) exploitation only, and does not extend to any other use, such as recordings.

Moreover, synchronization licenses may contain restrictions on video and cable exhibition. If you wish to use a musical piece that has been *recorded* previously, the AFM will charge a reuse fee.

A synchronization license lists the following:

- Name of musical composition.
- Name of film in which the musical composition will be used.
- Name of film in which the musical composition was used (if any).

You may run into some difficulty obtaining a synchronization license for any musical piece performed on screen (such as the famous tune from *Casablanca*); it is far easier and less costly to settle on music that has been used as background music.

There are no set price scales for prerecorded music. You may have to pay a few hundred dollars for an unknown piece, or up to hundreds of thousands for a well-known song.

In any event, the search for period music may be time-consuming, frustrating, and expensive. My advice is to forgo period music and to have appropriate music composed.

---

*If the copyright has expired and has not been renewed, you may use any music without paying a license fee.

Canned Music. The most inexpensive, least time-consuming, and often most highly effective way to "score" your film is to purchase canned music. While for some of the films I produced I commissioned music to be composed, for others I used a combination of canned music and composed synthesized music. Your sound lab can provide you with a wide selection of prerecorded canned music as well as canned ambiance sounds. You'll have to pay a small fee, which may range from a few hundred to several thousand dollars.

You won't have to worry about any licensing fees, since the sound lab owns all rights to the music, by either having purchased the music or having had it composed.

Of course, you do not own the music. You have bought the *rights* to use the music in your film, and consequently you may hear the same tune in your competitor's film. But that's a chance you'll have to take.

8.

Ways and means to finance your film: ten sources of money

y its very nature an "investment" refers to a venture that points to potential growth, such as promised by stocks and bonds, or provides an income as CDs do. Seen in this light, investing in a motion picture is risky business indeed. Unless a film was fortunate enough to garner sufficient "advance sales" to cover at least the movie's production cost, there is no guarantee and little promise that the investors will recoup their investment or earn a small profit. One keeps wondering why people still look upon films as sources of investment. After all, the Tax Reform Act of 1986 has all but eliminated so-called tax benefits connected to motion picture investment.

The answer to this question may be that in most of us there exists a need for adventure, that certain something that makes movie people work for little reward and makes others, fortunately, invest their money in the endeavor. It may be the inherent appeal of a gamble, it may be the lure of art, or it may be just the fun of getting a glimpse of the movie industry. Just as long as you are completely honest in divulging the high-risk nature of any motion picture investment, and depending on the world's economic situation, even the small-time independent producer will be able to interest investors in his/her project, if the:

- Producer has a track record of a number of films that recouped their original investment and earned some profit.

- Producer has a track record of bringing in films on time and on budget.
- Project features a recognizable star. The star does not have to be a blockbuster name, but ought to be recognizable among film buyers and distributors.
- Genre of the film is a popular one.

There are ten primary ways to finance one's project:

1. Partnerships:
   Joint venture
   Limited partnership
2. Corporation
3. Development Financing
4. Equity Financing
5. Foreign Financing
6. Investment Contract
7. Fractionalization
8. Grants (applicable only for nonprofit ventures)
9. Network Financing
10. Bank Financing

As you work on financing your movie, one or the other of two "financing tools" may come into the picture:

Letters of Credit (LC)
Completion Bond

Partnerships

JOINT VENTURE

In a joint venture (at times called joint partnership) set up for the purpose of producing a motion picture, any of these partners may pool their monetary, creative, and business resources:

Producer
Owner of lab (printing and developing)
Owner of sound lab
Owner of firm selling raw stock
Owner of equipment rental firm (cameras, lights, sound, and grip
  equipment)
Owner of firm providing opticals
Owner of sound stage
Screenplay writer
Director
Star
Composer
Art director
Cinematographer

In a joint venture all, or a combination of, the above-listed partners, are considered active partners. Every one of the partners has agency power—one partner can bind all members in a joint venture (joint partnership). In other words, if one partner incurs debts related to the project the partnership is involved with, all partners are liable. Partners are agents for each other:

- Each partner individually can perform any service necessary to
  conduct business (this includes borrowing money).
- Each partner is personally liable for the debts and taxes of the
  partnership; in other words, if the partnership assets are
  insufficient to pay any creditors and/or IRS claims, each partner's
  personal assets are subject to attachment.

A joint venture is a fiduciary relationship; partners cannot compete in business. All partners, as has to be stated in the partnership agreement, have certain implicit rights and duties. Unless partners have agreed to share profits and losses equally, they have to agree on a sharing ratio. (The equipment rental firm, for example, may have a smaller ratio than the lab providing developing, printing, and negative cutting.)

You see, a joint venture may be either a highly effective, a treacherous way to perform business. If you are considering setting up a joint venture, look closely at your prospective partner's reliability, commitment, and
Only if your project promises some profits will lab owners be interested

in participating in a joint venture. For this reason you ought to have some basic building blocks in place before you approach any of them:

- The producer must have a track record of films that came in on time and on budget, and made some profit.
- A screenplay dealing with a popular genre, and one that offers a strong promotional hook.
- Letter of interest from a reliable distributor.
- Letter of intent from a recognizable star.
- Letter of intent from a director who has a good track record.
- It helps if the producer has lined up some presales.

LIMITED PARTNERSHIP

Most motion picture partnerships operate on the principles of a limited partnership. Setting up and operating a limited partnership requires:

- Filing of a certificate with the secretary of state.
- Filing of partnership's name.
- Certain requirements regarding calling and holding meetings.

A limited partnership is composed of a group of limited partners (the investors) and one or more general partners (the producer, or producers). The limited partners, as long as they do not actively take part in the management of the partnership (production of the motion picture), have *limited personal liability*, that is to say, limited partners risk only the capital they invested.

If the picture goes over budget, the limited partners cannot be held responsible to contribute more money. It is the general partner (or partners) who has to come up with the necessary funds. If a limited partner, however, takes part in the management of the business (that is, takes over any key position such as production manager, or participates as actor), then he or she loses the limited partnership status and becomes a general partner.

Most investors interested in joining a limited partnership do so not as much because of the promise of profits to be gained from the venture but because of tax benefits.

If a limited partner's LC (letter of credit) is used to secure a bank loan, and *if* the limited partner participates in the payment of interest rates charged on the loan, then these interest payments are deductible.

Generally, under federal tax law, expenses in a limited partnership are considered *passive* (since the limited partners do not participate in the management of the business) and such *passive* expenses cannot be used to offset *active* (non-limited partnership) income.

For instance, James Bowers has invested in Eve Roberts's movie *Beach Party in Acapulco;* he is a limited, that is to say *passive,* partner. In addition, he has set up a professional corporation with other dentists. Now, James Bowers cannot deduct the monies he spent on the interest payments (on a bank loan he took to invest in the film) from the income he derives from his professional corporation (dental practice). Yet he will be able to deduct the interest payments for this Eve Roberts film from the profit he gained from having invested as limited partner in one of her previous ventures:

Limited Partnership Expenses (*passive*)
Limited Partnership income from previous film (*passive*)
Professional Corporation (dental practice) income (*active*)

If a film provides the limited partners with capital gain, such gains will be taxed as ordinary income.

Participating in a limited partnership means that the investor (limited partner) owns a certain percentage of the venture; in other words, the investor owns a *share*. These shares are considered *securities* in much the same way as stocks are considered securities. The sale of securities is regulated by the Securities and Exchange Commission (SEC) and by the individual state's Blue Sky laws.

It is imperative that you are protected by an attorney who is highly experienced in drawing up limited partnerships. If any of the SEC laws are violated, the investors not only can demand their money back but also have the right to bring criminal charges against the general partners.*

In addition, your attorney has to deal with IRS Regulation D, which protects *nonpublic* offerings. Regulation D sets up these requirements:

- General solicitation of potential limited partners is prohibited (yet you are permitted to solicit among persons you know).

---

*Check out the Blue Sky laws (so called because these laws differ from state to state) of the state you operate your business in.

- You may not advertise for limited partners.
- You may not accept more limited partners than allowed by the SEC and the state in which your limited partnership operates, or intends to operate.
- Rule 506 and Regulation D permit the offer and sale of limited partnership shares up to $5,000,000 and restrict the venture to thirty-five investors.

At times—and this needs to be verified with your attorney and tax accountant—more investors are permitted participation. These investors, called accredited investors, must be earning a yearly income in excess of a quarter of a million dollars. These prospective investors do not qualify easily, but have to undergo extensive IRS screening.

Generally, once the limited partners have recouped their investment, they split the profit 50/50 with the general partner.

Corporation

The following is a short discussion of some of the most important legal and business aspects regarding a corporation. Generally we are looking at two kinds of corporations: The corporation set up for a large company or conglomerate, and the corporation set up for the medium or small-time producer.

Every corporation, regardless of whether it may be a multimillion-dollar outfit or a small-time firm (S-corporation), has the right and capability to issue stocks. I must warn you, it might seem very tempting to raise production funds via stock issues, but in most cases it does not work, and in some cases such practice backfires severely.

First of all, no reliable stockbrokerage house will deal with stocks issued by a small-time corporation. In other cases (and I have seen them), a group of investors eager to get hold of a company that is large enough to have its stock traded, buys enough stock to be able to take over the company.

The type of corporation we will discuss is the so-called S-corporation. This corporation protects a company's president and directors from personal liability. A corporation may be set up for one film only, or it may be the home base for any number of films.

If you are interested in having an umbrella for a number of business enterprises, you may choose, as I did, to set up your motion picture company as but one "division" under an umbrella corporation. The name of my corporation, NW&H-Industries, serves as an umbrella for my film production firm "Ciara Productions, A Division of NW&H-Industries."

Needless to say, if you consider setting up a corporation, don't buy a do-it-yourself kit, but employ a knowledgeable attorney.

A corporation is a *legal entity*, and not a group of investors as the limited partnership is. This means a corporation can hold and sell property, can sue and can be sued, just like a person. In simplified legal sense the corporation *is* a person, and this means that the corporation and not its directors are liable for debts contracted by the corporation.

The information given in this section refers to California corporations, since according to the state you wish to incorporate in, rules and regulations change.

In most states three or more persons are required to apply to the secretary of state for permission to incorporate. After payment of the incorporation filing fee and initial state franchise tax, a corporation charter is granted. Such a charter provides the following:

- Name of company
- Formal statement of formation
- Type of business
- Location of principal office
- Duration (perpetual existence, 50-year life, renewable chapter)
- Names and addresses of directors

As far as stocks are concerned, the following information must be given:

1. Classes and preference of class of stock
2. Number of PAR (stated value of stock)
3. Stock structure

The corporation code requires a statement as to the number of shares the corporation is authorized to issue, as well as the breakdown of classes, if applicable (most corporations set up for the purpose of film production do not issue a series of stock).

SUBCHAPTER-S

If you the producer should decide to set up a corporation, but feel that corporate income tax structure provides disadvantages to your company, you may consider a closed corporation. At times companies deciding to incorporate are confused about the terms "close" and "closed" corporations. "Closed," at times referred to as "closely held corporations," is used to describe a corporation having a relatively small number of shareholders. While a "close corporation" issues shares, the average "closely held" does not, and has more or less been established to protect its directors from excess liability.

A subchapter-S corporation permits a corporation to retain the limited-partnership feature of being taxed as a partnership and not as a corporation. A subchapter-S permits corporate losses to flow through to stockholders, who can use these to offset active income on their income tax return. Strange as it may sound, a number of your stockholders might join your venture because of anticipated losses that may fit their tax structure. Yet in order for subchapter-S stockholders to count corporate losses against *active* income such as salary, the stockholder must participate in the corporation's activities more than five hundred hours a year.

As you set up a subchapter-S corporation, you have to be aware of these regulations:

- The subchapter-S corporation must be a U.S. corporation.
- All stockholders must be individuals, trusts, or estates. No other corporation may purchase stocks.
- A subchapter-S corporation may not admit more than thirty-five stockholders.
- None of the stockholders may be nonresident aliens.

DIRECTORS

Ownership in a corporation is evidenced by stock certificates, but ownership of stock certificates does not give a stockholder the right to participate in the corporation's management. Yet in many small corporations the owners of the business serve as directors and managing officers.

Section 204 permits stock corporations to eliminate the liability of the directors of the corporation for monetary damages. This is important to know. The provision reads: "The liability of the directors of the corporation for monetary damages shall be eliminated in the fullest extent permissible under California law." This provision, of course, has its potential application for publicly held corporations, and does not really protect directors of closed S-corporations.

VOLUNTARY DISSOLUTION OF CORPORATION

If you had set up a corporation for one film project only, it might be dissolved. The dissolution of a stock corporation is initiated by an election to dissolve. The corporation wishing to dissolve *must* file dissolution documents with the office of the secretary of state. The mailing of those documents to any other agency, state or federal, does not meet the statutory filing requirements. The documents have to be sent by certified mail with return receipt requested (always refer to the corporation number when submitting any documents for filing).

Setting up any corporation is not inexpensive, and you definitely need the services of a tax consultant, or even better, a tax attorney. (At times one can buy an existing corporation. This, of course, saves some money, but one has to beware that one does not take over the existing corporation's liabilities, tax and otherwise, as well.)

The segments dealing with limited partnership joint venture and corporation have been written to give you some basic information and advice. Yet rules and regulations pertaining to all types of partnerships are lengthy and at times complicated, and without any doubt, you need the help of an attorney and tax consultant to set up your partnership.

If you intend to finance your movie via a partnership or corporation, you'll submit an offering, as discussed in chapter 2.

It is difficult to tell whether a partnership or a corporation provides the producer with more advantages. Here are some advantages and disadvantages:

PARTNERSHIP

Advantages	*Disadvantages*
Limited partners do not necessarily have to put up funds, but *guarantee*	The general partner (you, the producer) are liable for a film's over

Advantages	*Disadvantages*
the bank loan by issuing letters of credit (LCs).	budget and other debts.
Partnerships are more easily set up than a corporation.	Limited partners are permitted to offset losses on other *passive* investment only.
Partnerships can be set up from film to film.	Limited partners lose their limited partnership status if they become *actively engaged* in the limited partnerships's business.
Among reliable partners, all working for the same goal, a venture makes a great production team.	In a joint venture, partners are agents for each other and liable for each other's debts incurred in the management of the business.
	Limited partner shares cannot be solicited publicly.

CORPORATION

Advantages	*Disadvantages*
In a corporation the corporation, not its directors, is liable for any debts incurred.	A corporation is costly to set up.
Tax-wise, a corporation may offer some advantages to stockholders.	A corporation has to adhere to stringent rules and regulations (stockholder meetings, directors, etc.).
Shares can be sold publicly, that is to say, a broker or investment counselor can interest prospective investors in your project.	

Development Financing

Every producer needs funds in order to develop his/her motion picture project. One has to spend money on optioning the literary property. A director and one or two stars have to be added to the project, and a budget and offering have to be written. In short, the entire package has to be assembled before any investors can be approached. And let's not forget the producer's overhead, office rent, utilities, secretarial services, plus costs for fax and telephone.

If you hire a WGA (Writers Guild of America) signatory screenwriter to either adapt the literary property you have optioned or to write an original screenplay, you'll have to pay a minimum of $25,000 for the script and director, and stars may charge at least $10,000 each to grant permission to have their names attached to your project. For miscellaneous expenses, you can add another $5,000. So, conservatively speaking, if you figure between $75,000 and $100,000 you're not too far off. Agreed, a small amount if one considers the millions spent on so-called low-budget films, ranging between two and five million dollars.

But you'll have to realize that none of the above fees will be recouped should the film fail to go into production. The money you have spent on developing your project is lost. And it is for this very reason that the producer faces great difficulties raising development financing. A film in production promises recoupment and maybe some profit, yet a film in development promises nothing. Understandably, investors hesitate to provide you with the funds you'll need to get your film's development off the ground. Most producers repay development investors (plus a percentage) after the production funds have been raised. Some producers, in addition, promise to pay a percentage of the net profit. Since net profits, as we have discovered, are of a rather hazy nature, such an arrangement, in my opinion, is not quite ethical.

As far as finding development investors, you'll be pretty much on your own. Understandably, since development funds are rather small in comparison to production funds, and since the "money finders"* earn between 3 and 5 percent of the located monies, they are most likely not interested in wasting time looking for development funds.

The usual suggestion of asking development monies from friends and relatives is poor advice. Borrowing money has ruined many relationships.

---

*An individual or firm who has been hired to locate funds.

It is far better to cut your development budget to the bone and pay for it yourself (or borrow the money from a financing institution). These are a few steps you might take:

- Write the budget and offering yourself.
- Hire a nonunion (but skilled) writer to write the first draft of your screenplay. By guaranteeing that the screenplay—if the film should not go into production—will revert to the writer, you may find a writer who will work for as little as $2,000. But don't fail to reserve the right to hire another screenwriter if the studio or investors should demand it.
- If you offer them a terrific screenplay featuring challenging roles, you may be able to convince stars and director to defer their development fees.

If you are in the process of searching for development money, or if, as suggested above, you have decided to finance your film's development yourself, be completely honest with yourself. Only a small number of projects in development will ever get into production. Even if a producer was fortunate enough to garner a studio development deal, he or she has no guarantee that the film will ever go into production. A studio executive may put a project into "turnabout," that is, discontinue the film's development, because too many development projects clutter the executive's desk, a better project has captured his or her interest, or (and this happens often) the studio executive in charge of your project has been dismissed and the new person arrives with an armload of development projects of his or her own.

Equity Financing

Equity financing applies only to films budgeted over ten million. Legally, the equity partnership is a limited partnership and has to adhere to all rules and regulations pertaining to any limited partnership.

Under an equity financing contract, a limited partnership hires a producer to develop the motion picture project owned by the partnership. The partnership has been set up for the purpose of financing the development of the project. Once the producer has raised the required production funds, the partnership dissolves and the partners recoup their investment plus interest. The partners, of course, are given the opportunity to form a newly set up limited partnership investing in the film going into production.

Usually partners who had participated in the equity financing and continue to participate as limited partners will receive a slightly higher percentage than other investors if they decide to continue their participation.

These investors, to be sure, will not participate in the film's profit, but do receive their interest regardless of whether or not the film breaks even. (Yet, the recoupment of the money is not guaranteed; they do stand the chance of losing their investment.)

Foreign Financing

During the past few years, once plentiful opportunities for foreign financing have all but vanished. As in the United States, many foreign countries have clamped down, if not even outlawed, once popular tax shelters. Still, if you are determined to acquire partial foreign financing, you ought to at least give it a try.

Before you give foreign financing a second thought, you should assemble:

- Completed screenplay
- Letters of intent from an acceptable director
- Recognizable stars

Your next step is to contact an entertainment law firm that has overseas connections, to inquire about investment firms operating in the country where you plan to shoot your movie. Find out as much as you can about overseas regulations and laws pertaining to partnerships (joint venture, limited partnership, corporations).

Setting up a partnership with a foreign country may give you the opportunity to take advantage of your partner's country's tax laws, which may, unfortunately, not be any more lenient than U.S. tax laws, and by the same token you have the responsibility to adhere to your host country's laws, customs, mores, and rules. Here are some suggestions regarding coproduction with a foreign country:

- You arrange coproduction with a foreign studio and/or an established production company.
- A foreign investment firm solicits investors.
- A foreign country underwrites your production (a rare event nowadays).

Regardless of the financing scenario, all foreign countries insist on the following:

- The picture must be a major production; in other words, a picture with a budget below $5 million has no chance to acquire foreign financing.
- The U.S. producer may bring an American director and two American stars to the foreign locations. All other actors have to be hired in the country coproducing the picture.
- All key personnel (production manager, camera director, script supervisor, art director, key makeup artist, wardrobe mistress) have to be hired in the country coproducing the picture.
- All key personnel must be citizens of the coproducing country.
- The film under consideration must not be detrimental to the host country.
- The film under consideration must have "national content," that is, the film's story must be related to the host country's history, social customs, mores, etc.

A producer offering to bring in half of the required budget stands a much better chance (read: only *chance*) to have the project considered by any foreign country.

Major studios and at times mini-majors, having the advantage of extensive presales in the major foreign markets, are able to arrange mutually beneficial coproductions with foreign countries such as England, Canada, France, Italy, Germany, Japan, Spain, and major South American territories. Some smaller countries—Hungary, Malaysia, and Poland, to name a few—do welcome the lesser-known production company. These countries, with struggling, or barely existing, motion picture industries, will welcome you, the producer who brings work and money into the country. Your coproduction scenario may look something like this:

Let's say you are proposing a film budgeted for five million dollars, and have signed a director who has a track record of acceptable films, and a star who, even though not of the first order, is recognizable enough. Let's further assume that your screenplay contains the demanded "national content" and will be shot in the prospective host's country. Still, you the producer have to come up with half of the production money—in our hypothetical case, the nice round sum of two and a half million U.S. dollars.

Generally your coproducer, the host country, will not come up with cash but will supply you with services. These services are provided either free or for a nominal sum, and may include lab services, use of sound stages and editing facilities, free hotel accommodations and transportation, and—if you press hard—free raw stock.

But think twice before you pack your bags and book a flight. Granted, at times if you need the mood and scenic background of the host country, a foreign coproduction is invaluable. Nevertheless, you'll have to be aware of the drawbacks you may encounter:

Language barriers. You might not be fluent in your host country's language, and obtaining production information is complicated if done via an interpreter. Moreover, your director will face the same difficulties in trying to explain moves and expressions to foreign actors.

Different working habits. You may have to accommodate yourself to a crew that might be accustomed to exceedingly long lunch hours, including siestas. You may have to pray for patience as you ask to have a prop such as a chair or small table moved from one side of the set to the other, and are forced to wait until the grip's assistant finds *his* assistant. You have to get used to local holidays, and you may even have to close your eyes to the fact that your crew brings relatives on the set during lunch hour.

Foreign actors. Since you are permitted to bring only two stars to your host country, you'll have to cast foreign actors for all other roles.

And this will prove a major stumbling block. First, you'll have to dub* these actors; second, you'll deal with stage-trained actors who are not necessarily used to working in front of a camera.

These actors tend to overproject, move too quickly, and have difficulties

*Dialog has to be rerecorded in English.

hitting marks (certain areas marked on the floor where an actor has to turn or stop).

So, unless you do require the foreign country's locale and mood, you are far better off to stay home and shoot within the U.S. borders.

If you are interested in a coproduction with a foreign country (not a foreign studio or production company), you should contact the respective country's consulate general (located in most major U.S. cities), ask for the federal agency—most likely called "ministry"—in charge of motion picture coproduction, and get in touch with said agency.

Investment Contract

Some investors who are wise to the fact that only a few movies show a profit, invest in a film to earn a percentage on their investments, rather than to participate in profits.

The investment contract works well for the low-budget film, if used either in lieu of a bank loan or as intermediate financing if you finance your film via fractionalization. The investment contract investors don't—as a bank will—take possession of your literary property as collateral. If collateral is requested, it should apply to the film in production only. Do *not* agree to put personally owned stocks, bonds, or real estate up as collateral. The investment contract works best as a "stopgap measure" in concert with other investment arrangements.

Fractionalization

Fractionalization means you are financing your film via advance sales.

For the small independent producer who can list a number of fairly well-selling (not terrific) films on his/her résumé and who is known as reliable, financing a low-budget film via fractionalization is a viable way of obtaining production funds. And most important, fractionalization permits you to avoid high bank interest and to gauge your film's profit scenario more realistically.

Furthermore, this particular way of financing a project lets you keep the artistic control over your film and cuts down on distribution fees and expenses.

But fractionalization is complicated at best, and should only be attempted by a producer who is well acquainted with the ins and outs of distribution.

And another word of warning: Even though fractionalization of movie rights does bring in sizable advances, you have to take into consideration that these advances may be the only money the film will ever make. Therefore, advance sales *must* cover the entire production cost, and, it's hoped, bring in some profit.

There are several steps to consider as you solicit production funds via fractionalization.

1. Have a project that promises to sell as well internationally as domestically. Keep in mind that comedies sell well in Europe but do poorly in Japan and Southeast Asia. The Scandinavian countries, as well as Spain and Germany, object to violence.

2. Unquestionably, to launch a successful advance sale campaign you should present your prospective buyers with:

- Completed (and final) script
- Recognizable star
- Recognizable director
- Budget
- Suggested ad campaign that focuses on the films
- Hook and sellable points

The funds needed for your presale campaign can be acquired through:

- Equity investment
- Short-time bank loan

3. Your proposed film will sell more easily (and make more money) if you can prove future domestic theatrical distribution. At this point a distributor for hire will get your film into limited distribution. His or her letter of intent (not "interest") is invaluable. (If you work with an independent distribution company and not a distributor for hire, make certain to grant them the right for domestic U.S. distribution only. Do not give them the right to sell your film for home video and cable.) You'll provide the distributor with a limited number of release prints (not more than fifty) and the usual promotional material:

- Theatrical trailer
- Radio blurb
- One-sheets
- Mats

4. Presell your film to cable. Contact the executive in charge of acquisition:

HBO
1100 Avenue of the Americas
New York, NY 10036

Movie Channel
1633 Broadway
New York, NY 10019

MTV (Pop Music)
1633 Broadway
New York, NY 10019

Showtime
1633 Broadway
New York, NY 10019

Viewer's Choice
10 Universal Plaza
Universal City, CA 91608

Cinemax
1100 Avenue of the Americas
New York, NY 10036

Disney
3800 W. Alameda
Burbank, CA 91506

Encore
11766 Wilshire Boulevard, Suite 710
Los Angeles, CA 90025

You'll arrange for a *negative pick-up deal*, a certain amount of money payable to you within a year in four equal installments.

5. Presell your film for an advance to home video. Lately home video distributors have come and gone rather quickly, but to the best of my knowledge these firms have been in the business for a long time:

Handleman Company
500 Kirts Boulevard
Troy, MI 48084
(Supplies the big retailers such as Blockbuster and Wherehouse)

Ingram Entertainment
1123 Heil Quaker Boulevard
La Vergne, TN 37086

Capital Records Video Distribution
1750 N. Vine Street
Hollywood, CA 90028

Vidcom
175 West 2700 S.
Salt Lake City, UT 85115

These are just a few names; for more information, I suggest that you consult these publications:

Video Review
902 Broadway
New York, NY 10010

Video Week
475 Fifth Avenue
New York, NY 10017

Video Business Weekly
345 Park Avenue South
New York, NY 10010

Film & Video
Optical Music Inc.
8455 Beverly Boulevard, Suite 508
Los Angeles, CA 90048

You'll receive an advance, and, if the film sells well later on, royalties. The amount of the royalty depends on the previously received advance payments, but usually will range between 10 and 20 percent of each tape's wholesale price.

6. Offer your film to those foreign buyers who have bought your films previously. Most likely you'll receive LCs to be used to secure a short-term bank loan.

Some producers, hoping to garner additional advance sales, go through the expense of attending one of the foreign film markets. I discourage this. Most likely buyers who have not bought your film before will be reluctant to invest in your proposed project. It is far more advantageous to take your completed film to a U.S. distributor specializing in foreign film sales, and have him or her represent your movie. True, you'll have to pay a distribution fee and expenses, but your film does earn some additional monies.

7. Pull your project together by forming a joint venture with a lab and sound lab.

8. Produce your film, carefully watching its budget.

9. Deliver the completed movie and collect your well-deserved reward:

- Cash in the LCs
- Collect the home video advance
- Collect the first installment of your cable negative pick-up deal
- Pay off your equity investors and/or short-term bank loan.

The above scenario takes into account that you will receive the funds arranged via presales after you have delivered the film. True, major studios and mini-majors collect the advance payments before commencing the production of their projects. Nevertheless, you the small-time independent producer will garner more advance sales if you choose the latter route.

Grants

Some beginning producers hope to finance their first project though grants. In order to do so, you ought to be aware of a few basic facts:

1. Most endowers fund nonprofit operations only. You'll have the choice of either setting up a nonprofit corporation, or applying through the channel of a nonprofit conduit that administers the grants. If a grant has been approved, the conduit retains an administration fee.

2. Your project must have been tailored for a low-budget film ($500,000–$2,000,000).

3. Your film must have artistic merit, or must be based upon a literary property of philosophical or social value.

4. The story must play in the United States.

5. The film cannot be sold, exhibited, or leased for profit.

You'll have a far better chance of having your project approved if you have some financing in place. Here are a few addresses you might be interested in:

Sundance Institute for Film and Television
19 Exchange Place
Salt Lake City, UT 84111
(in order to apply you must have some financing on hand)

National Endowment for the Arts
1100 Pennsylvania Avenue
Washington, DC 20506
(your project must have artistic merit)

National Endowment for the Humanities
806 15th Street
Washington, DC 20506

Applying for a grant is time-consuming and often frustrating. A project that might be right for one agency is wrong for another. Therefore, before you even think about applying, try to find out what the endowment office wants, talk to one of the officers, and get a general feeling as to whether or not your project might meet their requirements.

In a sense, the proposal you submit to an endowment is similar to the prospectus discussed in chapter 2. Stars are unimportant if you are applying for a grant (unless you apply to the Sundance Institute), and instead of the film's hooks you'll stress your project's artistic, philosophical, or social merit. Don't forget, an endowment is greatly interested in the script per se and the expertise of the people involved.

If you have been given a grant to shoot a documentary or educational project, you may want to consider setting up a nonprofit corporation.

NONPROFIT CORPORATIONS

Nonprofit corporations for religious, charitable, special educational, and recreational purposes are organized under the Nonprofit Corporation Law, Corporation Code, Section 5000. Section 4120 (d) states: "When submitting articles for a public benefit corporation, it is required that the client include an extra copy for transmittal to the office of the Attorney General by the Office of the Secretary of State."

If a nonprofit corporation plans to obtain tax-exempt status, it may do so under the 501(c) (4) Internal Revenue Code. If, however, the corporation does not plan to be tax exempt, it has to be established as a mutual benefit corporation.

If the nonprofit corporation is supposed to be tax exempt, you'll have to take the following steps:

- Pay the minimum state franchise tax and apply for exempt status immediately after incorporation.
- Hold for delayed filing until the exemption has been granted by the state tax board.

In both cases you'll have to submit to the office of the secretary of state the articles of incorporation, consisting of an original and four copies.

Network Financing

One way of linking up with possible investors is through computer-based networks. Investors list the deals they are interested in, and the networks search for companies that meet the criteria.

Most networks charge a listing fee to both investors and companies. The success of each search, of course, cannot be guaranteed. Networks search for deals, they do not consummate them.

It is most unlikely that a producer offering his first venture will find success, but networking is a rather new and innovative way of raising funds for the producer who can look back upon several successful films.

Obtaining venture capital via network financing is not an easy task. One may count on from about six to ten months to find investors. And, of course, finding an investor is still a matter of luck. Yet, since networks run continually new applications from investors and venture capital seekers alike, your firm sees continued introduction. Once an investor has been found, and venture capital has been obtained, networks charge no fee. This is, compared to the usual finder's fee of 3 to 5 percent, a very favorable picture indeed.

The bad news is that investors participating in network programs do expect an annual return on their money of 20 percent; they are not as patient as the institutional (limited partnership) investor, and are less focused—what is hot for them one year may be uninteresting the next.

Furthermore, if these investors actually become involved in your firm (strategic partners), they have the power to take over your firm. For this reason it is imperative to find strategic partners who understand and appreciate the motion picture industry.

Networks are neither investment advisers nor brokers, and since they are unable to evaluate or verify the accuracy of the submitted application you, the producer, have to check out your prospective investors thoroughly.

This is how networks operate:

- Investors submit their interest profiles, describing their investment criteria.
- Entrepreneurs submit investment opportunities, background of their firms, a business plan, and financial projections. (Tailor your proposal to the offering discussed in chapter 2.)
- Networks submit to investors only those entrepreneurs profiled that meet their investment criteria.
- After networks have introduced investor and entrepreneur, their role terminates.

What you should know about the investors participating in networks:

- Most investors are individuals of means.
- All investors invest only in products and services promising significant growth.

- Investors *never* invest in the absence of any business plan.
- Investors insist upon a management team of proven competence and background.
- Investors need a time frame as to when they can cash in on their investments.
- All investors must certify that they are accredited investors, as defined in rule 501 in SEC regulation D, or rule 506 of regulation D.

An entrepreneur has the best chances of locating investors' monies if he or she falls into one of the following categories:

- Entrepreneurs who require venture capital between $50,000 and $1,000,000.
- Entrepreneurs whose ventures promise substantial capital gains for investors.
- Entrepreneurs with a solid and proven background in their respective fields.
- Entrepreneurs who are referred to networks by accountants, attorneys, and bankers.

What the motion picture producer needs when contacting a network:

- Solid background in motion picture production
- At least one produced financially acceptable film
- An offering (as discussed in chapter 2)
- A distribution contract and distribution plan
- A script
- A recognizable director and/or stars
- Presales sale (helpful but not necessary)

Bank Financing

Permit me to begin this section with a warning: For you, the independent producer, financing your movie via a bank loan ought to be a measure of last resort, and should be attempted only if you have been blessed with a distribution contract that provides you with an advance equaling the production cost of your film, or if you were fortunate enough to negotiate a "negative pick-up" that guarantees you an amount in excess of the production cost (cable).

Banks traditionally grant loans on the basis of "ongoing business"; that is, they grant loans to a business promising "future performances" (future loans). For this very reason, institutions such as Bank of America, Wells Fargo Bank, and Chemical Bank provide lines of ongoing credit to major studios and mini-majors. Therefore, it is easy to understand why independent producers face difficulties obtaining a bank loan. But while it is difficult to finance a film via a bank loan, it is *not* impossible if you have the following in place:

- A distribution contract (letter of intent) with a major studio or financially solvent mini-major

or

- Sizable presales of your movie to foreign distributors, domestic home video, and cable
- A well-known star
- Completion bond
- A sizable budget. It is far easier to obtain a loan for a relatively high-budget film in comparison to its lower-budgeted counterpart. Administrative costs for a film budgeted at about $2 million are identical to the ones for a film ranging in the tens of millions, or so banks claim.

A few years back, and the opportunity may arise again, banks did consider smallish production loans, the so-called secured loans. A secured loan refers to a loan secured by collateral—by the producer's film. In many cases, however, banks also demanded real estate, stocks, or bonds as additional collateral.

Motion picture loans are high-risk loans, and since banks have been burned numerous times, they approach these loans cautiously and conservatively. For this very reason the producer who intends to produce a "rock-bottom budget" picture on a budget of about $500,000 to $750,000, should not even think of approaching a bank.

It is a fact that a bank won't finance a venture unless the loan is secured substantially by low-risk real estate, blue-chip bonds, and stocks. So, instead of putting up your (and your friends' and relatives') life savings for collateral, it is far more sensible to finance your film via a joint venture instead of a bank loan.

Policies regarding motion picture financing loans vary from bank to bank, and at times from film project to film project, but most likely the bank will protect its loan by requiring the following:

Rights to the literary property (screenplay)
Security interest
Pledge-holder agreement
LCs
Completion bond

Security interest. If a film is to be shot within the United States, the bank granting the production loan files its security interest at the producer's place of business (state and county).

If the film is to be shot outside the United States, the bank will file security interest in the respective country or countries. In addition, the bank will file security interest in all documents pertaining to the film (copyright of literary property, star contracts, and so on).

Pledge-holder agreement. In case of the producer's default, labs (and other service companies) have the legal right to place liens on the film they supplied services for.

Besides taking security interest in the film, banks secure their loans through pledge-holder agreements whereby the pledge holders subordinate their liens on the film to the bank.

Furthermore, if the labs are not suppliers but participants in the venture, they—as any other participants, such as investors, director, writer, and star—are considered *unsecured* participants who, in case of the producer's default, have no rights concerning recoupment. Wise to this fact, third parties often demand recoupment and/or profit participation from any monies that have been gained via advance sales.

If third-party stipulations exist, the bank must be notified at the time of the loan application.

Letters of credit. Occasionally if a mini-major finances your movie, or if you have secured funds via private investment (partnerships), letters of credit (LCs) enter the picture. If the mini-major keeps a substantial line of credit with a bank, the bank will accept the mini-major's LC for an unsecured loan. (An unsecured loan refers to a loan that is not secured by any collateral other than the LC.)

If, however, the loan has been granted to a partnership, and participants put up LCs to secure the loan, we are speaking about a *secured* loan.

In this instance the partners' LCs have to be secured by assets, such as deposits the partners may have at the bank or the partners' stocks, bonds, and real estate.

LCs are discounted in the same way as secured loans are discounted.

Most mini-majors and private investors would much rather furnish the producer with LCs than loans. An LC serves as a *guarantee*; in case the producer should default, the bank has the LCs and the assets they represent. On the other hand, the investor issuing the LC does not have to put up any monies, as the LC serves as collateral. Should the producer, however, default on repaying the monies owed to the bank, the investor's LC will be called in.

Besides securing a bank loan, the LCs serve another purpose. As we have learned in the chapter dealing with distribution, a foreign buyer who has purchased the rights to your film will issue an LC drawn upon his or her bank, with your bank. On the LC's due date, and if you have delivered all materials to the buyer's satisfaction, you'll cash in the LC.

Completion bond. Banks don't care whether or not your film makes any money. No matter what its profitability may be, banks collect healthy interest rates; however, they are very much concerned that your film may not be completed. After all, an uncompleted film spells a loss for them, and therefore banks require completion bonds to be in place before granting or even discussing a loan.

The bonding company, like the bank, makes stringent demands. The producer has to submit:

Screenplay
Budget
Star names
List of key personnel

Interestingly enough, it is neither the popularity of the star nor the excellence of the screenplay that determines whether or not a completion bond will be granted, but the producer's track record.

A completion bond adds about 10 percent to the budget. If the film stays within the budget—and it had better if you have hopes of remaining a working producer—most bond companies agree to refund a certain percentage.

The producer has to agree to have the bonding company's representative on the set. Even if somewhat disconcerting at times, the observer's presence is a blessing in disguise. An unbiased observer notices danger areas pointing to production slowdown or over budget sooner and much more easily than the producer does.

At times, reluctantly, a bonding company takes over a production that threatens to get out of control. Then the bonding company has the right to:

- Adjust and/or rewrite the script
- Replace key personnel (including the producer)
- Replace creative personnel (including the director)
- Adjust shooting schedules
- Omit special effects and/or stunts

Unfortunately, no bank will grant funds covering the entire amount requested. In the same manner as if you were to borrow money for a real estate venture, the bank "discounts" the loan. Usually the bank discounts about 20 percent of the assessed value (that is to say, your film's budget) and it is obvious that the producer needs additional financial sources, all involving third parties:

- The producer may go into partnership with a lab and sound lab, provided their services are part of their investment.
- The producer forms a joint partnership with investors.
- The producer forms a limited partnership with investors.

Securing a bank loan is costly. You'll pay between 2 and 3 percent above the prime rate. Considering that it may take between two and three years until the bank loan plus accrued interest has been paid off, you are looking at a rather sizable amount of money. For this very reason, do not fail to include the interest rates to be paid in your budget.

In the last analysis, and don't kid yourself about it, the producer assumes the responsibility for the loan—a heavy burden indeed.

Some Tough Questions You'll Have to Answer

1. *How much money do you need?* Be very specific about the amount of money you'll need. Before approaching any possible investors, have

a realistic, if conservative, budget on hand. And most important, be ready to discuss each item on your budget.

2. *How are you going to pay back the loans?* Be ready to provide a credible cash-flow projection that takes the risky nature of any film venture into consideration.

3. *Will the investors see any profit?* Do not make empty promises, but again point to the risks involved in investing in a motion picture. On the other hand, however, do not fail to stress your movie's sales potentials (cable, home video, foreign).

4. *How will investors be protected?* Make it clear investors invest (and gamble) in a high-risk venture. Don't be too ready to give any of them collateral rights in any equity other than the film to be produced.

Financing Terms

Angel. A private investor who is willing to provide some seed money to a venture.

Seed money. Funds used to start out.

Asset-based loan. A loan that is tied to a firm's accounts receivable. The lender has the right to seize the firm's assets if the borrower defaults.

Equity. Capital that entitles the investors to an interest in the firm.

Senior debt. In the event of default, the bank that granted the loan has seniority over other investors.

Subordinated debt. A nonbank debt that stands in second position after the bank's right to recover. These loans are also called unsecured loans.

Before you make a financing decision, here are essential points to raise with your accountant and attorney:

- Advantages and disadvantages of the corporation—PD agreement (pages 76–77).
- Advantages and disadvantages of the producer—PD agreement (pages 77–78).
- What to ask about the PD agreement (page 81).
- Specifics of the pick-up deal (pages 89–93).

- Things to remember about the independent distributor's distribution contract (page 97).
- How to find out about the independent distributor's strength (pages 98–99).
- What to know about auxiliary sales (pages 100–101).
- Foreign film market distribution fees and chain of sales (pages 103–105).
- What to find out about the prospective home video distributor (page 108).

9.

A special niche:

how to market your

home video

Two types of marketing are evident in the home video market: theatrical film rental and *sell-through*. Most nontheatrical home videos (exercise, how-to, self-help, educational, and children's tapes) are sold and bought like books or records. But in no way can the nontheatrical home videotape compete with the tape output of an even mildly successful film. At the time of this writing, the nontheatrical video market commanded only a rather small fraction of the entire video output. The average number of units sold ranges between five hundred and five thousand tapes.

The immense success of Jane Fonda's famous exercise tape is not a typical example. Jane Fonda is a major movie star, and her tape was one of the first exercise tapes on the market. On the other hand, there are hundreds of tapes on the market selling well, if in conservative numbers. To name a few:

The Secret Leopard
National Geographic
Vestron Video

Arnold Palmer
Course Strategy
Vestron Video

Michael Caine
On Acting
Ingram Video

If marketed ingeniously in specialty stores, drugstores, bookstores, and (depending on its wider appeal) in major chain stores, the attention-getting packaged and professionally produced nontheatrical video still brings in a respectable profit.

Therefore, before you decide upon producing your nontheatrical tape, consider its success factors:

Marketability
Outlets
Packaging

Marketability. Because of the relatively few units sold in each outlet, your nontheatrical video *must* attract a number of different markets. To arrive at an overall marketability picture of your video, ask yourself these questions:

1. Does my nontheatrical video fall within an easily recognizable category such as exercise, cooking, or inspirational, or does it deal with a topic that, so far, has escaped extensive video representation? How about thinking of a home video exploring your own expertise in crafts, sewing, modeling, interior decorating, painting, or any other topic that can be shown visually, and—maybe even more important—has escaped extensive video representation.

2. Has your video a promotional hook? In the case of the nontheatrical video, the term "hook" does not refer as much to the participation or endorsement of a major star as it does to a "presold" audience. For instance, a tape on dog training will appeal to a fairly large group of potential buyers, while a tape on lace making will find few, if any, aficionados. If you, however, *give lectures* on an esoteric subject, such as porcelain painting, and you sell the tape during your lecture, a handsome profit can be made from moving only a few tapes.

If you've answered the above questions affirmatively, you should think about the right marketing outlets for your video:

Home video distributor
Wholesaler
Direct sales to retailer
Catalogs

Self-distribution:
  TV and radio spots
  Magazine coupons
  Direct mail

Home video distributor. Home video distributors have to move large numbers of units within short time periods. These units, like books and records, must make a profit during their initial release. If a title does not sell quickly enough, it will be backlisted, that is to say, the title will still be carried on the packages of the distributor's sales pamphlet, but it won't be promoted any longer. Since distributors have to sell large quantities of tapes during a short period, understandably they are not interested in nontheatrical videos that sell slowly but usually have a long shelf life. Yet, you may have just the kind of tape a distributor wants to sell. As with a distributor who intends to sell your theatrical feature film video, you'd have to sign a distribution contract. Less complicated than the PD agreement, it still covers clauses worthy of your, and your attorney's, consideration.

Home Video Distribution Contract

1. *Exclusive rights.* According to the agreement, the distributor handles all areas. Have these areas spelled out, and if possible keep (after a reasonable window*) direct sales for yourself. (Remember, the distributor loses interest after your tape's initial surge, and your tape might languish in the company's warehouse.)

2. *Advance.* Chances are, the advance is all the money you'll ever see. Ask for an advance substantial enough to compel the distributor to generate sufficient promotion for your tape. Advances, in most cases, are not paid until the tape's *release date.* Have the distributor agree upon a specific release date. Distributors, hoping for a "hot property" to come their way, prefer to keep a tape release date rather vague. This is unfair; after all, the producer's funds are tied up in the tape. Should the distributor refuse to set a release date, have him or her pay half of the advance upon signing the agreement, and the other half upon the tape's release.

---

*"Window" refers to the time period that has to elapse before a show can move on from one medium to the next.

3. *Royalties.* Once the advance has been recouped, the distributor has to pay royalties to the producer. Royalties usually are based upon the nontheatrical tape's wholesale price. I suggest that instead of a percentage, your attorney arrange for a fixed dollar amount to be paid per unit.

4. *Returns.* The distributor understandably does not pay royalties on returned tapes. Expecting returns, the distributor holds back about 20 to 30 percent of the expected royalties. This sum is called a "reserve." A distributor likes to hold the reserve until all unsold tapes have been returned. It is a good idea to add a clause limiting the reserve period to six months.

5. *Delivery date.* Delivery date refers to the date the producer has to deliver the master tape and other materials to the distributor. Do not delay. Do not ask for an extension. Distributors are on tight schedules. They have to deal with graphic designers and printers (box covers, sell sheets, mats), tape duplication, and trade magazine advertising. The distributor cannot afford to miss any deadline, and neither can you if you want to stay in business.

6. *Agreements and clearances with third parties.* List all parties to whom you owe deferments, or who own points in your project. These parties may include actors, writers, labs, or private investors.

7. *Conditions precedent.* List of conditions that, if not met, render the contract null and void (have your attorney negotiate each and every clause listed).

8. *Indemnity insurance.* Most likely the distributor carries an umbrella indemnity insurance. The average how-to or self-help tape does not require such insurance.

9. *Legal documents:*

Copyright certificate (U.S. copyright registration certificate issued by the Library of Congress, Washington, D.C.).
Notarized assignment of rights (only if applicable).

10. *Governing law.* Arbitration and/or legal actions in case of disagreement.

11. *Delivery materials*:

Digital master in NTS Format
Digital video master in PAL Format.*
Music and effects track (if applicable)
Music cue sheet (if applicable and if composed music has been used)
Color slides
Black-and-white prints

12. The producer's rights to audit the distributor's books.

13. *Payment schedule.* If the producer receives an advance, you'll have to negotiate its payment:

Entire advance due at time of signing
Entire advance due at time of release
Half of the advance due at time of signing, the other half due at time
of release

14. *Royalty statements.* Usually royalty statements are due biannually.

The success of any nontheatrical video may be attributed to the producer's choice of distributors; in short, a specialized tape needs a specialized distributor:

Educational Tapes

Teaching Films, Inc.
21601 Devonshire Street
Evanston, IL 60202

BFA Educational Media
468 Park Avenue South
New York, NY 10016

Library Video Company
P.O. Box 4051
Philadelphia, PA 19106

---

*NTS and PAL formats refer to tape formats. If your tape is to be distributed domestically, you do not need a PAL.

How-to Tapes	Do It Yourself 712 Euclid Avenue Charlotte, NC 28203
Children's Tapes	Kid Time Video 2340 Saetelle Boulevard Los Angeles, CA 90064
	The Video Schoolhouse 167 Central Avenue Pacific Grove, CA 93950
	Crown Video 225 Park Avenue New York, NY 10003
	Children's Video Library 1010 Washington Boulevard Stamford, CT 06901
Cooking	The Kitchen 512 W. 19th Street New York, NY 10011
Inspirational	Faith for Today 1100 Rancho Conejo Boulevard Newbury Park, CA 91320
	Spring Arbor Distributors 10885 Textile Road Spring Arbor, MI 48111

Wholesalers. To sell your tape via a wholesaler requires that you not only produce the tape, have it duplicated, and packaged, but also supply advertising materials. You have to supply advertising materials such as posters, cutouts, sell sheets, and, if you wish to have your tape advertised in any of the video trades, mats.

My video film *Night of Terror* (Ciara Productions, Inc., and Westlake Studios) was marketed successfully through wholesalers. We supplied the wholesaler with the boxed product and usual advertising material (sell sheets, posters and mats, but no cutouts), and once the contract was signed participated in advertising the video with one-page ads in some of the leading video trades.

Video Magazine
460 W. 34th Street
New York, NY 10001

Video Software Dealer
5519 Centinela Avenue
Los Angeles, CA 90066

Video Review
902 Broadway
New York, NY 10020

Both production firms and the wholesaler participated in the advertising cost. After about three months the film had run its course, and the returns came in. Rather than have the video backlisted, the film, as had been arranged contractually, reverted back to us. So did the returned copies. For another six months we sold the film directly through discount distributors.*

But getting back to the nontheatrical video: Unless you have a "line of titles" (that is to say, a number of subject-related nontheatrical tapes), it is difficult to convince any wholesaler to carry your product. Generally, wholesalers prefer to work with big established distributors guaranteeing a constant stream of products. In order to interest distributors in your tape, you'll have to give them a deal they cannot refuse. A 50/50 cut between producer and wholesaler off the tape's wholesale price is considered a fair deal, and the 40/60 cut is not unheard of. On top of this, a number of wholesalers want you to pay for shipping charges to retailers. Stand firm on this issue; pay shipping charges to the wholesaler only.

How acquisition works. Start out by calling distributors and wholesalers to find out who is in charge of acquisition. *Never* send out your tape and letter of inquiry cold; contact the person in charge of acquisition by phone. I prefer to establish a phone contact because I think a phone call is more personal,

*See "Fractionalization," page 141.

and it tells me immediately whether or not a company is interested in my film or tape. (When you call, don't ever permit the receptionist to pawn you off to a second-string executive.) Most likely you will be invited to mail in your tape plus some information about your company. Don't ever approach any distributor and/or wholesaler with a demo tape that shows what the final tape will be like, but supply a finished and polished product. If you intend to sell your tape via a wholesaler you must be able to show box cover and advertising materials. But box cover and advertising materials are *not* necessary if you hope to sell your tape through a home video distributor. Once your tape has aroused the acquisition department's interest, you'll be invited to a meeting. This meeting will be a short one, and you'll have to push your tape's hook. Refer to the tape's most salient points only; do not permit yourself to ramble on about secondary issues. Remember, the acquisition department is not interested in your tape's merits, it is interested in your tape's sellability.

If acquisition has been properly impressed by your tape and your presentation, the marketing department comes onto the scene. Once you are dealing with marketing, prepare yourself to deal with pointed questions:

- Who will buy your tape?
- Has the tape been geared toward a distinct group of buyers?
- What specific feature, topic, or tool will attract them?
- Will enough tapes be sold to justify marketing cost and effort?
- How much will it cost to put the tape on the market?
- What is the likely profit margin?

Retailers. First of all, don't even *think* about selling your nontheatrical tape to your kindly neighborhood video store. True, this store—like any other video rental store in the country—does do a booming business. But it *never* buys from an individual producer; it orders its supplies from wholesalers And don't forget, your neighborhood video store is in the rental business, making a living by renting out tapes of feature films. A video retailer cannot afford to clutter precious shelf space with nontheatrical tapes renting only a few times. And besides, how many video stores will you be able to contact? Granted, there are mailing lists galore. You can purchase a mailing list, each giving about 200,000 names and addresses of video rental stores. But mailing out your nontheatrical video is nothing but an enormous waste of money. Generally, one expects about 1 to 2 percent return answers from a mailing list. I would not count on even that small number; the average corner video retailer does not buy from individual producers.

If your tape has strong general appeal, you may consider contacting large chain stores such as Montgomery Ward, Sears, K mart, Wal-Mart, and so on. Concentrate on their merchandise that ties in with your tape. Here are a few examples:

- Dressmaking in a jiffy—fabric chain stores
- Gourmet cooking, fast cooking, inexpensive cooking, inexpensive entertaining—housewares and/or appliance department
- Interior decorating on a budget—furniture chain stores

Give it some thought; there are hundreds of possibilities for the savvy producer. Contact the chain's corporate headquarters and ask for the executive in charge of the department you have targeted.

Naturally, as with selling to wholesalers you'll have to supply the chain with the duplicated tape, including box, as well as some posters.

The drawback is, if the chain store does not employ an internal distribution system, you'll have to ship your tapes to each and every individual store. And this, believe me, is lots of hard work. You'll have to concern yourself with getting the tape duplicated, packaged, and shipped,* as well as billing and collecting.

If you have produced a nontheatrical tape wide enough in general appeal to interest the countless minimalls dotting the country, you may want to get in touch with a wholesaler specializing in this field:

Handleman Company
500 Kirts Boulevard
Troy, MI 48084

On the other hand, if you have a highly specialized tape that may be combined with a book of the same topic, your best bets are bookstores. Here I would suggest that you do not try to contact the major chains (Crown, WaldenBooks, Bookstar, B. Dalton) directly, but work through a distributor highly experienced in this genre:

---

*You may, of course, select to have packaging and shipping done by a fulfillment house. We will discuss this method under TV sales.

Ingram Video
1123 Heil Quaker Blvd.
La Vergne, TN 37086

But be forewarned, bookstores expect 60 percent off the retail price, and they do have a 100 percent return policy. But, on the other hand, if your tape or book-tape combination finds enough friends, it will enjoy a long shelf life.

I successfully sold my nontheatrical tape *The Beginning Director's Guide to Filmmaking*, based on the book of the same title, through several chains specializing in home video equipment.

Catalogs. During the past years catalogs selling a variety of merchandise have become very popular. The most recent additions are catalogs selling home videos. To get acquainted with numerous catalogs you may check *Publisher's Source Book*, which you'll find in your local library, or write to:

Videotape Catalog
SMW Video Inc.
803 Russell Boulevard #2
Davis, CA 95616

I'd suggest that you call a catalog's acquisition department to find out whether the company is interested in your video's topic. If so, follow up with a letter stating:

- Target audience.
- Reasons why the target audience should be interested in your tape.
- Your tape's hook.
- In what way your tape is different (and better) from other tapes dealing with the same genre, or the reasons why a tape offering a new topic should find viewers' favorable response.

Don't forget to list a number of possible follow-up tapes; let the catalog company know that if your tape sells well you are ready with a stream of products. Catalogs, like wholesalers, are more interested in prolific producers.

---

*Walker and Company, 435 Hudson Street, New York, NY 10014

Catalogs are mailed out every two months, and your tape will be carried in one or two issues. You should expect to sell between 500 and 1,000 units. The producer *does not* participate in the catalog's printing and mailing cost, but has to supply the catalog with two or three color slides, mats, and two or three black-and-white pictures.

The catalog expects a 60 percent discount of the tape's retail price, and has a 100 percent return policy.

My company, Ciara Productions, Inc., in partnership with Udell Studios and a German company, Schau Mal TV, produced a made-for-video comedy in German, *Rote Tasche (The Red Satchel)*. The tape was marketed successfully through catalog sales. These catalogs were sent to German bookstores and specialty stores, as well as to individual customers who had purchased tapes previously.

Sponsors. A highly lucrative way of selling your nontheatrical video is sponsor tie-in. Granted, the process of convincing a sponsor about your tape's viability is difficult and frustrating. After all, your tape is supposed to make the customer choose the sponsor's product over another manufacturer's product or service. Therefore, you have to be specific about what the tape offers.

1. Exposure of the sponsor's merchandise and/or services.
2. Exposure of the sponsor's logo.
3. The promise that the tape will interest customers to buy more of the sponsor's services or merchandise.
4. The viewer's favorable association between tape and sponsor's service or merchandise.
5. The promise that the viewer has reason to view the tape more than once; this way the sponsor's name is kept in the viewer's mind.

As you are dealing with a prospective sponsor, do not offer a produced tape, but manufacture one to order. (It helps if you can point to a line of your tapes that has been marketed through catalog sales, distributors, wholesalers, or chain stores.) In any event, you must demonstrate your experience and professionalism in the field of the nontheatrical tape. Once you approach your prospective sponsor, you'll have to present a fully detailed outline.

For instance, let's assume you are pitching a tape idea on home protection. You'll not only stress the tape's topic but the following as well:

1. As the sponsor advertises and keeps booths at various home shows throughout the country, the tape (showing the sponsor's name and logo) will

be displayed prominently. The tape can be shown on a big-screen TV throughout the day.

2. The tape will show the sponsor:

- providing security guards for special events.
- providing special security for apartments, condos, banks, malls, businesses.
- providing twenty-four-hour security for private homes, and special security if owner is on vacation
- providing security (special telephone numbers and/or a calling device) for shut-ins and the elderly

3. In this way a client who has contracted one service will be exposed to the company's additional services.

4. Stress that a tape is far more successful and not more expensive than a four-color brochure, since it talks to the viewers directly. It acquaints them with the skilled and helpful people employed by your company.

This is the most important point of your presentation. The tape should not be viewed once and thrown away (as a brochure might) but should be *consulted* by the viewers. Therefore, the tape must contain information that warrants repeated viewing, such as:

- how to make your home burglar-proof
- how to make your home burglar-proof when you go on a short or extended vacation
- what to do and not to do when mugged
- how to avoid being mugged
- safety devices for your home, car, and on your person

You may encounter a sponsor that likes your idea but feels there are not enough video players around to make the tape-premium campaign successful. You counter with the answer that individuals and/or firms considering the firm's service or merchandise most likely own a VCR.

Once you set your mind to it, you'll find a number of sponsors to contact. Here are a few examples:

Sponsor	Suggested Tape
Banks (to new customers)	Saving and budgeting money

Sponsor	*Suggested Tape*
Health food chain	Nutrition and good health
Health spa chains	Exercise tape with a new twist

Before you contact a sponsor, find out whether your prospective client works with an in-house advertising department, or deals with an advertising agency exclusively. If the latter is the case, you ought to contact the agency before even speaking to the sponsor about your project.

Fractionalization. If you have signed with a distributor or agreed to have a wholesaler sell your tapes, don't forget to keep a window open, entitling you to direct and catalog sales.

Once your tape has run its course in a catalog, its life is not over by any means. Now the discount wholesalers come into the picture:

Budget Video
1540 N. Highland Avenue
Los Angeles, CA 90028

Discount Video Tapes
500 S. Buena Vista Street
Burbank, CA 91521

Movie Tape Exchange
9380 Route 130 North
Pennsauken, NJ 08109

Video Shuttle Nework
445 Eighth Avenue NW
St. Paul, MN 55112

Video Closeouts of America Inc.
261 Central Avenue, Suite 42
Jersey City, NJ 07307

Your profit margin, of course, is small. The discount firm sells your tape for about half of its former wholesale price.

Selling your tape via radio and TV spots. Both TV and radio spots can be immensely successful in bringing a product (your tape) to the public's eye, *if* your budget is big enough to carry the advertising expense, and *if* the number of units selling justify the expense.

TV spot. Producing a thirty-second commercial, conservatively speaking, costs between $10,000 and $20,000 even if you have no known star attached.

Naturally you want to bypass the prime-time spots and have your commercial shown at "preexemptible time," that is, during late-night hours. Rates vary. Naturally a commercial shown on a Scotts Bluff, Nebraska, TV station is far less expensive than one airing in Los Angeles or New York.

Radio spots. Advertising on radio is far less expensive than advertising on TV. Radio reaches a smaller but more specified audience, and before placing any spots you must know the demographics of the particular station—find out about the age and socioeconomic groups most likely to tune in. The best time slots are during rush hours, when drivers stuck in gridlock turn to their radios for solace.

TV and radio spots sell best if you provide the public with an 800 number to call. Flash the 800 number during the last ten seconds of your commercial. Make the number easy to remember; people do not have time (or in the case of radio advertisements, the opportunity) to get pencil and paper. Something like 1–800-GET TAPE might do the trick. For the very same reason *do not* list an address for customers to write to.

The 800 number, of course, demands that operators are on duty when your TV spot airs. This in turn demands that you work with a fulfillment house that processes the called-in orders and ships them out. Shipping charges change from company to company, but generally you'll have to count on:

$1.25 for processing order
 1.25 for invoice
 .25 for box and packing materials

The additional UPS charges have to be paid by the customer.

Mailings. Direct mailing used to be a highly effective sales method. But lately, as everyone faces an avalanche of advertisements, its appeal fades quickly. Most of the letters and brochures end up *unread* in the wastepaper basket. None of us has the time and inclination to read about goods and services we don't need and do not want to know about. The key to an effective direct mailing is that you obtain a list addressing exactly the clientele you wish to contact.

You may wish to contact the following publications:

Direct Mail List Rates and Data
Standard Rate and Data Service, Inc.
3004 Glenview Road
Wilmette, IL 60611

The Direct Marketing Association, Inc.
6 East 43rd Street
New York, NY 10017

The Direct Market Place:
The Directors of the Direct Marketing Industry
c/o Hilary House Publishers, Inc.
980 North Federal Highway, Suite 206
Boca Raton, FL 33932

Direct Marketing News
c/o DMN Corp.
19 W. 21 Street
New York, NY 10010

Direct mailing is expensive. First, you'll have to consider the cost of your brochure, which may run between $2,000 and $10,000. These costs include:

Copywriter (you may do this yourself)
Typesetting
Artwork (graphic art, color separation)
Printing

True, you may elect to design a single-sheet ad and have it photocopied. The cost will be minimal, but you'll still have to concern yourself with postage. And postage is sky high, if you consider that the average mailing list contains between 50,000 and 200,000 names. Further, you ought to consider that the average response to direct mailing falls below 1 percent.

Yet, on the positive side, direct mail permits you to build a basic group of clients interested in repeat purchases.

Magazine ads. Instead of direct mailing you might look at magazine ads that include an order coupon as a way to build your clientele. You will, naturally, advertise only in magazines catering to the specific clientele you